THE EMPTINESS OF THE MACHINE

THE EMPTINESS OF THE MACHINE

NIHILISM AND OTHER ABYSSES

5TH EDITION
ENGLISH TRANSLATION

ANDRÉ CANCIAN

Author's edition
2023

We're the insomnia of matter

SUMMARY

PREFACE

When we imagine a machine, the result is always something close to a mechanical system that works on its own. It doesn't bother us to think that she's nothing more than that. But how do we feel when we imagine a machine? Empty. We have the feeling that something is missing. And what is missing? What is a human being full of that is missing in a machine? Illusion. The emptiness of the machine is the awareness that our subjective world is a fiction; the awareness that our humanity is a delusion, that there is nothing behind what we are experiencing. We are machines, and our consciousness is a dream of that machine. Nothing else. Absolutely nothing.

André Cancian
2009

INTRODUCTORY CONSIDERATIONS

In my first work — *Atheism & Freedom* — I addressed atheism, seeking to clarify not only the topic itself, but also the various related issues. In this second one, I have the same proposal regarding *nihilism*, but with a slightly different writing style. This work can, in a certain sense, be viewed as a continuation of my first one, exploring its implications better, going inside with a more incisive look at certain issues that were addressed in it only in passing, but which deserve to be clarified and deepened. Even so, in this book the issue of religiosity will only be a marginal issue, because I think that, in writing an entire work on the subject, I have already dedicated enough space to lies.

I've always had the following curiosity: what conclusion would we reach if we were honest — really honest — about all the issues that we lie about constantly? This book is an attempt to answer that question, going through the most controversial, underground, and uncomfortable issues possible in the process, eviscerating the taboos that most terrify us. My intent is to understand and carry forward the implications of nihilism — all of them, and without ever making concessions. None. The intention is not to shock readers for needlessly, but to understand what reality would be if life itself did not exist, and then try to see ourselves as a fact, in the most impartial way possible — while also pointing that view to our interior.

The first chapter of the book, on nihilism, is also the most extensive, and constitutes the essential portion of the discussion, the rest being basically commentaries on particular issues, in the light of what was stated in that first chapter. Even so, the present work is not so much an attempt to justify nihilism in intellectual terms, but mainly a commentary on its impact on our lives. In this sense, *The Emptiness of the Machine* represents an experimental immersion in our own subjectivity in this critical phase of nihilistic disbelief, investigating how we deal with the death of our own beliefs.

ESSAYS

I

ON THE EMPTINESS OF EXISTENCE

NIHILISM

Nihilism can be defined as the implosion of subjectivity. Alternatively, and to be a little clearer, we can define it as a disbelief in any metaphysical foundation for human existence. It is not, however, something difficult to define, but to be apprehended. Because it is a fairly broad and abstract notion, there is a lot of confusion surrounding it. Let's look at some of the main reasons for this. *First, nihilism is vague in itself, since it comes from the Latin nihil, which means nothing.* The word *nihilism*, which could be translated as "swimming", immediately gives us no idea what it is. Second, nihilism has no positive content. Because it is a negative stance, we will only be able to understand it after we are aware of what it denies, and that is why the understanding of nihilism involves many other concepts; it will only become visible after we outline its context. Finally, nihilism has not historically received consistent employment either, and each thinker or movement interpreted it in a very particular way, almost always with an ideological background, in a short-sighted attempt to justify active and militant nihilism.

In general, we see nihilism associated with other ideas, denoting their inherent emptiness. For example, political nihilism would be more or less equivalent to anarchism, repudiating the belief that this or that political system would lead us to progress, which would be nothing more than a lying dream. Moral nihilism would be equivalent to the denial of the existence of objective moral references, that is, of good or bad values in and of themselves. Epistemological nihilism, in turn, would be the statement that nothing can be known or communicated. Therefore, we see that to associate any notion with nihilism is not exactly a compliment, but something like placing a sign next to it saying: there is nothing *here - especially nothing that is believed to be there.*

Nihilism, however, is not just a term that we juxtapose to any idea that displeases us, in order to discredit it. Its power to point out the emptiness of things cannot be used as a weapon, because when a shot is fired at nothing, the weapon automatically ceases to exist, and the whole thing loses its meaning. Nihilism, being a radical process of criticism, cannot be partially used. We cannot, for example, use moral nihilism to refute specific values, with which we do not sympathize, imagining that our own would survive. When we say that morals don't exist, it implies that there aren't any values — whether ours or those of our opponents. With moral nihilism, all morality is reduced to nothing, including ours. The reduction of morals to nothing, as we see, is based not on grammar, but on the assumption that morality is empty in itself, that it has no real and objective foundations. It is not a question of whether or not we sympathize with morals, but of the finding that it is a dream, a phantasmagoria invented by ourselves, and therefore not moral laws are more relevant than traffic laws.

We, however, will mainly deal with *existential nihilism*, that is, the position according to which existence, in and of itself, has no foundation, value, meaning, or purpose. According to existential nihilism, everything that exists has no purpose, including life. All actions, all feelings, all facts are empty in and of themselves, devoid of any meaning. From this point of view, living is as meaningless as dying, and we are here for the same reason as stones: none. This seems to be the most fundamental category of nihilism, in relation to which the other types take on the aspect of particular cases. Moral and political nihilisms, for example, can clearly be deduced from existential nihilism - because, if existence itself is worthless, this implies that nothing has value, including moral values, including progress.

* * *

The only way to understand existential nihilism is through reflection. The emptiness of existence could never be demonstrated through practice, or apprehended through immediate experience. If, for example, we reduced our planet to nothing with a nuclear bomb, that would not demonstrate anything. The sight of this planet being torn apart wouldn't prove anything either. Such a practical destructive stance makes little sense, since it is equivalent to trying to refute a book by burning it. Existential nihilism is demonstrated when we reduce man to nothing, and for that it is enough to have some intellectual talent combined with honesty, because the emptying of existence is the mere consequence of understanding it. We don't have to slaughter the whole of humanity to prove that life is meaningless.

To reduce man to nothing, and understand that this demonstrates existential nihilism, we must grasp the objective emptiness of existence - it being obvious that, as subjects, we can only do so subjectively. The problem is that, in the process of demonstrating that existence is empty, we are the very emptiness that we are trying to point out—we try to explain that we ourselves have no explanation. It seems paradoxical, but it's not. It will be enough for us to be able to understand ourselves as a fact, and nihilism will become practically a no-brainer. Only then will we realize that nihilism is not, as it may at first seem, an extreme stance involving some kind of revolt, but merely an honest and sensible view of reality — a view made possible in large part due to modern scientific discoveries. With some simple definitions and explanations, we can arrive at a reasonable notion from the perspective presented by existential nihilism. As the argument is a bit long, let's go in parts. Let's make some preliminary remarks about why nihilism seems so uncomfortable to us.

Many, out of prejudice, are afraid of the "emptiness of existence", but that fear, in itself, is something completely meaningless, since it is equivalent to fearing what does not exist; emptiness is not a positive threat. Otherwise, let's see: *There is no life on Venus.* Does anyone feel terrified by this statement? Hardly. *There are no banks on Mars.* Does anyone pale in the face of that? Not either. Suppose, however, that during all our lives we had worked hard, believing that all our effort would be converted into money in a bank on Mars. Now we would feel threatened by the statement that there is none on this planet, there never was any bank, because we lived because of that, we believed in this supposed Martian money as the thing that gave meaning to our lives. Therefore, what terrifies us is not the emptiness of existence, or the emptiness of interplanetary banks — what fills us with fear is the possibility of discovering that we were completely wrong in our beliefs about reality. It would be overwhelming to know that we have given great importance, of having dedicated our entire lives to something that simply does not exist. That's why we shudder at the statement that existence is meaningless, although that statement is as certain as that there is no money on other planets in the solar system.

We resist nihilism, not because it's false, but because reorganizing our view of reality would be too much work. Then, if we put our personal interests aside, we will see that what worries us about nihilism is the fact that it confronts us harshly with our own naivety, with the fact that we have allowed ourselves to be deceived so grandly that our lives began to depend on lies, on imaginary assumptions. So let's realize that when nihilism points out these lies, it's not destroying reality, but our delusions. From this point of view, nihilism is nothing more than an exercise in honesty and impartiality, and it only empties the reality of fictions that never actually existed. That honesty can be hurtful, but it's a sign of maturity. If existence, devoid of illusions, seems empty to us, let us at least know how to admit that it is our fault for having been filled with them. If we like to fool ourselves, that's fine. However, if our interest is to become capable of dealing with reality as adults, it will always be preferable to accept existence as it is in itself, even if that means giving up many of our most deeply held beliefs. It is better to live in a meaningless world than to believe in a false sense for the world, which points nowhere.

As we can see, the essential concern of nihilism is not to discover the truth, but to point out the lies and recognize the limitations. Describing the facts is the role of science. Nihilism only consists of the discipline of being honest in the face of those facts that we observe, understanding, and accepting their implications. In this sense, one of the areas most affected by nihilism are the "big questions" of existence. This is because the answers to such questions are, in general, much more obvious than we think - and often we even know what they are, but we prefer to continue accusing science of being "blind and limited" to justify our prejudices.

We affirm that such issues are too "profound" just as a pretext to deal with them in a superficial way; we say that they are "mysteries", "impossible to answer", just because we are afraid of the answers. Other times we leave these issues aside, not to protect our delusions, but because we thought that investigating them would drive us insane. Quite the contrary, this would only lead us to lucidity, it would allow us to live with our feet on the ground. But what is the floor? Now, what is under our feet. What is the world? Now, it's what we have before our eyes. What is being? Well, that's what exists. In large part, nihilism consists of the rare ability to see the obvious.

Let us ask ourselves, for example, *what is man?* Now, we are what we seem to be: machines. Just consult any basic anatomy book. There's nothing "behind". That "behind" is nothing more than a fantasy. It was invented by us in a childish attempt to humanize existence. Nevertheless, although we know perfectly well what man is, we still believe that there is a mysterious "something else" in the equation. We continue to deceive ourselves with the notion of the "depth" of knowledge, which makes us want to seek the "behind" the world. What's more, it makes us believe that the true reality lies in that "behind", which, precisely because it is an illusion, is equivalent to nothing.

When we study man as if he were not a machine, of course we could not reach any conclusion, because that is absurd. It would be the same as a rat investigating itself as if it were not a rodent, judging that the "reason for being" of its tooth cannot just be to gnaw on cheese. The supposed "intimate sense of reality" that man seeks based on his subjectivity is the same that this rat would seek if it had an intelligence similar to ours, assuming an entire metaphysical order "behind" the world that attributes to its tooth a "transcendental rodent sense" that refers to Absolute Cheese. Little wonder that science to date has never found what doesn't exist. Science can only investigate the natural world by the simple fact that the rest are metaphysical delusions. Abandoning meaningless problems is not an intrinsic limitation, it's wisdom.

✳ ✳ ✳

What is concerned with seeking what is "beyond" reality is not science, but metaphysics, which literally means *after physics*. But what is beyond physics? Now, the answer is obvious: nothing. Much less reasons. In a world where everything is physical, only what we invent can be metaphysical, at least if we understand metaphysics the classic investigation of "ultimate reasons". Beyond the scope of scientific realism, metaphysics has no function; it is absurd that it has a function. In the quest for objective knowledge, the baton was passed on to science. The metaphysics that investigates the world "deeply", through pure reason, is dead. This never led to anything, as we tried to discover reality, not by looking at the world, but at a mirror. The metaphysical answers to existence seem interesting to us because, obviously, they are based on the convenient assumption that human reason is capable of replacing experimentation and accessing a supposed "essence of being" through magical intuition, such as discovering the world by remote control. It seems tempting that we can explain reality in this way, but metaphysics is a long shot, something as useless as using the imagination to predict the future.

Let's look at the issue as follows: metaphysics was born at a time of igno-rance, when men didn't even know about the existence of bacteria. It didn't even occur to them that our brains were made of neurons. Even so, they wanted to rationally explain decomposition and thinking. Since they didn't have microscopes to see reality precisely, thus verifying the existence of decomposing microorganisms, they limited themselves to dreaming up metaphysical theories, speculating about "hidden realities" that rotted us in secret, and of course they didn't have the slightest idea what they were talking about. When they saw a decomposing body, for example, they imagined that this was perhaps due to some natural order of things that imposed decomposition on us as an "existential sense". Thus, by ignoring that bacteria are what rots us, they supposed that this would be due to the mysterious "decomposing essence of being". This type of delusional reasoning, consisting of rigorous stop-gap logic, is at the heart of metaphysics. It addresses all the issues of existence with that same degree of autism.

In this approach, instead of being investigated, the world must be *thought* of. Instead of observing facts, we should seek explanations based on pure reason, daydreaming about some supernatural essence that determines natural facts. Of course, if the being were rational in itself, something like a mathematical equation, truth would be something abstract that transcends the facts themselves, that is, the "essence of being" would consist of logical principles. But where do we get the idea that being is rational? And what is this "essence"? We don't know. The fact is that this delusional metaphysics would never have been born if we had given the Greeks a microscope and a periodic table.

Seen in this way, the most profound metaphysical investigations are a pure and simple waste of time, because they are searching for something that is simply not there — and the vast majority of the questions of existence, of the questions that we consider most important, are raised not by physics, but by metaphysics, by the most shameful inquisitive blablah. If such observations seem strong, this is because, even today, our modern view of reality still hides many metaphysical prejudices.

Let us think, for example, of the raison d'être of life. Where did we get this crazy idea from? Certainly not from experience, certainly not from the world that we have before our eyes. This is an unreasonable metaphysical question, since it is something that could under no circumstances be solved by the observation of the physical world, and this can be illustrated by the simple fact that the observation of the physical world carried out by modern biology, despite explaining perfectly well how life works, is not accepted as an answer to that question. Otherwise, let's see: we watch a sperm and an egg fuse; we see the cells multiplying; we see all the steps involved in the formation of another organism; we see life happening right before us; everything is perfectly clear. Even so, we continue to insist on the belief that there is something "behind" that reality, something that is more important than reality itself. That something, of course, is our metaphysical beliefs. Science cannot answer the question of the "reason for being" of life because this way of conceiving life does not correspond to reality. It would be the same as asking science to answer where the winged dragons that we saw after consuming hallucinogens are located.

To be at least reasonable, we have to admit that we've never had legitimate reasons to think that life has a "reason for being", because nothing in our experience in the world suggests that question to us. What kind of physical phenomenon could have hinted at this question? We looked at a flower and thought: oh, *how curious, there is a flower in that vase!* Why isn't there a vase in the flower? Why doesn't the flower have teeth? What a mystery! That can only be because it has a "reason for being" — the flower blossomed to fulfill a transcendental sense! Seeds and pollen have nothing to do with it: it is something deeper, much higher than the material world! Then we propose the challenge to ourselves: *I'm going to find out what that reason is!* After a few years, we returned from theological school and answered that only God knows.

In this type of investigation, we desperately set out to find the answer to a meaningless question, and we are still amazed that we never found it. Of course, that question could only be answered if the world were something like a human *playground*, made in our image and likeness by some bored deity. However, since the world does not behave according to our childish expectations, instead of admitting the obvious, of accepting that what is right before our eyes is real, we think it wiser to invent a second mysterious existence that carries the "hidden essence" of ours - a world that we can only imagine as an immense library full of dusty scrolls in which the "reasons for being" of everything that exists in the world in which we are in are noted.

Therefore, to transform any absurd belief into a glorious "metaphysical investigation", it is enough to put a question mark at the end of it: we will have before us another "unfathomable mystery", another proof of man's profound ignorance in relation to the world in which he lives. *However, let's be frank: weren't we ourselves the ones who, without any respectable reason, invented that the flower has a "reason for being", that it must have a reason?* We transformed this circular reasoning into something so grandiose that, when investigating it, we have the illusion of walking in a straight line. We get lost in daydreams, and we call this "transcendental meditations", "the search for the inner meaning of being", something that is nothing more than a man running around his own ass in search of reasons that inflate his vanity. Faced with this hidden something that makes us so monstrously naive, the question of the mystery of the world seems like a matter of lice.

Let's come to our senses. If we pay some attention, we will see that the flower's true raison d'être is not really a reason but a fact: the fact that it sprouted and blossomed; that's all. The rest are meaningless metaphysical questions, mere interrogative nonsense that lead our investigations to an imaginary world that has nothing to do with what we are trying to understand.

* * *

It should already be quite clear why the nihilistic stance is uncomfortable, so let's move on to the next topic. As nihilism is linked to a change in our metaphysical conception of existence, we should outline what metaphysics is today - and especially what it was. The metaphysics that we criticize here is the so-called traditional metaphysics, which, based on anthropocentric assumptions, launches into investigations without feet or heads, seeking something that does not exist to explain what exists. Modern metaphysics, on the other hand, seeks only to outline a coherent vision of what reality is, leaving science the role of discovering what exists. Instead of dreaming, she thinks based on the facts that we know, but without making aberrant extrapolations. The contrast between the two will help us to better understand the context of nihilism.

Metaphysics is an area of philosophy that seeks to investigate the most fundamental aspects of existence through reason. It deals with what is not immediately accessible to us through the senses, that cannot be investigated directly and experimentally, that is, through science. It asks questions such as "what is it to exist?" , "what's the reason?" , "what is reality?" etc. Metaphysics asks such basic questions that science cannot answer them directly, and the practice of science itself presupposes many subjects that only metaphysics investigates.

Science only observes facts and records them methodically — it investigates with the eyes; metaphysics, with reason.

When we say that "all living beings are born, grow, reproduce, and die", we make a scientific statement, which can be observed. When we say that "life has no meaning", we make a metaphysical statement, because it is something that we conclude from a process of intellectual abstraction, and abstractions, in theory, cannot be observed. Therefore, when we conceptualize reality based on facts, we are doing philosophy, not science. Science doesn't think, but we need to think in order to do science coherently, and that is the role of metaphysical reflection in the modern context: to guide our investigations. For the most part, modern metaphysics has become a means of avoiding the naive errors of traditional metaphysics.

As we saw above, traditional metaphysics is Essentialist, that is, it supposes that everything that exists has an "essence" that makes it what it is. The role of metaphysical reflection would be, from this perspective, to rationally investigate this "essence", since the observed facts would be nothing more than its manifestation. It has already been said that this essence is fire, water, numbers, reasons, gods, etc.; today it is said that this essence is foolishness. Such metaphysics is not concerned with understanding the world in which we are: it seeks to understand a transcendental world of imaginary essences of which ours would be the result. His investigations presuppose an order of things that is extrinsic to being, that is, supernatural. It seeks to discover an essence that is also an explanation: the reason why the world exists. This type of questioning, obviously, would only be compatible with a world that had a "transcendent essence", something that refers to the idea of a "subjectivity behind the world". That is why we say that traditional metaphysics has a theological orientation, since it confers divine attributes to existence. So this type of metaphysical inquiry seems like philosophy, but it's actually theology.

Modern metaphysics, on the other hand, investigates reality, not from a transcendent perspective, but an immanent one. Instead of speculating about what is "behind" the horizon of existence, it seeks to understand what is the existence that is under our feet, not on our pillows. In other words, it treats the question of the "essence of being" not as something that is outside the being itself, referring to "ultimate reasons", but as an order of things that is intrinsic to being, that is, natural. Based on the facts that we know, we seek to understand the here as a function of the here, not of a supposed "beyond".

The very scientific notion that we have of reality is based on metaphysical assumptions — just think of objectivism and naturalism. Objectivism affirms that, outside our heads, there is a reality common to all of us. Naturalism affirms that the world works on its own terms, that it does not have any supernatural essence that determines it from the outside to the inside. It may seem strange that modern science starts from metaphysical assumptions, but they are necessary so that we do not fall into relativism, so that we have a reasonable point of reference for what the world is. To investigate the world scientifically, we have to suppose what the world is, and that is a metaphysical assumption. Furthermore, we must conceptualize what knowledge is, differentiate subjective knowledge from objective knowledge, define what proof is, and why evidence is valid, as well as by what criteria this validity is established - which is the task of another area outside science, epistemology.

Without seriously investigating such issues, we would not know how to interpret the results of our observations or how to structure scientific experiments in order to know the reality. The function of modern metaphysics, from this point of view, would be precisely to establish a theoretical foundation to guide the investigation of sensitive reality carried out by the sciences.

A point of view that indistinctly rejected metaphysics would not allow us to make any assumptions about reality that were beyond immediate experience. We could not, for example, justify the assumption that there is an objective reality, and with that we would fall into relativism, perhaps even solipsism. If there was nothing objective, all reality would be reduced to a social construction — including matter, gravity, electricity. The creation of a world map would be as arbitrary as a novel, since everything would be nothing more than a subjective fiction. Relativism is good at emphasizing our limitations, but taking it seriously would be as unreasonable as stating that a scientific publication is as arbitrary as a comic book.

There is, therefore, no pejorative sense in saying that we make a metaphysical statement by supposing that the world is natural and objective. It is something metaphysical just because we talk about the basic constitution of the world, something theoretical that we need to base the sciences. Of course, the discoveries of science perfectly support such assumptions, but they do not cease to be metaphysical, since they are something that can never be demonstrated directly through sensitive reality, but only conceptualized, thought out.

* * *

Metaphysical assumptions about reality are important to guide us, to give us a global view of reality, but since this is a speculative terrain, we must be very careful about what we assume about the world itself. Metaphysics thinks in the dark, and can easily be lost in daydreams. If we suppose, for example, that the world is "rational in itself", we will begin to think that everything in it has a "reason for being", that there is an intelligible reason that explains, say, why gravity attracts bodies instead of repelling them. What kind of reason would that be? It is not known, but bodies falling at 9.8 m/s squared would be the result of this "reason". But why doesn't this essence cause bodies to fall at 15 m/s cubed? What is the reason for this? We don't know where to look for such reasons, but it comforts us to think that the world is rational, and that's all we need to be convinced. The fact is that there is no metaphysics in gravity. We know that gravity attracts bodies because we've seen it happen. This is a scientific, empirical statement, not an abstract rationalization.

Purely rational arguments, after all, only reflect the way we use words. If we can't verify them, they don't say anything — just like the "first cause" argument says nothing. When we ask why "reason" gravity is like that, we are assuming that it could be otherwise, and that it is how it is for a reason that can be understood. This presupposes that natural laws are rational, implying that reason, in some way, is at the essence of reality. But gravity wasn't thought out, it was observed. It's not a theory, but a fact — and we don't need to think when we can see. Therefore, metaphysics has no function here.

Raising metaphysical questions about natural facts is equivalent to humanizing existence, assuming that there is a "rational intention" behind what exists, as if the world had been designed by human or superhuman beings. But where do we get the idea that being is rational in and of itself? The most plausible explanation is this: from ourselves, because this has never been demonstrated by any observation of reality. Again, we see that this search for the "hidden sense of reality" is just theology in disguise. To illustrate, let's realize that asking the "why" of the natural world would be the same as asking why the Sun shines. Of course, when asking this kind of question, we put ourselves in the place of the Sun, thinking about the reasons why we would shine if we were that star. Based on this, we answered, for example, that the Sun shines "to warm the Earth", and of course this assumption cannot be demonstrated, nor is it in the least consistent with the discoveries of Astronomy. This type of response is clearly anthropocentric, since it seeks outside of man, in reality in itself, something that only exists in our subjective universe: intentionality.

The sciences, by arriving at the same results from independent observers, can justify the assumption that there is an objective reality, independent of us. Since we have never seen changes in the laws that govern phenomena, we can also justify the assumption that the world is natural. But how can we maintain that reason exists outside of man? We would only be allowed to think of existence as possessing a "reason for being" if it had been created by an intelligent supernatural force, if there were many indications of this in the facts we observed, but there is none.

This type of reverse reasoning, which seeks intentionality in things, is only admissible in subjective matters. For example, just as buildings have founda-tions, concrete columns, steel reinforcements, elevators, windows, floors, doors, and just as each of these elements has a structure and purpose, if the universe had been designed, there would also be an intelligible "reason for being" that constitutes its essence and that explains why everything is as it is, and not otherwise. The essence of the world in itself, in this case, would be equivalent to the intention of the engineer who designed it - and only from that perspective would this type of metaphysical investigation make sense, but we would have to assume that it had a creator. This allows us to better understand why traditional metaphysics has a theological orientation: it asks questions that are only admissible based on the assumption that the world was created intelligently to fulfill a purpose. Therefore, in the end, traditional metaphysics boils down to the attempt to reverse engineer the divine project.

✳ ✳ ✳

When we place reason before observation, instead of investigating the world, we investigate our own reason, our own subjective universe. We closed ourselves off from the sensitive world and began to seek not observable facts, but "ultimate reasons", "intentions behind the world", and that investigative stance never reached anywhere. Investigating the natural world with a meta-physical approach would be equivalent, let's say, to trying to discover the geography of the continents, not navigating around it and writing down what is observed, but locking ourselves in a room and meditating on the reason for being, on the essence and purpose of the whimsical twists and turns of each continent. With this approach, not only do we not know what the world is like, but we are also spending all our energies on useless investigations about anything.

We realized the error of investigating the world rationally, through pure reason, and began to investigate it with our eyes, through empirical procedures. We investigate reality through scientific experimentation, and we call natural laws the patterns that we can discover about how the world works. Since such patterns are independent of a subject's perspective, we say that they are objective. Thus, when we put observation before reason, we begin to investigate what we want to discover. Instead of daydreaming, we went out into the world, circumvented the continents and wrote down what we observed, and we only used reason to know how to structure our investigations, not to dispense with the need for boats. This stance provided us with useful maps, which serve to guide any navigator, instead of just thick books with metaphysical speculations about the transcendent essence of fine sand. Once the empirical observation is over, all metaphysics can do is affirm that there is a world to which the map corresponds.

Since the purpose of science is to know the world, and not to understand the whys of its supposed creator, we had to readjust our metaphysical concep-tion of the world, reducing it to what we had before us and that was subject to investigation. Our knowledge then became the objective description of the facts — rather than an attempt to explain them as the result of the subjectivity of a higher being. From then on, we gave science the role of investigating the facts, of exploring the world, and metaphysics was left with only the role of conceptualizing the world based on those facts that we observed, adjusting one to the other to allow an increasingly precise and coherent knowledge. We began to use reason not to understand or explain the world, but to make knowledge possible, to justify the validity of science as objective knowledge.

As can be seen, today the field of metaphysics is much more modest and seeks only to understand what reality is and how our relationship with it occurs. It seeks to explain how it is possible to understand the world objectively, not from the subjective perspective of the "absolute being", but from the subjective perspective of man, which is contained in the natural reality itself, and not above it. Thus, what we now call metaphysics is not the attempt to investigate what exists "beyond" physics, but beyond immediate *experience*. It seeks to distinguish what exists in itself - and that would exist even if we didn't exist - from what exists only in our minds. With this approach, we are no longer trying to justify the world, but knowledge. Instead of distinguishing between being and essence, between inside and outside of physics, we began to distinguish between subjective and objective, between inside and outside of man. We abandoned the idea that there would be an ineffable "transcendental essence", as we realized that this essence was just our subjectivity projected into the outside world.

This naturalization movement has profound implications for how we think about the world and the place of man in existence - and, since this change of perspective is relatively recent, we still carry many metaphysical prejudices inherited from traditional essentially metaphysics. The relationship between nihilism and metaphysics, in this case, would be precisely the attempt to understand the implications of reducing man to the natural. Existential nihilism denies that there is any sense in seeking a subjective meaning in the objective world, outside of man. In other words, the investigation of natural reality can never involve subjective issues, since we cannot investigate them through the observation of natural facts.

To take these subjective questions forward, investigating, for example, the "reason for being of man", we will need to naturalize that question, that is, approach it within the context of a natural world governed by impersonal physical laws. The problem is that, by naturalizing subjectivity, the issue is as unreasonable as seeking a physical basis for Christmas to take place in December. Understanding our subjectivity as the result of a natural process renders most of the questions we raise about the world itself illegitimate. Thus, when the scope of metaphysical reflection is tied to science, experimentation, and natural facts, the result is that metaphysical investigations that do not relate to what was observed in the natural world are no longer admissible. To state that man cannot seek for himself a meaning that is not based on natural facts is, of course, equivalent to destroying the idea of meaning at the root - with investigations about the meaning of life being restricted to natural facts, such as the survival of the species and genetic perpetuation, for example.

As can be seen, nihilism plays the uncomfortable role of "executioner of senseless investigations". It's not really an ideology, an approach with any "positive" objective, but an attitude of analytical and rectifying reflection. Nihilism does not seek to explain or guide man, but to place him impartially within what is known through science. From this point of view, since the end of traditional metaphysics is equivalent to a radical break with theology, we can say that nihilism plays the role of a gravedigger of meaning: it seeks to bury all the issues raised based on the assumption that there would be a "reason" for everything that exists. The beyond disappears, leaving only the here.

In this approach, what we call *the emptiness of existence* would be precisely the vacuum created by this drastic reduction of our metaphysical conception of the world. We thought that what existed within us, our subjectivity, also existed outside of us, reflecting the "ultimate principles" of reality, something like a "spirit of the world". Now, reducing the world to physics, to natural phenomena, that essence has become equivalent to physical laws — something that we thought was just a small portion of reality. When we began to see the world as something natural and objective, we also became something natural and objective, and this greatly disappointed us - it being the role of nihilism to keep man disappointed until he decides to abandon his existential childishness.

Understanding that physical laws are, so to speak, the "essence" of reality, the most interesting observation to be made is the following. Is the existence of man a physical law? No. Is there anything in the natural world that makes man's existence as necessary as gravity? No. It follows that we are not part of the natural world as men, but as matter. Since there are no subjective natural laws, our subjectivity has no essence. Rather than necessary, man's existence is contingent: we are an accident. The naturalization of reality imploded subjectivity, and man was reduced to nothing.

✳ ✳ ✳

Having made these observations, we see that nihilism places us in a rather strange situation, as if we were visitors to the world, temporary guests of matter - and that is exactly the case. We are a natural phenomenon, and our idea here is to completely review ourselves as such, clearing our understanding of reality.

Up to this point, we have been busy explaining that the emptiness of existence stems from recognizing the non-human character of the world itself. From now on, we will dedicate ourselves to outlining more clearly what this non-human world would be, distinguishing it from our subjective universe. Our first observation will be about the search for knowledge. This misses one point from the subject, but it's important. Then we will begin to outline the distinction between objective and subjective in detail, and we will give some examples of the "application" of nihilism as an analytical procedure.

There's no doubt that understanding the world has always been our greatest philosophical ambition. However, except for curiosity, in the process of understanding it there is no safe starting point, and that has always bothered us. Many solutions were proposed to the problem of uncertainty in our knowledge, but all of them proved inconclusive — even today we are not sure. What hardly occurs to us, however, is to question the point of arrival: the certainties. If we don't have any safe starting point, why do we think it's safe to say that certainty is the point of arrival? Now, certainties are the objective of those who seek security, not knowledge. The problem of uncertainty arises simply from our anguish - it is not something to be solved through research, but through painkillers.

It should be noted, then, that it makes no sense to seek certainties in the world, since the very concept of certainty was invented by ourselves - and not with the purpose of knowing the world better, but of feeling more secure. We repudiate certainties because we want to understand the world, not justify our anxiolytic roundabouts. The belief in the need for certainties distorts our understanding because, upon accepting the notion of certainty, we begin to investigate physical reality in search of those same certainties, in an obviously circular process. This goal of achieving "absolute truths" was never demonstrated as valid, only supposed as desirable by medieval philosophers inspired by mathematics.

In these circumstances, if we cannot assume that we must seek certainty, we no longer have a starting point or an arrival point, which is great. Freed from these prejudices, we can begin to build an unbiased vision that is not committed to "peace in the soul" as a criterion of truth.

Just now, leaving that circle, abandoning all expectations, our starting point becomes to observe what is before us. We open our eyes, we see that there is a world, and that we are in it — nothing more. This is the most basic and neutral stance we can adopt. Starting from complicated and confusing positions makes everything complex and confusing, so we start from our existence in the world, which is the most elementary and immediate thing to which we have access. Of course, we don't have "faith" in that, we don't think it's an indisputable truth. Maybe we're wrong to think that we exist. Maybe existing is an illusion. There are *infinitely many* theoretical ones, but we also want our reasons for doubt to be based on facts, not on innocuous metaphysical assumptions.

Since we have no reasonable reason to doubt our existence, we don't. We think we exist because we're here, and that's all. This is not an issue that we can solve through metaphysical meditations—we have no way of investigating it. What leads us to accept the existence of the world as a fact is the fact that we have it before us. That's all we can say. We know that existing is absurd, but it's an absurd fact, not just speculation.

In this way, existing is not a metaphysical belief: it is simply about opening our eyes and seeing ourselves happen in this something that we call the world. Our stance would be metaphysical only if we opened our eyes believing that we should seek certainties or ultimate reasons. Instead, we just open them, and that's what we see. If existing is an illusion, it is the illusion that we are faced with, and we want to know it, whatever it may be. This basic uncertainty about existence is something that we simply have to accept, otherwise we will addict our investigation right from the start, starting to walk in circles like theologians.

∗ ∗ ∗

Having clarified that point, let us now turn to the distinction between objective and subjective. For our purposes, we will define objective reality as that which exists by itself unconditionally. The activity of this reality, in this case, would be what we call phenomena, that is, what happens. If existence, for example, were a clock, objective reality would be its cogs, its hands, its structure as a whole. The movement of these gears would be the phenomena. But from a nihilistic perspective, this would all be meaningless, that is, the hours would not exist - these pointers would turn for no reason and point to nothing.

To understand more clearly, let's use another example closer to our daily lives: a party. We pass by a place and see that any festive event is being held there. The next day, we stopped by the same place, but found no trace of the event. The place exists. People exist. Not the party: it was just happening. That's the idea. Now it is enough to extend the time involved to realize that people don't exist either: they all have a duration, that is, they are also happening. The more we advance in this reasoning, the more the implications become extreme, until we realize that eventually everything will be lost in this eternal recycling - and the only thing that remains is the way in which it all happens, that is, physics, the matter from which all this is made.

So far, everything is quite clear: the world exists, and we happen through it. However, now, to demonstrate why the humanization of reality is an error, and also to explain how this error occurs, we need to distinguish between objective and subjective reality, between the world itself and our awareness of that world. We have some difficulty in understanding this distinction through intuition, but we can explain it, at least preliminary, as follows: what exists independently of us, and that will continue to exist even after we are dead, is objective reality, the being itself. On the other hand, what exists only within our minds is subjective reality. This subjective world is created by ourselves, something that, after our death, will cease to exist without leaving any trace.

Let's continue the matter inside. We are machines, and our consciousness is part of a reality recognition system that has the function of guiding our bodies. The reality that we have before our eyes is a subjective mental construction, a partial representation of objective reality. Sounds, smells, colors: all of this is constructed by our brains from what they capture through a sensory apparatus. There's no *me* behind all this. We are our brain. And around that brain there is a body that allows you to walk around the world, and connected to it are sensory organs that allow you to perceive the world.

Each species has a different type of brain, and each type interprets reality in a particular way - and there are, of course, species that have no brain at all. As humans, we have a brain with five senses, and also the capacity for abstract reflection. It is through this, and that alone, that we can know what reality is. It should also be noted that our reason, although magnificently versatile, has no access to external reality — which is why pure reason is as useless for investigating reality as eyes closed for seeing it.

Our consciousness of the world is, then, a representation of the world, a particular point of view of a brain of a particular organism. Our perception of the world is not the world itself: it's just the way our brain presents that world to us. This reality, therefore, instead of being immediate, is immediate: it is for the world as a road map is for the roads. It is an approximate reproduction, a more or less equivalent translation, not a direct transposition.

Of course, our bodies, our brains, our mental processes exist and happen objectively. However, the world that presents itself before us through consciousness, through the senses, is a merely *subjective* reality that depends on us to exist. That's why it varies from subject to subject. What we see as a blue color, another individual may see as a green color. What smells rotten to us presumably smells wonderful to vultures. There are infinite ways of interpreting the same sensory information, and that depends on how our brain works, on how it is programmed to translate the information it receives through the senses. Thus, reality itself is not accessible to us: we can only apprehend it indirectly, in the form of representation.

This gives us a reasonable idea of what we mean by stating that in our heads there is only one representation of reality, a limited construction based on information that does not exhaust everything that exists. Our senses are programmed to capture just a specific range of information. Our eyes capture a specific spectrum of electromagnetic waves, representing them as colors. Our ears pick up a specific spectrum of sound vibrations, representing them as sounds, and so on. Thus, at first, nothing would prevent us from tasting with our eyes or from smelling with our ears - it would be enough if our brains were designed to translate reality in that way.

Then, based on physical material processes, our brain creates a kind of "virtual reality" that only exists within our minds, just as a television creates images from electronic components. The activity of our brain circuits creates our consciousness and, within it, a subjective world. That is our way of existing. Our brain, through the senses, continuously receives information from the environment and, based on that information, it creates a subjective representation of objective reality.

Thus, instead of accessing reality directly, our brain reads the raw data that arrives through the senses and presents to our consciousness a summary of its most relevant aspects. That's what brains do, that's their function. Through the senses, they are informed about reality to know how to guide the bodies in which they are installed. Naturally, the better our capacity to represent reality, the better our chances of surviving, of avoiding enemies, of finding food, sexual partners, and the like. Our capacity to reason is just a refinement within all of this, allowing us to distinguish subtleties. Such things, in turn, are designed as a function of genetic perpetuation. That's why we feel pleasure when having sex, why we feel pain when being assaulted, etc., but that matter will not occupy us at the moment.

So, we are real, but we don't see reality itself. Conscious life, however, is not an illusion. As machines, we are beings as material and objective as the world that surrounds us. We exist objectively, our consciousness is a real phenomenon. However, despite being real, our consciousness does not have immediate access to reality itself. This contact is mediated by the senses. As a result, we are limited to the subjective representation created by our brains, with our senses being the only point of contact with the outside world. This results in the impression that to exist is to be alive, even though life is just a rare species of chance.

As our contact with reality occurs through this partial perspective, created by ourselves, two problems arise. First, our representation of reality is committed not to science but to survival. Second, since being aware of all this is not biologically relevant, we do not distinguish between one thing and another, and the subjective seems to us to be something objective, as if our consciousness, our mental representation of the world, were the world itself, something that leads us to humanize what we observe, transposing our representation of reality, which is inner, to the outside world.

It seems to us, for example, that colors exist by themselves. Colors seem to us to be an intrinsic property of the objects we observe. They seem to be something external, independent of us. When we observe a red object, it seems beyond doubt that that color is in the object, and not in our heads. But all colors are created by our brain from the capture of electromagnetic waves. That's why we see colors in a world where there's no color at all. The fact is that there are no green or blue objects in and of themselves. It is our brain that creates colors in the process of transforming the light energy reflected by such objects into mental images. Seeing colors is just one way in which we represent reality, and they only exist because there is a brain that creates them. If we want proof of that, all we have to do is close our eyes.

Electromagnetic waves, on the other hand, are objective, since their existence is unconditional. They exist by themselves, whether or not there is a brain to capture them and translate them into mental images. The same goes for things like love, joy, pleasure, pain, anguish, etc.: they are something that only exists in the biological context of our bodies.

Thus, everything that happens in our consciousness has its beginning and its end in the consciousness itself. Outside of consciousness, everything is unconsciousness; outside of life, everything is dead. Naturally, since we are living beings, we have the impression that life has an "intrinsic value", but this is as illusory as thinking that atoms have feelings.

* * *

As we define, objective reality is that which exists by itself unconditionally. However, since our subjective existence, the content of our consciousness, is purely conditional, nihilism, when applied to ourselves as subjective beings, reduces us to nothing. Not only colors, but our entire subjective universe is now viewed as a "fiction", as a virtual reality created by the subject. From this perspective, when we say that "everything is nothing", by this we mean that our subjective view of existence is conditional. We mean that our consciousness happens inside our brains as a result of a material process, so that objective reality is not in the consciousness itself, but in the neural activity, in the material brain that creates that consciousness. If we blow our brains, only our awareness of the world will disappear: the world will continue to exist.

Because the world itself does not have any of the characteristics of human subjectivity and, at the same time, that we are beings that exist enclosed in a virtual world created by themselves, we can say that our subjectivity is similar to a kind of psychotic outbreak of matter.

Once the distinction between objective and subjective has been made, nihilism begins to be situated more clearly in our minds, allowing us to relativize our anthropocentrism. Thus, when stating that everything is nothing, that existence is empty, we refer to the absence of meaning inherent to that objective existence - because meanings, intentions, and objectives are something that only makes sense in the context of our biological machines. We should not, therefore, understand nihilism as a "denial of reality" or as an "existential pessimism". We must understand it as the view according to which objective reality is something that just exists and is free from any subjective traits. The subjective, on the other hand, must be understood as something that exists only inside our heads. Thus, objectively, the being exists, and nothing else. But what about what happens? What happens, happens, and nothing more. Whether it happens inside or outside of our heads, it doesn't matter.

This justifies the statement that, outside our subjective universe, nothing has meaning, everything lacks meaning, since such things are created by the subject himself. That's why the problem of the "meaning of existence" has no solution, since it's not even a problem, just a fact.

* * *

At first, it's not very clear what it's for to understand all this. Nihilism, as a theoretical stance, has no trace of practical utility. However, intellectually, it is a very interesting analytical tool, provided that it is used in moderate quantities. An *overdose* of relativism will only make us anxious that we are not sure of anything and that we have rejected every reference point from which we could deduce anything useful. We would be paralyzed by the simple fact that "maybe we could be wrong", that "we can't be sure of anything". But obviously, because such a stance consists of the certainty that we are not certain at all, it refutes itself, without offering us any promising perspective on how to come to know anything.

Radical skepticism is just an intelligent way of stating, in philosophical terms, that we are limited and stupid, in which the person who makes the statement places himself as an illustrative example of shooting himself in the foot. Apparently, this kind of skepticism is just anxiety disguised as philosophy. Sure, we could be wrong. However, if we are, we will correct the error as soon as we discover it: we are not interested in dreaming up terrible hypothetical errors, because that is just paranoia.

* * *

As a destructive agent, nihilism will not allow us grandiose discoveries, it will only clear the ground so that we can build a more coherent vision of reality. Thus, when applying it to any subject, we should expect nothing more than the annihilation of the object we are analyzing, that is, its reduction to nothing. Nihilism operates a kind of "sterilization of the being", eliminating all its subjective elements: it takes from the being all life, all movement, all meaning, all meaning, all meaning, that is, it dehumanizes it, mischaracterizes it to such an extent that it becomes indistinguishable from anything else. This allows us to have a raw view of what we analyze, seeing it stripped of anthropomorphisms, reduced to its raw objective existence, which is equivalent to saying *reduced* to nothing, that is, to nothing but itself.

Nihilism, as can be seen, seeks to remove us from the equation so that we can conceive something close to what reality would be objectively - the purpose of this is to prevent our knowledge from becoming a humanization of existence. Thus, by adopting a nihilistic perspective in relation to any subject, it is as if we were dehumanizing that issue, dissecting it. Once we have erased its subjective qualities, any distinction between one thing and another will cease to exist, regardless of the level at which we have established such distinctions — such as value, meaning, meaning, identity, etc. — and we will have to reconstruct our understanding of the subject from that very severe perspective. In the process, the delusions die, the facts remain.

As this idea is a bit abstract, let's think of a more palpable way of putting it. For example, *what is a man*? We can define it, *roughly speaking*, as a mammal with a bulky brain that walks in an upright position. This definition distinguishes man from all the rest, especially the rest of the animals. It gives the human being a distinctive character compared to existence. Therefore, from this subjective perspective, we have a definition from which we can affirm that man is something, that man exists. However, what would happen if we now adopted a nihilistic stance towards man? There would be a series of questions that would eventually deconstruct this whole notion, denying the distinction between man and other things. Let's look at something simple that illustrates this idea.

Humans are composed of approximately 70% of water. As long as that water is, say, in your brain as a component of the chemical reactions that keep you alive, or in any other part of your body, you will also be a man. So water is human insofar as it composes the biological system that plays this previously defined role. The same is true for the remaining 30%, which are proteins, fats, sugars, nucleic acids, etc. We know that man only remains alive under the condition that the matter that constitutes his body is permanently changed. Then at some point the water that was in your brain, and that allowed you to think that you needed to cut your nails, will be expelled from your body. What will water cease to be a man to be precisely what? Exactly what it was before it was ingested: nothing; just a collection of oxygen and hydrogen molecules, as it always was, as it never ceased to be.

Unless we think that atoms acquire some magical aura after absorption and lose it after excretion, we must admit that the subjective concept of *man*, which we ourselves invented, is something that creates a subjective and qualitative distinction between that *man*, which is a specific arrangement of matter, and other things, which are arrangements of matter arranged in a different way. Both things, in the end, are exactly the same thing: matter. All we did was classify, give names to the bits of atoms that seem important to us, and the distinctions we created with that are just conventions. This distinction that we see between man and non-man could never be objective because, for example, the water molecules in the river, in the rain, or in the brain are, objectively, of the same nature. Whatever the situations in which they find themselves, they do not exhibit any discernible difference in their physical behavior.

If this applies not only to water, but also to everything that makes up man, and if man is composed of the same matter that constitutes the rest of the universe, where exactly could we find an objective basis for the distinction between man and the world? Between the water in your blood and the one in the faucet? Between the oxygen in your blood and that in the atmosphere? We can't — or the rivers would already be humanized by our urine filled with essences and greater realities. *All we do is create conventional subjective definitions, in which what we take into consideration is the practical utility of designating this specific arrangement of matter by the term man.*

Therefore, analyzing man from a nihilistic perspective is equivalent to denying his objective existence - but only as a being endowed with a supposed "objective subjectivity". This does not mean that we do not exist, that we are not here, but that it cannot be said that man exists objectively, in the same sense in which water exists. This is because, unlike colors, sounds, feelings, water is not created by our representation of reality. Of course, water arises due to chemical reactions. We know that its elements can be decomposed, but this is all independent of a subject's perspective. If we broke down water using electricity, electrolysis wouldn't occur in our brains.

Thus, when we accept that man is composed of the same matter that makes up the rest of the universe, and that it behaves in the same way, whether or not it is in his body, this implies rejecting the distinction between man and non-man. From this point of view, if a man were seated on a chair, his body and the chair could not be viewed as distinct, objectively different things. Everything is now seen as an indistinct soup of atoms. The distinction between man and chair only emerges after outlining subjective classification criteria, which are completely arbitrary. Not that such criteria are useless, as they are not. The fact that something is subjective is not an objection to its significance, just a condition of existence: the condition of existing as a subjective phenomenon, as the perspective of a subject, not as an "essence of being". In no sense could this be used as a justification to remove the value of the chair or of man, since things such as value, meaning, meaning only exist within the subjective sphere, never in the objective world.

Faced with this, someone could say: *how can it be said that, when looking at this object, there is no person seeing this object!* Of course, for all intents and purposes, there is a person seeing that object. But the person, as a mechanical biological system, as well as its remarkable capacity to convert light energy into mental images, is a phenomenon, and as such will cease to exist - or, better to say, to happen - as soon as the material chain that gave rise to the phenomenon ceases, resulting in a wake. With the death of the individual, that subjective universe in which there was a person who saw objects ceases to exist - and when a subjective universe disappears, there are no traces left of it, just as there are no traces of movies left when a television is turned off.

✷ ✷ ✷

It can be said that, in the example above, we "niillify" man, that is, we deconstruct him, emptying him of any subjective qualities. When we suppress the subjective aspect of man, we begin to see ourselves as a fact, as something indistinct, that cannot be separated from the rest of reality. We are then reduced to a bunch of atoms—and we see that our own thinking is nothing more than the activity of those atoms. Through this intellectual process, we were able to glimpse what a man is in himself, in an objective sense. If we were to ask the same question — what is man? —, we would answer, now, *man is nothing*. Since the reduction to nothing is an intellectual process, not something practical, a bullet was not needed to carry out this action - although it serves to illustrate that after death nothing will remain of our subjectivity.

The fundamental utility of analyzing something from a nihilistic perspective, as can be seen, is to verify its consistency, that is, its relationship with reality, its life - and, to test the vitality of an idea, nothing more reliable than destroying it and then verifying whether it has the strength to be reborn from its own ashes.

Even though we deconstructed the man in the example above, this idea has not ceased to have life, because we can completely reconstruct it from subjective reality, and it doesn't bother us at all that we have to do it ourselves, without any external authority. Since we are men, this is a concept that we simply make a point of cultivating, and it is completely contained in the human sphere of reality.

It is also important to remember that this deconstruction did not cause us distress just because, from the beginning, we didn't have any metaphysical fantasies about man being "special" or "something beyond" matter. Thus, even though it was unconstructed on a conceptual level, our existence was still a fact. And the same could be said of colors: even though we know that colors are just a subjective fiction, we continue to cultivate this concept, since it is useful for decorating the walls of our homes. If colors do not lose their value because they do not have a "transcendental essence", why would man lose?

We judge such observations to be obvious because we know that we are just a specific model of biological machine to which we give the name man. If the human species did not exist, the concept of man would not exist either - our essence would not continue to exist in a hidden corner of the cosmos. Thus, nihilists can deconstruct the concept of man as much as they want. That just erases a definition, but it doesn't change the fact that we're machines that like to name things. Nihilism only prevents us from losing sight of the fact that, ultimately, it's just grammar that distinguishes us from the rest of existence.

✶ ✶ ✶

The man, as we see, survived the criticism. However, if we reduce to nothing a concept that has no reality behind it, there will be no way to reconstruct it. When, after undergoing such a process of criticism, the concept is unable to rise again, this indicates that it was already becoming a ghost, which had ceased to correspond to an explicitly human reality and took refuge in nothingness in the form of an impersonal metaphysical dogma, supported only by tradition or faith. So, for example, if we reduce morals to nothing, what will be left of reality in that concept? In other words, from what can we reconstitute it, bring it back to life? Just from ourselves, because there wouldn't be any other reference. So if we can't explain where we get our values from, they can't continue to be sustained. We cannot claim that they exist "by themselves" if we cannot demonstrate them as a natural fact - and if there is no beyond, we will only have to defend them as a subjective value, invented by us.

Suppose there had been a tribe that believed in two moral laws: that it is wrong to eat faeces and that it is wrong to eat lettuce. In an archaeological excavation, we found these two laws written on some artifact. In this situation, only the first law would be something intelligible to us, a moral value that could still be reconstructed as something related to the world. The other law would be seen as a meaningless superstition based on some fanciful assumption of these people regarding the disastrous nature of lettuce leaves. No sane person would think that we should stop eating lettuce, nor would it make sense to eat faeces to mock the values of this tribe. However, if we were to discover that the lettuce that this tribe cultivated was a variant that, due to some genetic mutation, became poisonous, then we would consider the prohibition it was defending perfectly reasonable.

In another example, reducing criminal laws and the Ten Commandments to nothing, only the former could be reconstructed with our own hands. We could reinvent criminal laws from scratch, because we know where they came from and what they are for. They are human moral values, and we know how to justify them: common interests and the police. This would obviously not apply to the Ten Commandments, since no one could demonstrate the reality of the metaphysical legislator who created them.

In this situation, all moral values that have ceased to have roots in reality, that have been converted into pure abstractions and outdated idealisms, die when they are demolished by nihilism, and that is because of the simple fact that there was no living reality to sustain them. These values, now without context, no longer defend us, do not represent us. They are not supported because there is no one to support them, and their death can only be delayed by appeals to authority.

As can be seen, the process of nihilistic criticism would be equivalent to gathering all the paper money we have and all the gold that supports its value. Destroy all paper money banknotes and then, verifying the amount of gold we have, reissue the banknotes, knowing that, now, there is a reality supporting their value. Dogmas, that is, ideas without value or content, harm our understanding of reality just as bottomless checks harm the economy. *This analogy makes it clear that nihilism, far from representing a drastic measure, is nothing more than a procedure for monitoring reality, emphasizing not the destruction but the transparency of our knowledge.* Thus, those who are confident that their ideas have a solid foundation will have nothing to fear. However, those who issue empty, fraudulent judgments will have no way to protect them.

* * *

Morals are a very controversial subject, but it is evident that we ourselves invent all moral notions. We filled them with ideas, then emptied them with criticisms, and so we walked. A set of moral notions plays the role of guiding our behavior in life in society. As we are beings in constant change, the creations that originally appeared as our reflection should accompany us in these changes, but it is quite common to end up crystallized in notions that are apparently sufficient in themselves. In other words, they lose their meaning, their origin, their function, and now they say nothing, nothing more than the echo of a forgotten voice. However, instead of dying, it is common for them to remain alive anonymously according to tradition and authority. It is as if a subjective element had "caught the tangent" and transposed subjectivity itself, placing itself now in the objective sphere that we, mere mortals, cannot reach. They become angel values. This, of course, is impossible, but that is how the absolute authority of certain values is established, at least in our heads. An excellent example of this is the cult of ancestors - because, obviously, if such values were justifiable, it would not be necessary to defend them using the history of the dead.

What do we have here? Incomprehensible values, which point nowhere, and whose foundations, instead of being something, are nothing. In the afterlife, they are everything. In here, they're nothing. They are reasons whose reason no one understands, but even so following them is "absolutely necessary" - for reasons that no one knows how to explain. If we were to admit that all this is nothing more than blind and irrational inertia, that's fine. However, when we try to rationally justify the preservation of these dead theorists, we have metaphysics again trying to graft reason onto what has no reason. It's things like that that nihilism destroys, and we don't see how that could be a bad thing.

Despite establishing seemingly safe references that free us from relativism and uncertainty, metaphysical morality only uses a circular device to shut up the matter and allow us to move on with our lives as if the issue were resolved. This metaphysical morality, in large part, is concerned with the solution of imaginary problems, such as the sex of angels or the navel of Adam. However, when it deals with solving real problems, the result can be - and often is - harmful, because it locks our understanding of reality within dogmas and throws away the key. Everything remains explained by an untouchable and incomprehensible reason, which we must obey without hesitation. The same wisdom that, in other matters, is normal, becomes a crime when directed at these issues. This is how a subject becomes "profound", and the more profound the more palpable its incoherence is.

What could be more ridiculous than to subordinate our entire understanding of reality to the belief in absolute values and concepts that everyone respects, but no one knows how to explain, and that inhabit a reality in which we are not? And what could be more inconsequential than considering such a submissive stance as something reasonable? We simply magically removed from the top hat a fantastic explanation for something that often doesn't even exist. Then we tried to justify this leap of faith by calling it a "mystery", the "inner meaning of things", the "moral order of the world", and the like. We are guided by this as if it were an ultimate reality, something that, in the end, is equivalent to walking at random, despising the ground itself.

Allowing metaphysics to infiltrate morals may seem like harmless childishness, allowing it to proclaim its irrelevant moral imperatives with foolish solemnity, but it is noticeable how much it hinders a clear understanding of the values that effectively guide us as human beings. This metaphysical atmosphere causes us to begin to see everything from a constantly false perspective, and since we are forbidden to question that perspective, we increasingly lose contact with reality. In a short time, we lost the capacity to make moral judgments in the first person, because we gave metaphysics the role of dreaming them for us, receiving in return a morality that was lost from the facts. It's true that nihilism is a cold and uncomfortable presence, but we never get anywhere trying to overcome it with metaphysical nonsense - if that doesn't result in a delusional transcendental dogma, it will at best be a table of commandments that force us to be even more incoherent.

Metaphysics is not even justified as a preventive measure against the supposedly "pernicious" implications of nihilism, because nothing cannot be put into practice. Nihilism destroys only delusions, and that is only intellectually. There are no direct practical implications. To clarify this point, let's think this way: has anyone ever heard of a holocaust committed in the name of uncertainty? Of martyrs who gave their lives out of disbelief? Now, nobody kills in the name of doubt, nobody sacrifices themselves for reality. All the wars we fight are based on some certainty, and all the certainties are metaphysical beliefs to justify our absurdities. Only convictions are dangerous. For this very reason, nihilism does not pose any danger. Those who say otherwise are the ones who are trying to protect their delusions from the most basic facts. Such individuals would never fear nihilism if their beliefs were justifiable facts - after all, no one tries to protect the seriousness of nihilism, fearing the disintegration of the universe; no one invokes universal imperatives to defend that it is wrong to have blood transfusions between incompatible types; no one needs to have faith to affirm that it is wrong to shout in libraries. No healthy morality needs to be defended by metaphysical anemia.

Many also claim that nihilism seeks to destroy the "social order", but that is another misconception. What nihilism seeks to destroy are our lies. However, if our social order is based on lies, of course it will be refuted by nihilism, but that is only an indirect consequence of being honest. Even so, that was never explicitly the objective. All we did was refute — and not target — what can't be supported. Furthermore, since nihilism is not intended to point any path, it can also never serve as a pretext for social militancy, since nihilists have no certainty, ideal, or truth to defend. Since nihilism is a negative stance, when we adopt a positive stance, embracing any cause, we stop being nihilists and become defenders of that cause.

The harmless nature of the nihilist stance will be even more clear if we are careful to observe that a practical nihilist would not be a mad person involved in the promotion of some social apocalypse, but a person in a coma, in a vegetative state. The idea of trying to "live" the emptiness of existence is similar to a mental disorder, since this emptiness can only be thought of. Nihilism, at most, can make us feel distressed by the death of our delusions, but it doesn't mean anything, except that we don't like to be wrong.

∗ ∗ ∗

The observations made so far served to give us a clearer idea of exactly what we are talking about when we affirm that something is "nothing", since, at first, the idea that nothing can actually exist and, consciously, deny its own existence seems contradictory. When we talk about things like "nothing", "emptiness", it's actually not in the same sense as "that which doesn't exist", of "non-being". Nor does this have anything to do with pessimism, that is, with distorting reality negatively just because we don't like it. The terms "nothing" and "emptiness" are used only to designate that which disappears when the being is stripped of that which is not objectively proper to it. The initial confusions disappear when we understand in what sense these terms are used.

Therefore, to say that existence is "empty in itself" does not mean that nothing exists in it, that it is the purest vacuum, but only that, removing from it all the qualities that relate only to our subjective world, we are not even left behind. All that is left over is that situation in which everything is indistinct, and thus it makes no sense to claim that this or that piece of matter is "special" because it constitutes a man full of life, because, from this perspective, matter constitutes a living man, a dead man, or the earth that once had the form of a man and that now feeds flowers in the garden is completely irrelevant to our purposes.

So when we talk about nihilism, this brings us back to that uniformly sterile reality, to the contrast between objective existence and subjective existence. Of course, it should be clear why nihilism can only be theoretical, never practical. The closest we can come to understanding existential nihilism is the apprehension of this emptiness as a condition of existence; that is, understanding that the same being that constitutes everything that we are and everything we think is the same that constitutes rocks, stars, cigarettes, walls, etc., and that the fact that we are thinking about it, of this may distress us, does not change anything, because this anguish is happening in our brains with the same need with which electrons turn on a lamp.

Whenever we cross the circle in which human subjectivity is circumscribed, we fall into that void of objective reality, in which we cannot even recognize ourselves. Because to conceive man objectively is, in essence, to imagine him as a portion of matter delimited by dotted lines. There are no colors here, there are no sounds, there are no sensations, there is no thought, there is no life, there is nothing: we have just another indistinct phenomenon in the tangle of the meaninglessness of existence.

We can try to conceive an image of existence from a perspective outside of life itself, but in general we haven't arrived at anything much more than a version of the world in which everything is composed of semitransparent clouds of atoms of different densities. A more reliable perspective may be the one we had when we weren't yet born, although it's difficult to conceive of that kind of thing. Perhaps just imagining the universe without any form of life having arisen in it is the easiest way to conceive from the perspective of nihilism at first. Then we will only need to add life as something that appeared in this universe and that will probably disappear at some future time without leaving any trace.

Since the being does not include the adjectives that we love to give it, the function of nihilism is, let's just say, non-adherent: to prevent our understanding of reality from being polluted by our anthropocentrism. By reducing something to nothing, destruction occurs only in the subjective sphere of existence, reducing it to a "virtual reality" within the material world. From this perspective, we began to understand our consciousness as if they were "movies playing inside our brains", not as existence itself. It is clear that such an understanding does not change anything in practice, it only helps us to discern the facts more clearly.

* * *

Since we cannot change the basic behavior of the reality in which we are, our only option is to understand it—and, that being the case, taking refuge from nihilism is nothing more than to entrench ourselves in laughable convictions. If we honestly ask ourselves why nihilism bothers us so much, we will see that the reasons are never more than personal pettiness and prejudices learned in childhood. It's already a big deal that we can understand how the world works: to deny it because it doesn't work up to our personal expectations is simply to condemn ourselves to ignorance.

Thus, after dismantling our numerous pretexts for "doubt", we generally realize that we have a pretty good idea of how things are, and that in fact there is no longer any grandiose mystery in existence - we have already answered the big question. We know what life is and how it works. We know what our planet is and how it formed. We know what the sun is and why it rises. Today we know everything that philosophers have ever wanted to know, or almost everything. The world itself is something physical and impersonal. In human terms, reality is the most complete void, and it's great that we know that.

As can be supposed, existential nihilism adopts this "emptiness" as a starting point and, since there is nothing to be done about it, also as a point of arrival. It's the kind of thing that we know there's no escape from, although we can't live very well with the awareness of it either. Be that as it may, we must at least learn to deal with the facts, pleasant or not, because the other option is to be delusional. Nihilism, of course, has no great practical importance. However, as long as we insist on thinking that there is something very spectacular to be found "behind" the world, nihilism will continue to be necessary to show us that this is just a fantasy.

Even though nihilism is perfectly defensible in intellectual terms, it doesn't make much sense to try to "live" because that is a type of perspective that simply stifles us. The awareness of the nullity of life comes to us like a paralyzing vertigo - and the biological constitution of man itself does not favor this type of approach to reality. Since ignorance is no impediment, mussels go through existence without philosophically understanding their condition, and it would be difficult to imagine reasons why that understanding would bring them any benefit. And the same applies to most men: it doesn't even occur to them that their navels are not the center of the universe. If you want to remain ignorant, that's fine. We know how to recognize that it does not concern us how everyone governs their lives. But we chose to approach it from an enlightened perspective, which takes into account the way in which reality works.

So if we're asked how nihilists live, what could we answer? Now, they live as they please, but with their eyes open. Nihilists emphasize objectivity, but that doesn't mean that they despise subjectivity. They just have the prudence to relativize it enough to realize that it's not all that exists. In any case, we are subjective beings, and we can only live as such. We just have to keep in mind that our feet step on an objective reality, which is what really determines our lives. From this point of view, if life is a dream, nihilism would just be an attempt to make it a lucid dream.

✶ ✶ ✶

From what has been said, although there is no hope as to the possibility of envisioning a practical and constructive sphere in nihilism — in addition to its theoretical utility as a screwdriver of reality — this does not lead us to the conclusion that being a nihilist paralyzes practical life, since both things are located in completely different spheres. The accusation of hypocrisy commonly launched against the nihilist, in which it is supposed that true honor would consist of blowing one's brains out in the name of coherence, is quite superficial - and the very truth of this statement can be found in the fact that the shooting would not produce honor, but merely a mess that some unfortunate person would have to clean up. One cannot put as a theoretical objection the practical fact that nihilists are still alive despite considering that life, like everything else, is equivalent to nothing, since suicide is not an argument, just as blood is not honor. Faced with an objection of this nature, we can only suppose that individuals of this kind, for some devious reason, think of themselves as a "company", an "investment" of the being: as if the atoms that make up their bodies were shares whose value fluctuates on the stock exchange of existence depending on how much they believe it is worth. Apparently, refusing this idea is just a sign of common sense. Beliefs don't change facts.

In and of itself, nihilism is worthless. Its only possible value is relative, and consists in the fact that this perspective allows us to identify predictably disastrous delusions. The usefulness of this lucidity can be illustrated by the difference between a drunk man and a sober man. In this sense, its nature is similar to that of atheism, which also has a negative character in the face of an illusion that is clearly harmful to our understanding of reality. Explicit atheistic disbelief could, in this sense, be understood as a particular case of nihilism.

Thus, there is no reason to be "proud" of being nihilists, other than because it is an indication of wisdom. An enlightened nihilist, guaranteed to be stepping on solid ground from the bottom of the well, is aware that his values, objectives, and himself are things that do not actually exist, but only condition-ally, and finds no problem in suspending any effort to place himself in the "essence" of the objective world. Even because, by trying to do this, we would be doing nothing more than creating an imaginary world in which atoms smile when they see us - or worse.

APPENDAGE

There is another way of coming into contact with nihilism, although it is not the most pleasant. It's not about trying to understand the emptiness of existence rationally, through reflection, but about feeling that emptiness affectively. The very fact that there is such an unexpected point of contact between a purely theoretical view and a universally encompassing facet of human subjectivity makes the issue, if not more interesting, at least more worthy of consideration.

It is the situation in which the everyday vision of life, immersed in fantasies and closed in on itself, is shattered by the confrontation with a disconcerting situation, causing the world to be reduced to something poor and empty. We are talking about *grief*, that is, the natural reaction of every human being to the loss of something affectively important, such as a loved one, a romantic relationship, close friends, including ideals, or anything else with which one had a close emotional bond.

Obviously, we are not referring to the ritual of wearing black clothes or to minutes of silence, nor to hysterical moans or to rivers of tears, but to what occurs subjectively in the individual's worldview, to the state of mind brought about by the loss. Common symptoms of grief are sadness, depression, despondency, lack of interest in the outside world and, what is especially interesting in our case, a penetrating lucidity. This state in general can be described as the feeling that everything "loses its meaning" or that "nothing has value". In no other situation is the meaning of the term "in vain" better understood.

When we look for something that, in practical terms, corresponds to nihilism, we see that grief is a strong candidate. This is because the impression one has is that the bereaved individual becomes temporarily nihilistic by a kind of "emotional emergency". In emergencies where our physical integrity is at stake, the body's automatic reaction is to trigger the fight or flight command. Likewise, when the integrity of our psychological world is at stake, we experience grief as a stop-and-think reaction, as if the brain, by "reducing our subjectivity to nothing", was physiologically preparing us for a cold and calculated review of reality.

Since, in this case, the individual is not only daydreaming about the emptiness of existence, but feeling it intimately, is the practical experience seriously hampered by anguish and depression, making life seem completely meaningless - and isn't that, in the end, just the case? Isn't it strange that most individuals have to go to such an extreme to learn that kind of truth? Because every time we try to find "reasons" that justify or give meaning to life, we always come to the conclusion that there are none. As there is no way out, no one insists too much on this point. Sooner or later, we recognize the null nature of this type of undertaking and, without protest, we limit ourselves to letting ourselves be guided by will, employing reason as an accessory that is at your service.

The problem is that, when transposed into practice, nihilism has the aspect of a mental illness, of something that paralyzes us, and has even been characterized by psychiatry as a form of delusion in which the subject denies the existence of reality, in whole or in part. The idea that the everyday reality that surrounds us is worthless, that it doesn't even exist objectively, is perfectly logical and justifiable. However, when nihilism contaminates our affective world, it forces us to admit that we ourselves are nothing, it makes us feel that nothing — and when both things coincide, they converge on an incredibly sound logic. The only way out seems to be practical suicide that will solve a theoretical problem.

Of course, most people are not so dominated by rationality as to commit suicide motivated by syllogisms. However, we have to admit that feeling empty is something quite disturbing, especially when we have the full understanding that this is not a delusion, but a state of mind in which we can clearly grasp one of the most basic truths to which we have access. Only if we were not content to merely apprehend this nothingness intellectually, but also wanted to orchestrate our entire practical life based on it, living like paralytic mummies, then we would have become perfectly delusional beings. This is physically impossible, and rightly constitutes a mental disorder.

Thus, not being able to act according to this truth, the most reasonable escape would be to admit that understanding reality and living in it are things governed by different rules. Although, in essence, what is done in both cases does not differ much: in one case we will be fantasizing in a private world and, in the other, in a public world. Both solutions arise in self-defense, but only one of them does not cause us to lose contact with the reality that surrounds us, that is, with society.

* * *

Everyone fantasizes about the world to be able to endure it, including nihilists. We flee from the void to be able to live, but we must bear in mind that the abyss does not cease to exist just because we look away and the vertigo passes. In any case, intellectually, this fact does not bother us, because there is a big difference between knowing that there is an abyss and being in that abyss, just as it is different just knowing that lions are dangerous and being face to face with one. Therefore, we only need to look for ways to divert the affective eye from the nihilistic perspective, because our logical view, as long as it remains sane, will never be able to do so - since that would be tantamount to denying reality. Not that this isn't done, but it's really regrettable to find the door in the face of truth in the only place where we can receive it.

From this perspective, grief could be understood as a kind of *psychological nihilism*, in which we apprehend the emptiness of existence not directly, through reflection, but indirectly, through affectivity. The depressive state provides us with a dry and direct intuition about objective reality, reducing the subjective to nothing - and we can see that this is equivalent to a procedure for monitoring the reality of our psychological world carried out involuntarily by the brain itself. In these convulsive situations, we are forced to face reality naked and raw, and even the most optimistic individuals are kidnapped by lucidity. While the individual is bereaved, they lose the capacity to deceive themselves. That's why nothing we say will be able to console him; that's why religious people also cry at wakes, something that doesn't make much sense at first. The fact is that, upon seeing their loved one being embraced by worms, every religious person realizes that their belief in spirits and reincarnations is, in the end, a joke that tries to deny the obvious. Your beliefs will only come back to comfort you once you've overcome the loss.

✳ ✳ ✳

There are only two situations in which we can be impartial: when our interests are not involved, and when our interest is the truth itself—that is, when our partiality, for personal reasons, coincides with impartiality. Within that, depression, in and of itself, has nothing relevant. What's interesting is just the fact that, in depressive phases, we kind of "turn our backs" on life, starting to see reality with disinterest. Thus, the perspective of depression, because it is dispassionate, allows us to be unbiased, representing a rare opportunity to see things as they really are.

This explains why, during depressive phases, nihilism seems to us to be a viscerally coherent vision, with which we can identify ourselves both in intellectual and affective terms. On the other hand, when we are in a normal phase, pursuing our everyday dreams, that same perspective seems somewhat distant from our way of feeling reality, from our experience - even though, intellectually, nihilism continues to have the same vitality. Considering that everyday tasks make us superficial and that depression, as a rule, makes us realistic, it seems quite logical that this should be the case. We know that existence has always been, will always be empty. Whether this distresses us depends not on philosophy, but on our affective disposition, on our brain chemistry — ultimately, on whether or not we are able to deal with reality.

With these details in mind, we can understand more clearly why nihilists are often thought to be suicidal. This happens because our own vision of the world is so loaded with affective values that, if destroyed, even partially, it would lead us to grief, which is pain. And hardly any worldview would remain intact after undergoing a beautiful revision that would take into account a criterion as fundamental as the distinction between the subjective and objective spheres of reality. But, logically, every individual who calls themselves a nihilist has already overcome this phase of mental reorganization and, therefore, no longer feels threatened by the fact that everything is empty. However, if we place ourselves in the position of someone who affirms that nihilists are suicidal, we will have no difficulty understanding the reason why they think so. The idea of intentionally losing something for which we have deep affection sounds so absurd, so self-destructive, that it would be similar to the idea of killing our own friends just to learn how to deal with the loss of loved ones. In other words, a great sacrifice in the affective sphere that is in no way compensated by the gain in the intellectual sphere. More than natural, it is inevitable for any individual to protect themselves from an idea capable of causing damage of this magnitude to their affective life. Faced with such a threat, your profound regard for truth boils down to this maxim: may *the truth be* shattered!

* * *

So, for someone with a somewhat flowery vision of reality to see their remarkable garden wither, a confrontation with philosophical nihilism is enough, which, from this perspective, can no longer be considered something so harmless. Because it is possible that, through thought, when we understand our condition, we may enter into a state of mourning for the "death of reality", so to speak, since for us reality is our understanding of reality, and the destruction of the foundations of our worldview can be something quite difficult to manage, and it is common that there are episodes of anxiety and anguish in this indigestible process.

On an emotional level, when we begin to understand the world as a physical system, as something impersonal, it is as if by doing so we were "killing" reality. As an example, let's imagine the following situation: we were searching in a library and, by chance, we found a document with our name on it. As we read it, we discover that all our family members are actually not human beings: they are machines pre-programmed to live with us. They like us automatically, right from the start. Even your feelings are calculations of your central processors. That's what we read in the document. Well, even if such an understanding didn't change anything in practice, wouldn't knowing it be emotionally devastating? The feeling that everything was never more than a fantasy overwhelms us. Now it's enough to realize that this is not any fiction: they really are machines, and so are we. Everyone is. Life is a dream inside a machine. Faced with this, we were stunned, perplexed, and "mourning" is the best word we can think of to describe this feeling that something died, although we don't know very well what.

Whether the reason for this emotional state is the loss of a loved one or the destruction of our vision of the world, the central difficulty consists in adapting to a deeply painful loss, in going through a phase of transition lacking references, in which we must carry out a radical change in ourselves. In this transitory state, the way in which we think and view the world corresponds exactly to nihilism, in which everything loses its meaning and life is, as it were, "suspended in nothing", perfectly aware of itself and of its precarious condition. Subjective reality is repudiated for different reasons, but the same perspective is arrived at: the nihilistic abyss, the obvious.

Of course, facing objective reality requires a lot of courage, and most individuals are only capable of this in extreme situations, where lucidity is essential. In other situations, we live in a kind of state of torpor. That's not necessarily a bad thing. Subjective reality may cause us suffering, but running away from it will bring us no comfort. It will only make us perceive the truth even more harshly. As there is nothing behind our delusions, lucidity quickly becomes unbearable. The awareness of the indifference of reality comes to us as something corrosive, like a silence that mocks all our dreams.

There is, therefore, nowhere to flee: we must face our condition of existence in our element, subjectivity. It would be foolish to think that escaping from planet Earth and launching ourselves into the void of space would be a great relief from the earthly problems that afflict us. We would just be floating in nothing. This detachment may allow us to see things with some impartiality, but we cannot remain in that situation for long. Asphyxiated by boredom, overwhelmed by the awareness of the nullity of life, we soon return to our subjective bubble, certain that there is nothing very interesting outside of it.

* * *

It would also be useful to understand why there is so much suffering involved in such changes in our worldview. To our unhappiness, there is nothing special about this adaptation, although it is common to hear the contrary. The fact that such a process is painful, sometimes overwhelming, is a natural unhappiness to which we are all subject, both mentally and physically. Serious damage caused to a limb, for example, in addition to being extremely painful, also requires a long recovery time, as the injured tissues will have to be literally rebuilt by the body, cell by cell. Likewise, a drastic change in our worldview or in the circumstances in which we are used to living entails a physical change in our brains. Many important connections between neurons will have to be made and others undone in order for our nervous system to adapt and be able to deal with the new situation, and suffering is nothing more than an indication of how physiologically inconvenient this is, of the amount of resources needed to carry out such an "update".

Since during this adaptation process we find ourselves somewhat lost and disoriented, the resulting depression and lucidity can be seen as preventive measures so that we do not take action before our brain is familiar with the new situation, thus avoiding actions that are inadequate and possibly dangerous to our immediate well-being. It would be as if we had always been used to driving only cars, but in a twist of fate, we were placed in front of a vehicle that we have no preparation to fly, such as an airplane, for example. In this situation, our primary reaction would not be to step on the accelerator and expect everything to be as before, as we know that this would be suicide. Lucid, we delved into the instruction manual for a long time, pondered over all the relevant issues and, as soon as we felt prepared to take control of the vehicle, took action, returning to living normally. Undoubtedly, it is something that requires time, and in this, too, there is a great similarity with tissue damage.

* * *

Because, in the long run, nihilism is incompatible with maintaining life, it is quite common to hear that it is just a "provisional state", something to be "overcome". And that's correct. However, we shouldn't confuse overcoming practical nihilism with refuting theoretical nihilism—flirting with that optimistic relativism that seems like a compliment to dementia. The question is only what can be done despite existence being hollow, despite all nothingness, without running away from the question like cowards. And overcoming nihilism is nothing more than thinking of ourselves as the ultimate source of value and meaning of all things. Let's get used to dealing with such issues without going beyond the sphere of our own subjectivity.

In practice, we have to overcome nihilism because reality doesn't care about us—it will never sympathize with our misery. Whether we're right or wrong, we'll still need to keep our bellies full and our bodies warm, and that means that overcoming it is a biological issue, not a philosophical problem. If nihilism paralyzes us at first, it is only because, in large part, they are delusions that move us, and it is inevitable that we will be temporarily stunned when we realize this. However, going back to walking is not equivalent to overcoming nihilism, but rather to the acquisition of the capacity to better separate our knowledge from our practical needs, until both things work normally again, but more independently.

Thus, overcoming nihilism concerns its practical paralyzing effect that makes life morbid, not its logical incoherence; it concerns the fact that it is impossible to justify a subjective life through objective nothingness. And this, let's say it once and for all, is achieved through *madness,* the only way by which we can live rationally in an absurd world. However, we shouldn't expect anything too extraordinary from this, since life, in itself, is a completely crazy system. This "madness" is not the same as an unrestricted right to stupidity, it's not the same as losing your mind. The madness to which we refer is something that crosses life from end to end: our nature. In other words, it is something that we know very well. It's our little human fantasies that, despite all the nothingness, allow us to carry on with life, even if that doesn't make any sense.

II

ON REALITY AND KNOWLEDGE

MEN ARE DIFFERENTIATED
BY THE MISTAKES THEY BELIEVE IN

RELATIVISM

When we are driven to nihilism, we are hit hard in theory and, indirectly, in practice. This is because our theoretical view of the world also influences practice, although not in very fundamental aspects, which are almost exclusively biological in nature, thus escaping our control. It may be painful, but it's a way of clearing our eyes, of getting rid of intellectual rubbish. We become more lucid, more aware of our condition. However, in essence, our practical life doesn't change much, just our way of looking at it. The essential loss are the references that we thought were objective, external to us, but which were actually internal, subjective. In this regard, there is no hope — everything dies, everything vanishes, and we have two options: to forget what died in us, to adapt to the change, focusing the responsibility on ourselves, or to embrace the vocation of intellectual gravediggers. Assuming we have some common sense, we'll stick with the first one.

In that case, we have to live in a situation where there is no starting point, or arrival, outside of ourselves. Stripped of safe references to guide our lives, it doesn't take long for us to notice a shadow of relativism over our heads. However, since the main issue has already been resolved, that is, how do we know that running into nowhere and seeking answers is not a solution, but a meaningless escape, the situation in which we find ourselves is no different from that in which we find ourselves when we go to a restaurant and have to choose something to eat, based solely on our need for food and the dishes available. Even though it's not a very sophisticated example, it's pure relativism, and only someone out of their mind would revolt against the menu, adopting that sweaty stance of radical skepticism while doubting a growling belly. There is no need to fear the presence of such relativism in practical life, since it is nothing new and does not cause any problem worth considering. However, this kind of almost simplistic serenity in the face of uncertainty is not something that we can find very well distributed around the world.

Undoubtedly, everyone can exercise the right to have their own opinions without this being an affront to everything we know about reality. We have quite a vast area so that our imaginations can fly freely. However, after that point, all that remains are individuals sowing completely unreasonable ideas under the pretext that "everything is relative". That's in the subjective field. In objectivity — that is, in nothingness — there is not even a way to admit the presence of any humanized idea, however tolerant we may be regarding individual freedom, because that is an area that simply does not concern us. In this context of reality, we merely limit ourselves to describing, under harsh penalties, their physical behavior, and nothing more. Feel free if you are willing to waste time listening to theories from individuals who claim to have a *VIP* badge behind the scenes of reality, while the most extraordinary scientists remain limited to their superficial materialistic descriptions that do not answer the "important" umbilical questions. Let's see, for example, how interesting the theories are about how the brains of certain individuals, endowed with hidden superpowers, violate the laws of physics because of their paranormal curiosity about what is sealed inside a letter - with content that is invariably irrelevant. Now, since the capacity to mentally influence our own bodies has already been more than proven, and the capacity to influence anything beyond that has already been more than refuted, we should be at least suspicious when we see individuals making claims that are not only extraordinary from a logical point of view, but also extraordinarily complimentary to themselves.

Just as we have Occam's Razor, as the logical principle according to which, when explaining a phenomenon, we should not seek unnecessarily complex solutions, but, on the contrary, stick to the most modest hypotheses, provided that they are able to explain it well enough, it is admissible to propose, as a mockery, the Cancian's Razor, as the subprinciple according to which entities should not be praised unnecessarily. In other words, the more a theory praises its owner, the more likely it is to be wrong. You should not massage your representative's ego beyond what is strictly necessary. In fact, it would even be recommended to start with the most detestable and insulting premises that we can sustain, since they invariably correspond to the simplest and most probable. An example of its application: when we hear a certain individual claim that they have the capacity to transgress physical laws, what should we think? The individual says that, if you are focused enough to channel certain mysterious, unknown, and undetectable energies, you will achieve the impossible - even with irrelevant purposes, such as talking to the dead. In other words, it claims to be capable of doing what no one has ever been able to prove. We have two possibilities before us: 1) this individual's neurons are actually capable of causing spatiotemporal seizures and accessing a parallel reality in which there are disembodied dead people willing to chat; or 2) he is an idiot. What is more likely?

✳ ✳ ✳

Having said these initial considerations, let us return to the subject that interests us. Science is, without a doubt, the area that suffers the most attacks from relativists. However, at first, it is not exactly clear why so many individuals feel dissatisfied with the material vision of reality offered by modern science, since it describes the world in an incomparably better way than any other approach. Based on the most probable hypothesis, this is because science is a cold objective description, not a comforting subjective explanation that places us in the heart of the world. Also because it solved certain questions for which we already had our own answers, and we don't like to hear scientific explanations when they don't meet our expectations, crumbling them up.

Tantrums aside, the fact is that, now, there is little room left for us to cultivate our own answers in person. Science orchestrated the understanding of reality on an industrial scale, and it did so well that our hunches, opinions, and beliefs became simply and simply unnecessary. The most beautiful monument that we built to house knowledge is exactly the one that ignores us, and for many this indifference is unacceptable. However, those same people who protest against the imperialism of science are those who lost their old jobs in the manufacture of explanations, and still had to remain silent because the explanations offered by science are much more well-finished and efficient than their own. There may be a lot of issues at stake here, but the truth isn't one of them. These are just envious individuals who would like not to correct, but to take the place of science.

Even if everyone is keen to take advantage of the latest technological innovations that science provides, they remain, for the most part, ungrateful for the enormous expenditure of energy on absurdly complex research and studies to arrive at the final result of being able to speak to any corner of the world in real time. They embrace all technological innovations, but look with disdain at the theories that made them possible, because they do not want such "coldness" to contaminate their personal lives.

Keeping in mind that science has brought extraordinary benefits not only to knowledge but also to our quality of life, it seems paradoxical that, for such petty reasons, we do not feel adoration, but only indifference to such a fruitful field. Its value is invariably reduced to technology in favor of our personal fantasies, and science goes unnoticed as a banality, as a development of the "poor physical world", which should not be taken too seriously, just used to facilitate our daily activities. In this situation, since science doesn't say what we want to hear, we're not willing to listen to it either — and the result is that we don't see scientific knowledge as something that relates to real life.

Sometimes this blindness that causes us to give more value to personal beliefs than to proven facts creeps into science itself. Forgive the cultural relativists, but the idea that the moon is made of cheese does not rise to the same level as the scientific description just because some forest-people believe in it and build curious commemorative props to demonstrate it during ritual dances around bonfires. Science is about objective reality, which is the same for everyone, in every culture. Proven facts are not relative cultural phenomena. Thus, we should not respect the statement that the moon is made of cheese, just the sad right individuals have to believe this absurdity, if it pleases them.

We are told, however, that we are wrong to think so, that we should view them as equivalent and equally valid statements. Our answer to that is the following: thinking like that is crazy. Culture and knowledge are very different things. Respecting different cultures and their particular customs is one thing, and we don't see anything wrong with that. However, when we hear a cultural relativist make a claim as insipid as that an educated doctor, when it comes to medicine, is as worthy of respect as an ignorant healer who diagnoses his patients by feeling the viscera of animals, what could we think? Now, this can only be a desperate attempt to value one's own profession. We know that meaningless rituals heal because of the placebo effect, not because of their equivalence with modern pharmacology — and that statement is not a judgment. The rituals may be inserted in a different cultural context, but they are in the same reality - and we are evaluating facts, not beliefs. Because then, despite their undeniable anthropological value, they are still ignorant superstitions.

It is commonly answered that this is a Western prejudice, but it actually seems more likely that the case is the prejudice of hypocritical cultural preservationists trying to find someone to blame for the disappearance of their beloved object of study who, amazingly, allow themselves to be seduced by theories that work.

The fact is that cultural relativists, like most religious people, don't really believe what they're saying, and it's easy to prove it: when they get sick, they turn to modern medicine. None of them use gods or healers as the first option, and this makes it perfectly clear that they are not being completely sincere in their statements, otherwise they would act according to what they say.

✷ ✷ ✷

63

Let's try to identify the root of this problem by addressing it from another perspective. In theory, there shouldn't be so much discord, so many different opinions about the same facts. If there is only one reality, and if we know it reasonably well, then why don't all men agree among themselves? The reason is obvious: because we interpret and misrepresent the facts in favor of our interests. What we call "personal opinion" is nothing more than our particular way of distorting them.

Thus, men disagree with each other because their opinions are based on subjective interests, not on objective facts. Logically, there is consensus only on issues that we were unable to distort in our favor, and of course such issues would be worthless in a discussion. We value only what we can distort and subvert with subjective interpretations, the rest being useless for our private purposes, since it applies equally to both parties. Science is sidelined in these disputes precisely because it does not prostitute itself easily. However, when she happens to be close to our opinions, we praise her like a goddess, and this makes clear our blatant tendency to partiality.

In practice, the value of a point of view is never judged by its veracity, but by how much it benefits us personally. In defending our personal opinions, we do not do so as scientists, but as lawyers. Trying to scientifically hide a personal opinion is nothing more than a sophisticated and painstaking way of ridiculing oneself. So, since we know that in these matters reason will never be on our side, nor on anyone's side, we are forced to act like crooks, like everyday lawyers. This explains why we argue so much about personal matters, but never about impersonal matters; it explains why we disagree about moral laws, but never about physical laws. The problem is that discussing subjective issues subjectively is always a circular procedure, since it is equivalent to searching for the foundations of what we ourselves invented. In this process, the objective is not to achieve the truth, but to skillfully twirl around to try to demonstrate to our opponents that we have the right to be wrong to their detriment.

As can be seen, relativism has its true origin not in uncertainty, but in the fact that we are competitive, egocentric, and hypocritical mammals. As a philosophical stance, it is something completely ridiculous; as a social stance, it always draws the attention of police officers. Relativists always "doubt everything", always "analyze all sides", but they never discover anything at all, and that should not surprise us. Since the intention is not to know, but to convince and enrich, being right has always been a marginal issue - revealing that none of this ever had anything to do with knowledge. It is merely a maneuver by means of which individuals try to legitimate their interests under the pretext of searching for truth. So, really, there's no relativity at all: what there are are monkeys wanting to get along. We know that true relativity is in our navels, and we know that we have to lie about it to have a chance of winning the case. The very fact that we see the freedom to profess free opinions as an inalienable right is nothing more than the admission of our unavoidable need to lie and deceive, of the glacial maturity of our cynicism.

Virtually all of our personal opinions are unjustifiable. If we could prove them, we wouldn't call them opinions, but facts. However, in the position of lawyers in our interests, we must do everything possible to demonstrate that we are right, even if we know that we are completely wrong. In general, we politely argue with modest and unlaughable fallacies. Becoming relativistic, however, is equivalent to losing the fear of ridicule, turning the tables and trying to win the case by questioning the authority of the judge himself. Since, in subjective matters, there are no final judges, the relativist also seeks to transform objectivity into a purely subjective issue, since then it becomes lawful for individuals to declare, with the air of an expert, what they want about anything.

Once this is done, relativism leaves the scene: it is only invoked to justify this old trick, so that no one can judge the relativist for an absurdity that, under any other circumstances, would deserve nothing but laughter. Relativism, from this point of view, is equivalent to an intellectual magic trick: it is only adopted for a brief moment in order to create a convincing illusion that favors us personally. We used it as a feint, justifying an unjustifiable change of perspective. Even so, such a change will not apply to everything, just to any particular case that we want to distort. Of course, soon after, reality ceases to be relative, because authority, as we wanted, is now in our hands, and everything becomes absolute to the exact extent that it favors us.

* * *

As we can see, the point is that relativists only relativize reality for one simple and unique reason: to start occupying its center. Nothing more, nothing less. Thus, by challenging the authority of science, they know very well who their enemies are, how and when to fight them, and to what extent it is appropriate to sustain that relative view. In short, we are faced with hypocrites who appropriate philosophical and scientific concepts as a means of slandering what immediately and triumphantly refutes them. Despite their skeptical style, it's obvious that relativists never question what's in their favor.

In the hands of private individuals, the relativistic stance normally takes the form of a cross-sectional skepticism that uses doubt as a tool to confer respect on notions that violate any common sense, such as those who spent their entire lives waiting for a chance to take revenge on this villain. A conditional skeptical stance is adopted, that is, they are questioning only theories that conflict with their own. However, they desperately hold on to those that, in some way, serve to back them up. To be skeptical about one's own theory is absolutely out of the question, since the real issue is that they are right, leaving only to find a way to prove it, even if it involves blatantly lying.

Let's see what their practical behavior is like. The beginning is quite modest: pretending to be authentic thinking beings, these charlatans are allowed to enter the theoretical world, claiming that they have no great pretensions, and are just passing through the forgotten corner of the ridiculously unlikely, where life is good, and common sense cannot bother them with its whims, such as coherence. But their modesty is just a pretext: of course, they pack up halfway and camp in the commercial center of the theoretical world, and there they set up their precarious little stalls full of mystical gadgets, basing their ideas as possibilities justified by uncertainty, thinking that this will be sufficient for them, by right, to become owners of the occupied land, since their hypothesis, being intangible, is also irrefutable. This avoids the evidentiary taxes paid so that a hypothesis can be established in the real world. However, as in the real estate world, in the scientific world the value of ideas is also determined by the same three elementary criteria: *location, location, location.*

Any corner of the real world where there is some truth to be extracted is an extremely disputed point by scientists, and the struggle is waged with great violence, and only the best theories win the right to be established, and this is only provisionally, as another one always appears to challenge it. In any case, the simple fact that they have a fixed plot means that they have won all or almost all of the competing theories, and that gives them respect. They are recognized because they have proven to have more value, that is, greater explanatory capacity than the others. *Those who try to challenge them without having any structure, using, for example, relativistic nonsense, will be crushed as easily as Coca-Cola crushes teenagers with socialist inclinations.* In other words, it will not be necessary to do anything, just wait for them to mature enough to realize the ridiculous role they are playing in challenging a fortress with an ideological slingshot.

Those who do not give up on investment or those who, because they love their ideas too much, are unable to admit their absolute incompetence, are forced to move to another place where there is not so much competition based on weapons as powerful as logic, knowledge, reflection, research, consistency, and honesty. Some take their humble bundles of theoretical scraps and throw them with force, a lot of force — so much so that this takes their fluttering little bundles to infinity, and beyond, transcending all known reality. Falling exactly where? In nothing, which becomes the center of everything. Of course, its representatives remain firmly grounded in the unreal earthly reality while trying to sell not to scientists but to the unaware the actions of their theory, which now occupies the terrain of objectivity in the form of a metaphysical company. This is how they came to outsource the services of the Almighty, one of the most well-established metaphysical companies in the world beyond, with many branches on Earth, although this does not earn him a grain of respect from traditional companies.

Nothing being a lawless land, no matter how anemic the ideas are: they will be immune to any and all criticism. Since they have no reason or facts as their foundations, they constitute real disembodied ghosts, and attacking them with sensible material weapons is as useless as shooting a hologram. Some theories feel so secure because of the immunity they enjoy in their own circle that they naively venture to show up in the real world, but it's not long before they are chased away like tricksters, since, instead of accepting the rules of the game, they only bring a letter of recommendation signed by themselves, according to which they are so trustworthy that they don't even need to be put to the test — that would be an insult to their sublime transcendental principles. Thus, instead of evidence, they present us with smiles, catalogues of virtues, and testimonies of spiritual happiness, trying to impress us with credentials that are only valid in the world of their heads. Such nonsense, not to mention useless, at least renews our stock of jokes.

But there is an artifice that they employ to be able to establish themselves theoretically in the effective world, obviously not as a traditional theory, but as a virtual theory embedded in an irrefutable hypothesis. The easiest way to become happy owners of a theory of this kind is to acquire a relativistic *firewall* that works as follows: upon detecting that reason suspected its consistency and comes against it like a mad buffalo, it assumes a questioning *persona* and raises doubts that are thrown like a moral bomb against the reason itself, which, unable to ignore the rules, since this is the prerogative of metaphysicists, is obliged to comply with the bureaucracy of clarifying in detail all the controversies to make sure that there won't be any injustice.

The reason says: *Routine inspection; supporting documents, please.* The theory evades: *What is a document? What is a test? How can I be sure that rationality is reliable? Isn't this other document, authenticated by faith, valid?* In view of this, the unfortunate reason, hands tied, must do its official duty, going to fetch its uniform, its badge and a search warrant, equipped with all the documentation that explains exactly all the details involved in the theoretical legalization process. The virtual theory, however, wants to be a special case: it exercises its right to remain silent and remains on a vigorous skeptical defense. By the time reason arrived, authorized to carry out the survey, the alternative theory had adapted to the threat and burned all incriminating evidence. Reason ends up empty-handed and the alternative theory smiles cynically as someone who seems surprised to have raised suspicions. This goes on indefinitely.

This is how metaphysical crooks immigrate to the real world without having to pay any supporting tax for the place they occupy. They are, of course, treated as illegal immigrants by the native population, that is, by wise scientists, but this ruse is sufficient to prevent their deportation to the waste basket. In this situation, there is no appropriate legal measure. If we decide to take the law into our own hands, we will be convicted of moral harm, since we have no concrete evidence to justify our accusation. Since such charlatans, with their crazy motives, can indefinitely extend the deadline for submitting the evidence, we must remain silent while they say that their theories have every right to exist, as well as any others, since no one refuted them within the terms of science.

∗ ∗ ∗

Doubt, as can be seen, is an excellent pretext for keeping hopes alive in a coma. Thus, after any theory - and the hope that it was real - is impaled by facts, scattered by evidence, mocked by common sense and abandoned, lacking logic, in the gutter of mistakes, let us not think that it will have its sad end in oblivion. Even the stupidest of ideas will have its representatives — is there, in fact, another explanation for the existence of theologians? Theoretical slums are constantly popping up in every corner, and no matter with what rights. Lacking any explanatory capacity, all of them always limit themselves to defending themselves, since they have no structure to grow organized, like an organism, but only chaotically, like a cancer. Their goal is only to survive in order to continue to overcome the affective deficiencies or ideological delusions of their inventors and sympathizers, and to do so, all they have to do is amalgamate a handful of brazen plagiarism to their amorphous structure, distilled from the most recent discoveries of the hated official science that proudly refuses to see the value of those leech theories that want to be revolutionary because they confused what so much work had been done to clarify.

If there are doubts as to whether relativists deserve so many weighty adjectives, let's essentially see what their discourse consists of. First, some smart guy would gather any ideas and align them so as to appear to be plausible. Then he takes that theory, frames it and places it beyond the reach of any analysis - *e.g.* a trillion-dollar check issued by himself who, by chance, is also the owner of the bank which, in turn, no one knows where it is. He then builds a museum where everyone can observe it from a distance and also buy miniaturized replicas and fantastic alternative science books, in which bottomless checks are the latest news. Good news: another absolute truth was born about the world. *Now your representative will cross the seven seas giving lectures about your fabulous discovery, in which your innocuous ideas will be evacuated in reflective consider-ations, preceded by a flatulent one, it is not impossible that...* Such a representa-tive, of course, always wants to be respected with the pedantic discourse that it *is not possible to deny the remote hypothetical possibility* that... , but that's just the beginning. Then the real horror *show* begins: explaining that your money actually exists, although there is no remotely tangible evidence of that.

We can illustrate his speech as follows. Hypothesis A: *the money is under your mattress, but it is in a parallel dimension accessible only through meditation; hypothesis B: the money is the check itself after being energized by the inner power of external charity. The legend continues for hours on end and, after explaining at length through countless tortuous and obscure paths that it only seems to be wrong because it is the victim of a universal conspiracy by the scientific community against its flying check theory, it will launch the ridiculous hypothesis Z: money doesn't exist! — but that's according to the same people who claim to have come from an explosion that turned into a monkey that* became people. And the audience laughs, feeling inflated by the feeling that they are part of a select group of enlightened people.

Looking at it this way, it's an invaluable privilege: the whole world is wrong, and they just discovered it first-hand. They didn't have to think or even open a book to become the owners of the truth, and that's absolutely wonderful. The only truly sad fact is that scientists, in their narrow-minded attachment to the material world, are reluctant to recognize their wisdom. The scientists' motives, yes, are ridiculous: there is nothing, absolutely nothing, no measly trace of evidence in favor of their theory. However, for them, this proves nothing, other than that scientists are stubborn and stupid.

Faced with something of this nature, it only remains for us to cheer. We cannot deny such a "remote hypothetical possibility". Then, since we can't handle them, let's join them, also giving free rein to our imaginations. Knowing that the truth is only accessible to the pure, we fast and pray at length to sanitize our spirits. We retired to the wilderness, to a simple and solitary life, and stayed there for long years. *After many obstinate efforts, countless abyssal reflections, and subsequent flaming meditations, we finally mastered the art of reversing our peristaltic movements, and thus found a way to repopulate the world burned by doubt: perhaps existence is not completely empty and meaningless — perhaps it has 10% of the filling of philosopher's guava and its meaning points to the right.* Through the skies of the infinite sandwich! If that kind of theory had any dignity, she would shoot her own head - but her host won't allow it, because the bullet could hurt her pride.

Of course, at first glance, it might seem like it, but it's not absurd. From a relativist perspective, the theory that the meaning of existence points to the right is as respectable as the theory of the evolution of species. That is his enlightening message.

This rule of law to *nonsense* is due to the anarchy established by relativistic discourse, that is, to the convenient absence of authority regarding truth, regarding reality. We don't need much life experience to guess that any space, even the intellectual desert of nowhere, would not be unpopulated for a long time, but would quickly be invaded by legions of small parasitic ideas that are justified by no one having legal means of kicking them out. The settlement of nothingness is, unfortunately, as inevitable as human foolishness, and it shows that certainly nihilism should not be rejected in the intellectual sphere, if not out of integrity, at least as a health measure.

* * *

The remarks made above allow us to identify what is wrong with the relativistic stance. Faced with doubt and uncertainty, relativists never adopt, as scientists, a positive and constructive stance, seeking the best ways of knowing reality, but a negative and destructive stance, seeking the best ways to ridicule what they disagree with, what ultimately goes against their convictions and tears them apart. Of course, in any debate, your convictions are always conveniently omitted to avoid suspicion as to the legitimacy of your motives.

As a rule, relativists are just individuals who resent the fact that science does not corroborate their beliefs. We know that having the support of science is your biggest dream. To illustrate it, just think of the case of religious people - in their own way, they are also relativists. Religious people repeatedly state that faith does not need to be proven by science; they attack it when it develops theories that go against their convictions, such as heliocentrism and evolution- ism; they say that science is extremely partial, limited and dubious knowledge. Everyone knows that speech. Let us suppose, however, the following situation: science has demonstrated the existence of God. Black and white, it's there: God exists. It's a fact. The discovery is all over the papers, and atheists blush with shame. In view of this, would religious continue to defend such a relativistic stance, arguing that science is "intrinsically limited", and that, even if proven by irrefutable facts, the existence of God remains very doubtful? Well, of course not — they would become, albeit for the wrong reasons, the most staunch defenders of science. They would brag around the world that their beliefs are facts. In other words, they would no longer need to have faith, because believing in God would become as normal as believing in gravity. The same would apply, for example, to parapsychologists, if it were proven that the human mind has paranormal powers; to reincarnationists, if the existence of evolving spirits were demonstrated; to astrologers, if the influence of heavenly bodies on our behavior were established. If there were facts in favor of their theories, such individuals would immediately embrace science, abandoning the burden of incoherence that made them relativistic.

A final example that illustrates very well the true interests behind relativistic discourse are the criminals who, through any legal devices, seek to be exonerat- ed from crimes of which they know they are guilty. Of course, if they were innocent, they would have nothing to lose with the truth. On the contrary, they would help to seek it out of self-interest. However, since they are guilty, telling the truth is not appropriate. So if they want to remain free, their only chance is to confuse everything that is meant by truth, at least as far as the evidence that incriminates them is concerned. That is why they never show any sincere interest in ascertaining the facts, always limiting themselves to the minimum necessary for them to get away with impunity. Thus, instead of taking an open stance, emphasizing an unrestricted search for evidence, they simply look to the side in the hope that no one will bother to investigate further - because it would only be a matter of time before they find evidence that incriminates them. This is the reason why all the culprits are strangely exempt from curiosity: they know very well what will be found behind the appearances. They must, therefore, relativize the evidence that points to their guilt and also discourage further investigations in order to prevent new evidence from being found, as they could easily weaken, or even make indefensible, their alternative version of the facts, according to which they are innocent.

Suppose they charge us with some kind of crime. As heinous as this crime is, if we don't commit it, reality will be in our favor. Thus, if confronted in this regard, instead of defending ourselves with delusional speeches, relativizing the whole reality, fiercely attacking our accusers, planting treacherous doubts in every argument that they direct us, we will, on the contrary, be the most interested in cooperating with any proposed investigation, so that the truth can be reached as soon as possible, and thus the evidence will demonstrate our innocence. So, if we are innocent, our greatest interest will be in being honest, because, no matter how much is discovered about us, this will only confirm our version of the facts. That is why the distinctive sign of honesty is a clear conscience. This sincere interest in the search for truth is the exact position expected of any scientist: he is aware that being honest is a personal interest because his objective is to achieve the truth - and any other interest that is inserted into this equation can only harm him, which is why any individual who has nothing to hide with his personal interpretation of the facts will always see relativism as an enemy, never as an ally. So if reality is on our side, we have nothing to hide. It doesn't matter that new clues emerge to be investigated, it doesn't matter that all scientists in the world investigate the issue for decades and decades with the most advanced technological tools - the more we investigate, the more our innocence will be proven.

However, if we are guilty, doing so will be the exact recipe for being arrested. Evidently, the relativist does not resort to reason and evidence because he knows that he is wrong, he knows that the facts are against him. Then, since you cannot prove that you are right, you will at least try to prove that you are not wrong. Thus, for the sole purpose of preserving their beliefs, the individual strives hard to deny evidence that, under any other circumstances, he would calmly accept. In this process, it doesn't matter if the contrary evidence is true or false: it must be denied simply because it is against it. Of course, if they are false, the better: it will be easier to tear them down. In this case, like a true scientist, the relativist will refute all false claims with valid arguments, clear reasoning, and concrete evidence. What evidence will that be? It doesn't matter: they will also be declared false when they are against him. The same evidence that you use to refute contrary arguments would never be valid to prove the falsity of your own point of view. Even so, it is useless to point out this type of incoherence: it will continue to the end with its alternative version of the facts, since its interest lies in the practical result to be achieved, not in the truth.

The relativist, as can be seen, faces the hard task of arguing against reality. He knows it's wrong, but he desperately wants to preserve his beliefs—and his only alternative is to deny the truth to the brink of absurdity. In this process, relativists act exactly like criminals who claim innocence in the hope of remaining free. The criminal lies because he is more interested in freedom than in truth — the religious, in faith.

All the truths that are not on our side are relative: this is the exact psychology of relativism. With their stance of doubt, they are only trying to protect their faith, not to reach the truth. That is why their behavior is invariably defensive and unproductive. Whatever the topic, relativistic discourse is never disinterested. Behind their chatter there is always some secret conviction, some absurdity that, because they cannot prove, they at least want to excuse, and they do so with their unjustifiable stance of deconstructive doubt.

Relativism cannot be supported because it is not enough to doubt for free: there must also be justifiable reasons for doubt. Physical facts cannot be jeopardized by crazy interrogations. Since relativism is a position that defends a metaphysical doubt, since it is not based on any demonstrable fact, but only on daydreams about hypothetical misconceptions, here is our reason for rejecting it, the same reason why we reject radical skepticism: it is nothing more than faith in doubt.

IRREFLEXION

Critical and rational thinking isn't for everyone, nor should it, just like athletics isn't for everyone. It is unfair to demand that others have a logical and coherent view of reality that exceeds the minimum necessary to satisfy their immediate personal needs, especially when such commitment would require a great deal of effort from individuals whose lives are essentially practical. Such a commitment would result in a laughable benefit for the majority and could only be established artificially, through force. For the same reason, no one is forced to maintain physical conditioning beyond what is necessary to survive, no matter how flabby their bodies become. It doesn't sound reasonable to think that we must, during our entire lives, cultivate the minimum conditioning to, say, run ten kilometers uninterruptedly, for the simple reason that athletics is supposedly wonderful in and of itself.

Harsh physical activities are not for everyone, and neither are severe mental activities. Thinking is a tiring, strenuous occupation. The brain needs to be trained, conditioned, exercised so that we can practice reflection. Those who are not used to running long distances get tired quickly; in the same way, those who are not used to thinking are unable to reflect, to engage in intellectual debates for long periods. Without prior preparation, muscle aches and headaches begin in a few moments. The parallel helps us to understand that such observation is not a prejudice against thoughtlessness just as it is not against a sedentary lifestyle. It's just a matter of choosing, or at least accepting, what is most in line with our possibilities.

Similarly, if the objective were to guarantee our personal safety, we would have the choice of spending our entire lives practicing some martial art or simply buying pepper spray. If the goal were to achieve a state of profound serenity, we could spend ten years meditating at a Buddhist retreat or simply go to the nearest pharmacy and buy, for a few bucks, a peace in the soul pack. In this way, unless our objective is precisely reflection, it is more coherent to leave it to scientists, philosophers, and sympathizers, just as we leave the toothache to the dentists and continue to deal with what really matters to us, if it's nothing like that. We have every right to be ignorant and limited in areas that don't concern us, and that's not a shame.

Even so, it is not correct to conclude that all non-thinkers are naive fools just because they do not seek answers in philosophical reflection and scientific knowledge to an issue that, as a rule, cannot be solved. *In certain situations, reflecting at length on existential issues is not even the most worthy way out, since after a lot of effort, it offers nothing more than what any popular metaphysical system provides with the same efficiency as a drive through.* Just as we have snack bars for those who don't want to cook, we have religions for those who don't want to think. In them we find ready-made explanations for the most varied tastes. Just choose and believe it: the matter will never have to be digested.

Disinterest, however, is not the same as incapacity. Just as those who eat lunch at restaurants are not necessarily a spice donkey, consumers of ready-made systems based on dogmas are also not necessarily reduced to no-brainers, unaware of the philosophical problems raised by the human condition. It is common to invoke the idea that all supporters of popular systems blindly believe in canned answers to the questions that afflict them, but this is a mistake, and it's easy to demonstrate. For example, let's select a group of individuals with very heterogeneous beliefs: one believes in a personal god, another in evolving spirits, a third in the all-one, yet another in the god-nature, and so on. Then, in the most polite way possible, let them describe how important and true and comforting their belief is, allowing them to go on for as long as they want until they feel certain that we don't see them as fools for professing unfounded beliefs. Then, as a remote possibility, let's throw in the air the hypothesis that their beliefs are simply and simply false, giving them a scarecrow to hit, so that they don't feel the full weight of what they say on themselves. What will be the result? It's not hard to imagine: a purely nihilistic, absurdly realistic, cruelly honest discourse by individuals who may have never studied philosophy or science, having learned all this only through life experience. Your reasoning will basically be: "if God doesn't exist, we're here for nothing"; "if Allah doesn't exist, life has no meaning"; "if there's no immortality, we're just stardust" — and they're absolutely correct. In view of this, we have the impression that everyone, deep down, knows that existence is hollow, and their beliefs are just a way of protecting themselves from the facts.

Assuming that the idea of meaninglessness has arisen in everyone who has sought a solution for it, even if a simple solution, the conclusion is that most individuals have the capacity to at least conceive it. This indicates that almost everyone recognizes this emptiness of existence and intuitively protects themselves as they can, which means, as a rule, practical protection, the most practical of all: not thinking about the matter, taking it as resolved by faith. Naturally, this fact influenced society, with repercussions in the form of generic official or traditional solutions to provide some sense of security to those who feel afflicted by the lack of meaning and do not have the time or resources to investigate it in person. Those who are unable to conclude for themselves are forced to buy ready-made systems, and this generally means incorporating in a more or less passive way the popular ideas of the environment that surrounds them, such as those who get used to having lunch at the nearest restaurant for convenience.

Just as, in the past, believing in Dionísio and dedicating heavy drinking and orgies to him was perfectly respectable, since everyone did the same, today it is very normal to believe in Christianity and pray rosaries. As long as the belief has sufficient living representatives, it is justified as a kind of group irrationality. The greater the number of followers of a given doctrine, the greater its immunity from criticism and the greater the sense of security it provides to its adherents. Today freedom of worship is guaranteed as an individual right. However, belief only gains the *status* of reality if there are a sufficient number of faithful. An individual alone, naked in the middle of the street at three in the morning, praising the holy jabuticaba, will probably be arrested for an obscene act, even if he claims to be professing his personal faith, whose right is constitutionally guaranteed. However, if this were a custom firmly established within our society, whereby thousands of individuals undress in the middle of the night in praise of this fruit as what gives meaning to their lives, no one would dare to disrespect them, just as we don't disrespect Carnival. The law, therefore, only walks on eggshells on the subject of freedom of worship when there are a considerable number of representatives for whom such praise is important. In the name of social welfare, we respect the thoughtlessness of those who profess beliefs without feet or heads, even if they are uncomfortable for those who do not follow them.

Although the answers that such popular systems offer are not exactly personally satisfactory, when we see a legion of individuals showing such certainty about them externally, we are pleased to leave the question aside, not because the answer is satisfactory, but because the objective is precisely to take their minds off this existential misery and move on with life, and for that purpose the rest are an excellent pretext, whether with the belief in deities or in sacred fruits. Thus, the leaders justify themselves in the crowd of followers, the followers are justified in the leaders, and everyone in the other. None of them feel perfectly satisfied with their beliefs, but they pretend otherwise so as not to be excluded. When everyone does the same, the resulting impression is that only we are foolish enough to raise doubts, since it doesn't seem possible that everyone is faking it, but they are. Almost invariably, we end up following the example of others who, like us, are enacting their beliefs. Collectively, things work in a self-help system in which we see everyone protecting each other from doubt with that silly affection of someone who gives other advice that even they don't even believe in. As is supposed, these systems always strongly encourage socialization, since the central idea is that individuals suggest one another. That's why we'll never find a solitary parapsychologist who reads minds to pass the time. All of these things are displayed, staged, and minds are read exactly in this process of misunderstanding the facts.

Although it seems strange that a scheme of large proportions is sustainable through hypocrisy, it works very well, even if we are slightly coerced to omit our most intimate doubts. It works because, in groups, humans become highly impressionable, allowing themselves to be guided by what they believe to be the opinion of the majority, of which they desperately want to be a part. Being part of a group provides us with security, it makes us feel protected and justified in our opinions because there are a large number of individuals who think the same. Since the objective in view is well-being, the very veracity of the belief becomes a marginal issue, and lying about this becomes natural. This hypocrisy is not much different from what we see on a daily basis in the workplace, where we are forced to perform an entire theatrical *performance* in order to transmit a certain image to the clients. These conventional lies work because they both know the truth but no one dares to tell it. For this reason, both lie, but neither of them feels deceived. *This is the famous conventional hypocrisy, commonly referred to by the term professionalism.*

We can say that, just like most individuals commit their hearts to their family and friends, those who don't think compromise their intelligence with their beliefs. They know that, in the end, this is all a mere accident, but it's their chance. If they were born in another family, their loved ones and friends would be different, their beliefs would most likely be different as well, but none of that matters to their owners. The fact is that every man, to a greater or lesser degree, has some appreciation for his ideas, and that is because of the simple fact that they are his own. They're something they hold on to in search of safety, not reality — they're like their children. This happens in matters such as nationality, religion, culture, tradition, etc. Individuals are proud of their country simply because they were born in it; they follow their religion only because it baptized them; they respect their tradition just because it justifies their customs and prejudices.

It's all very inertial in the minds of those who don't think. They follow passively, absorbing environmental influences like a sponge. They defend their country, their tradition, their faith, for the same reason as their favorite soccer team. In groups, it all boils down to a kind of brawl between fans. They ridicule the customs of other countries like those who never thought that they could have been born in them — their fault is not thinking like us because they happened to have been born there and not here. Such individuals never choose what they defend, they simply embrace the first thing that appears in front of them and never let go of it again, they never think about it. Confronting them only makes them hold on to their beliefs even more firmly. So, even if you disagree with each other, there's nothing to debate — your ideas are always right just like your children are all beautiful and intelligent. Of course, they cannot explain why, because honesty would require them to abandon the partiality that allows them to live lightly. When they say that they don't need to explain themselves to others, they're just trying to avoid the embarrassment of publicly stumbling over the most obvious realities. That's why they avoid discussing the subject, which is why they often get irritated when discussing it. In the end, they are ashamed of its incoherence, but they need it to live in peace.

From the point of view of biological fatherhood, it is normal for parents to initially have the illusion that children are their property, but it is a belief that will sooner or later be contradicted by reality, since children will also become independent beings. However, in the field of ideas, many parents choose never to allow such independence to occur. They never launch their children, their theories, into the world, taking pride in the fact that their offspring are capable of surviving on their own. It never allows them to find out if they're actually ugly and stupid kids. Like owl parents, they constantly intervene in the life of their ideas to avoid being contradicted by reality. It turns out that such theories never overcome their own childishness, they never get rid of the subjectivity of their authors to move on to adulthood, that is, to objectivity. Dependent on the external care of their owners, when left to themselves, their fate is certain death.

As we can see, they are essentially occupational theories that distract and protect individuals from the anguish of doubt. They replace reflection with faith in a make-believe game in which the north is chance and the truth is the number of followers. Such childish perspectives are forced to remain eternally immature to satisfy their owners' need not to think. Thus, after a long life, their bodies are already old, their children have already become independent, but their beliefs have not yet come out of the diapers. They are overprotective parents so that they themselves remain perfect children.

✳ ✳ ✳

Naturally, this all happens as a more or less harmless theater. Thoughtlessness is quite justifiable for individuals who just want to lead their lives inertially, without paying much attention to what they are doing, since the more they observe, the more perplexed they are. In this case, lying is not harmful, since its owners recognize its personal character, its existence merely subjective—they do not feel entitled to impose it on others by force. When they have to make serious decisions, they never take into account their playful beliefs; they leave them in the background because they know that such facts are just a fictional reality that pleases and comforts them personally. They pretend to themselves in search of peace, and to others to keep up appearances. It's nothing more than a big neurosis, and everything's fine.

However, some individuals actually believe in the actual existence of their theoretical pimpoles, many even give them precedence over physical reality. They're the ones we know as fanatics. It is common to imagine fanaticism related only to radical religious groups, but it is something that we can find under the most varied disguises, from the classics religion, sports, and politics, to philosophy, science and other more sophisticated and little known positions, although equally important for the salvation of the world. Since fanatics give priority to their private worlds also when dealing with others, they are truly crazy beings, with whom coexistence is unbearable and often dangerous. It is certain that we will never find fanatical thinkers, because fanaticism presupposes thoughtlessness, not as a mere absence, but as an incapacity for critical thinking: it is far beyond a mere adult tantrum. They are too passionate about their ideas, like those who, on a daily basis, have to inject them into their veins and live them, no matter how absurd the implications may be. In this situation, the individual becomes completely biased and dependent on belief. Because of its fragility, this is always a more urgent issue than reality itself, which is why many become violent in its protection. Even if it seems paradoxical, in your minds everything makes sense, because you are being guided by a personal reality.

The distinctive sign of the fanatic is the constant mention of the importance of their personal beliefs for the well-being of others. This often takes the form of fiery speeches and apocalyptic prophecies, waiting for someone to take the trouble to pay attention. Whether they are listened to or not, they will never change their opinion or the subject. Of course, normally only fanatics pay attention to each other, since they are vying for the physical monopoly of an imaginary world. As they defend personal truths in search of the same space, all fanatics hate each other, and their struggles basically consist of the fact that some say 2+2=5, others that 2+2=3 - but the enemy they hate in common are the disbelievers, that is, the normal ones, who do not see the supposed relevance of their fantasies, and live on the fringes of their delusional worlds. As if keeping a very important secret, they believe that everyone needs to be aware of the epic battles being fought, because the fate of the world is at stake. Someone who is indifferent to something so great can only be an abominable individual who must be converted or destroyed. It's not an option to let him live in peace.

When, from a negative personal position, one tries to draw universal positive implications, we have the general case of fanaticism. In other words: *without me, woe to the world!* For example, when imagining a world in which there are no objective moral values, a fanatical moralist immediately loses his composure, predicting every kind of calamity based on clumsy syllogisms. However, since there was no actual physical destruction of objective morality, all we have is the death of an unfounded belief, that is, something personal, negative and subjective. It would be foolish to try, from this, to infer universal, positive and objective implications, such as the whole world sinking into a chaos of crimes and orgies, but that is exactly what happens in the minds of fanatics, because their beliefs come before reality.

If we were fanatical cartographers, when drawing a world map, we would begin to demand that it be the world itself. If there was an island that escaped our observation, we would consider it more reasonable to dynamite it or sentence everyone who visited it to death than to include it in our map. Of course, the world doesn't start to work differently just because we began to understand it in another way, and that explains why beliefs and theories need lawyers, but reality doesn't; it explains how we could "replace" Newtonian physics with the theory of relativity without the entire world wriggling into space-time convulsions; it explains how the Earth "started" to revolve around the Sun without us all falling from it when we adopted heliocentrism. However, the modesty of having just one *vision* of the world is not something that satisfies our need for greatness, especially when it borders on megalomania. We prefer the idea that if we're wrong, not only will our beliefs fall, but so will the whole world. We like to think that our theories are what allows reality to exist with meaning, without which it would fall apart like a dry tree.

Naturally, that kind of stupid arrogance is what underlies everything. A fanatic is nothing more than an individual who lives according to their autistic beliefs, having permanently severed their relations with reality when it comes to such issues. So, if the theory of relativity were in the Bible and, let's say, someone saw light traveling at a speed greater than 300,000 km/s, the reaction of fanatical individuals would not be to update the scriptures. Since they will not be able to burn the light at the stake, it will be likely that they will find an alternative solution, such as burning the witnesses or claiming that the photons were summoned to the illumination of a divine intervention. So, if the world doesn't behave according to your theories, it's the world's fault. In his heart, the fanatic believes that the world needs him and would not survive the death of his convictions. Then, for the good of all, he declares himself the savior and sets out on his mission to destroy everything that threatens them.

This delusional character of his personal view explains why the morals of fanatical individuals are so inflexible. In their minds, moral reality, invented by themselves, and objective reality are one and the same, and this bases their personal missions objectively. Violating a moral precept becomes as unacceptable, as unthinkable as violating physics. However, since, in this case, the material reality itself will not ensure that this never happens, they take the position of guardians of morals: they themselves become the law that guarantees the physical consequences of moral transgressions. In this way, at the cost of the devastation of everything that contradicts them, they preserve the integrity of the alternative world that they have in their heads.

If we want to measure someone's fanaticism about any idea, we just need to hear their predictions about what would happen if it were wrong. The more external consequences there are, the more fanatical and megalomaniac the individual is in their belief. For example, "if life had no meaning, no one would wake up in the morning to go to work", "if everything didn't happen for a reason, the world would be a complete disorder". On the other hand, conclusions whose consequences are personal are often just signs of wisdom. For example, "if life had no meaning, then I would only be deceiving myself." In this case, the individual has not yet lost contact with reality, but neither can bear it very well.

The difference between the predictions of a fanatic and those of a sober person is due to the fact that the former calculates them according to his beliefs, of a personal world, and the other according to the facts, of the reality common to all. So, on the one hand, if we asked a reasonable individual to make a prediction about what would happen if scientists discovered extraterrestrial life on a distant planet similar to Earth, he would say, for example, that this would confirm that we are probably correct in our understanding of the mechanisms responsible for the emergence of life. In other words, in essence, nothing would happen. What would happen if we discovered that our understanding of how life began is incorrect? Nothing. We would just have to find another way of understanding such a phenomenon. Normal individuals know how to differentiate their own reality from their mere vision of reality. They do not consider their knowledge as something that should be imposed on the world. On the other hand, when we ask a fanatical individual to predict what would happen if they were wrong, say, about a man possessing paranormal powers, we can expect that the consequences of this — for reasons incomprehensible to the uninitiated in his dementia — will even affect the intimate constitution of the corkscrew.

Whether we are wrong or not, the fact is that nothing happens when a simple vision is wrong, and many believe that this constitutes proof that they are correct, because, if they were wrong, the consequences would be devastating. So, for example, if we have an armed nuclear bomb in our hands and we are the only ones who know how to deactivate it, there will be reasons to feel responsible for others. Of course, no one will fear that we are wrong, but that a nuclear explosion will vaporize their lives. However, who would pay attention to an invisible bomb that never explodes, no matter how wrong we are? Just psychiatrists. Meanwhile, in the real world, everyone goes to work in the morning, and the fact that we believe that this has something to do with the meaning of life doesn't change anything.

Requiring a fanatic to be tolerant of other points of view is unthinkable. It would be like asking Superman not to save the world out of discretion. How could the chosen one allow himself to be reduced to anonymity because of good manners? In his mind, his war is crucial to the future of humanity. Your delusion must flourish, even if the whole world perishes.

TRUTH

It is normally thought that the knowledge achieved with the scientific description of the material world is just a preliminary process, an outline that will be improved until we reach the ideal truths. However, there are no ideal truths in the world, only real facts. In terms of knowledge, existence is not an idea to be grasped, but a reality to be described. When we whine that science is limited because, to date, it has not yet found reliable truths, this presupposes that there is that kind of truth; there isn't. Through abstract philosophical models that define truth as something perfect and virginal, we lose contact with the real world—we distance ourselves from it by thinking too much. Reality now represents an "appearance", a shell of the true "hidden essence of the world", which must be achieved through the exercise of pure reason.

Therefore, by disregarding the achievements of science based on notions of knowledge of this kind, we are placing ourselves in an imaginary world, since, in ideal terms, the world is nothing. We start from a kind of philosophical dogma that leads us to despise knowledge based on observation because in it we cannot find the certainties we seek, that is, it does not fit the ideal knowledge model that we predetermined as the only valid one.

We are faced with a false objection, born of the search for the ideal within the real. We condemn any project of knowledge of physical reality when we demand that it have ideal foundations. We asked him for something he can't offer. Science cannot achieve something that doesn't exist. Undoubtedly, ideal truths seem safer. They are sure of eternity. However, they exist only in our heads.

In addition to certainties, we also have ideal uncertainties, that is, radical skepticism, with which all knowledge is supposedly nullified through doubt brought to the extreme of uncertainty. Equally, it only exists in theory. The fact that we can doubt everything does not mean that we do not know anything, but only that there is no untouchable knowledge. However, for idealists, the slightest doubt is a categorical refutation — we have everything or nothing. If we can't reach the ultimate foundations, even appearances aren't reliable. Partially perfect knowledge is completely false. We seek the truth unscathed. We are not content to describe the operation of a machine: we want the original project, with all the details, the same type that would have existed if we had designed it. In the absence of this type of instruction manual, we declare everything false, uncertain, imperfect, superficial, misleading, etc. We want everything ready, chewed up, explained and definitive — preferably with a dedication from the designer.

In the search for an ideal truth, we have basically two antagonistic points of view. Some say that we can know everything, others that we cannot know anything about the ideal essence of the world. Obviously, since one seeks something in the world that does not exist in it, nothing has ever been achieved with it, only to great bickering between philosophers who try to defend their autistic theories.

The starting point of this search for truth is to sit in an armchair, close your eyes and reveal the ultimate principles of existence through thought. We ramble at length about hypotheses that make perfect sense inside our heads, we convince ourselves of them, and that's all. We could never seek a real truth because it comes to us corrupted by the senses, so we want to make it born directly from pure rationality. Sitting in opposing armchairs, skeptics limit themselves to seeking obstacles that make such truths inaccessible. After much debate, they come to no conclusion, and that's right until another philosophical coffee starts.

At the affirmative and negative extremes, we have ideal positions just *stated* about the real world, never discovered. Naturally, we were unable to achieve such positions in practice, as they ignore it: their beach is pure abstraction. Getting hands-on and discovering the real world is too vulgar, left to smart technicians. Thus, depending on what we expect from the world, we lean one way, the other, or we simply worry that both are unsustainable.

Let's throw some rocks at these metaphysical ghosts and see what they tell us. On the affirmative side, we have the old and monotonous concept of an absolute reality to which we have full access through thought. On the negative side, we have skepticism and the complete denial of any possibility of knowledge. The movement and the countermovement: a little peck of our kind. Some part building windcastles, another part demolishing them, and most just piling or knocking down bricks without really understanding why they're doing it.

Theoretical masons are the first, with the certainty of a concrete and universally accessible reality that reveals itself unreservedly to us during philosophical discussions. It can be loosely inferred based on the fact that we can rationally conceive the natural laws that govern phenomena. Our minds, therefore, reach the essence of reality, the eternal truth behind the world of sensory appearances — an error, of course, or at least an undemonstrable assumption, a leap of faith. Not that knowledge of natural laws is useless, but that simply doesn't matter in this matter. The fact that we are able to predict and represent the behavior of reality through mathematical equations does not mean that we have understood the core of anything, since we can describe various phenomena correctly from different theoretical models. The fact that theories work is an argument in favor of the technique, and does not make them absolutely true as to the ideal foundations of the world. The value of such knowledge is practical, and has much more to do with our biological well-being and the need for certainty than with the demonstration of the validity of this concept of ideal truth. It is a philosophy that tries to demonstrate itself ideally by piggybacking on our real needs. Their best argument is technology.

Outraged, the opposition stands up and rages: this cannot be sustained! They ridicule any possibility of knowledge, partial or total, about the world and its principles. We can't guarantee that our senses aren't deceiving us. We don't even know if we exist: we just believe in it. If the very fact that we exist is undemonstrable, all the rest of our knowledge is even more uncertain. In the process of knowing, therefore, we start from absurdity, walk on delusions and arrive at falsehoods. We will remain eternally oblivious to pure reality, and our knowledge is just a wild dream, a sophisticated way of remaining ignorant.

With skepticism, our capacity to apprehend any reality is rejected; everything that is taken for granted is thrown away; any possibility of the contrary is laughed at. The very reality we are in is called into question as a subjective fiction. We cannot say that we are alive, because we are not absolutely certain about anything. Thus, faced with the illusion of hunger, we eat non-bread with perhaps butter: hunger passes, but we still do not know if there is a direct causal relationship between the facts.

The defenders of such impossibility justify their destructive stance by the fact that, by pointing out the error, they are merely freeing man from his delusions. Criticism only destroys what cannot be sustained. They're not getting anything out of it; they tear down the buildings without intending to build anything on the ruins. Out of simple honesty, they declare all paths that lead to true knowledge as forbidden to man.

However, in this matter any denial is no less chimerical than an affirmation. Uncertainty itself, when affirmed as certainty, contradicts itself: it is hardly surprising that absolute doubt is equally unsustainable. They deny the world but remain with their feet in it. They need to live, of course, but it's false — everything is false! The need only seems to exist, but one can be sure that it is only the shadow of a phantom imagined during the materialistic ideation of a weak degenerate who, in desperation, believed in the senses.

This stance, in the end, does not exceed a moral system adapted to ulcerated pessimists who constantly spew how much we should hate everything that exists just because one day they believed that there was something much better to be found behind reality. Their philosophy is a kind of revenge with which they express their resentment, their frustration stemming from obvious and unavoidable impotence. Resigned, they bury the world and spend their whole lives mourning the deceased who died too young. Your doubts cry out for what you would like reality to be, but it can never be.

In this position we find not only radical skeptics, but also those who rejoice in rejecting the "wisdom of this world" because it is not perfect as they believe it should be. They are all bitter individuals who despise life because it cannot give them what they truly want: theology. Therefore, they dedicate themselves exclusively to slandering and defaming it in every possible and imaginable way, and with that their lives gain a purpose, that is, to be a pain in the shoes of those who are in fact seeking knowledge.

All we have left is silence, in the form of nihilism. It is the least incoherent position, since at least it does not shoot itself in the foot when committing itself to absurd and undemonstrable positions, according to which knowledge is the objective and the world must behave as a premise, as an assumption that makes it possible, interpreting the world as something that exists and appeared with the purpose of being known. While the suspension of trial has a paralyzing effect, no one is discussing the means of becoming the philosophical employee of the month. Refusing to work in an undertaking with no future justifies inaction, because if two identical abysses are neighbors, any predilection would be stupid. Therefore, with good reason to refute both positions, nihilism suspends judgment on the issue. It neither affirms nor denies the possibility of ideal certainties about the world because it also does not accept that the world has an ideal essence. Because, after all, what they seek so much has never even been demonstrated, merely supposed to be the most desirable objective for our efforts to explain the world.

Nihilism, of course, is also an uncertainty, but not in the form of a positive affirmation of our unavoidable ignorance about everything - a mature, serene uncertainty, free from childhood trauma. It doesn't mean complete indifference, as this can only be found on morgue racks with chips tied around the fingers—a prudent, enlightened indifference, justifiable by the lack of anything better.

We want to understand the world. However, since there are no reasonable grounds to be adopted as a starting point, one starts without any foundation, without the purpose of one day finding them. With that, we finally accept uncertainty with maturity. We stop hating the world because it's not what we dream for ourselves. We began to move towards knowledge on our own, without guarantees and without considering what we know as the provisional version of a supposed ideal.

How could we be naive enough to believe that the world could be reduced to a handful of metaphysical definitions and concepts on ultimate foundations? And that, in the impossibility of achieving them, the most wise thing would be to deny the world in favor of such concepts? Idealisms concern only our minds. Ideas, abstractions, are mammalian mental processes. We're right, not the world.

Today we know that we should not judge the value of ideas by how profound they seem, but by how much they relate to reality. However, for a long time, philosophy insisted on the error of trying to become profound in a world where everything is superficial. Its tradition was sunk into theological prejudices, losing contact with the world in which we are, filling books and more books with profound irrelevant considerations about how good it would be if the world were what one thinks of it.

With metaphysics, we investigate the world as someone who questions a person, a subject, the mind of God. Basically, it is nothing more than a disguised theology, with which we try to approach divine perfection through ideal reasoning, as we imagine to be those of the Creator. The search for ideal certainties, therefore, is based on the commendable assumption that man is a child of God. That has always been the fundamental error of metaphysics, always carefully concealed.

That is why, from this perspective, nihilism could be understood as a kind of existential atheism: a disbelief in everything that is metaphysical, in everything that was born from theology. From this point of view, atheism itself is reduced to a small point within nihilism, since it is nothing more than an absence of belief that has a name. There are no words that designate those who don't believe in elves, but for those who don't believe in God there are: atheists. That's the only difference. Most disbeliefs are simply anonymous.

By looking at the matter with some attention, we will see that the logic that justifies nihilism is the same that justifies atheism. When we turn our critical eyes and enquire not just deities, but all subjects, the entire existence with the same honesty, we have nihilism. That's why every nihilist is an atheist. It follows that, in theory, every atheist should be nihilistic, but few have the courage to do so, few endure such lucidity. Atheists, for the most part, continue to embrace the wreckage of what they don't believe because they fear the emptiness of existence - in which they believe.

Our cowardice about life, however, is a different matter. The fact is that the perspective that results from nihilism is equivalent to removing all theology, all the superstition that is mixed with our knowledge. Nihilism uproots this weed in the bud, it purges not only the belief in deities, but also all the implications and ramifications of this, all the metaphysical garbage that remained hidden in the depths of our knowledge as what "gave meaning" to reality, and that made us believe in the absolute necessity of that meaning.

By proceeding in this way, rejecting this religious stance in relation to knowledge, we overcome the dogma of an ideal reality. Through experience, we discover that the world exists, but not in ideal terms — its core is not a concept. The truth is not achieved by the apprehension of an idea-essence that underlies reality. Ideal certainties, as well as ideal uncertainties, are philosophical-religious delusions.

Therefore, for the same reasons, we also reject radical skepticism, which is based on this ideal vision of the world to affirm that man can never become similar to God: therefore, let us be humble, let us remain ignorant. Instead of investigating the world, let's open our Bibles and have faith. His true objection to knowledge is sin: man's senses are too limited and imperfect to understand the Lord's designs.

Metaphysics never sought knowledge, it always ignored all the realities before it. *It led man to wander for a long time in conceptual deserts in search of a revelation.* With its collapse, the depth of knowledge ends. Man ceases to seek the essence of the Earth in the heavens. We stopped believing that the ultimate foundations of the world are perfect ideas because we understood that this was an invention of metaphysics, of that impostor who tries to transform man into a blessed ignorant person. With good reason, she was kicked out of philosophy and returned to live with her real mother, theology.

Philosophy finally regained its lucidity and gave the responsibility of the search for knowledge to its most responsible daughter, science. Metaphysics continues to be kept alive, even if consumed by insanity and absorbed in itself. During her crises, as she throws herself against the walls of the absolute, we hear her scream that her greatest shame is to have been replaced by something so superficial. We didn't listen to what she says: she deceived us while she could, and she deserves to be despised for that.

✳ ✳ ✳

The man leaves the dark room of his beliefs and begins to observe the world with his own eyes. You're empty-handed. He didn't carry under his arm an instruction manual that would teach him how to interpret everything he saw. The first thing you see is that there is a world outside your head, but you lack words to define it. You feel your helplessness, your abandonment. He cries because he's alone. He does what he can with what is presented to him, but he still prays that he is wrong.

Many, hoping that nihilism will be a transitory condition until we are reconciled again with God, prefer to define existence as something intrinsically incomplete. So *the world is—just*. This is so that we are led to believe that we must complete the sentence for science to have full meaning. We are tempted to open the back door to allow metaphysics to return.

Let us have the petulance of placing the last nail in God's coffin. To bury this last hope, let us affirm, with a firm and precise hammer, that *the* world is nothing. With that, we burned the divine book to write the book of man. We opened a blank book and wrote down the first thing we were able to observe: the world exists and we are in it, nothing more.

With the end of metaphysics and the reduction of the world to nothing, we abandoned our ideal objectives and returned to seeing the world with the eyes, not with the intellect. We went back to walking using our own legs. We accept that if we want a manual, we must write it ourselves. To this end, we become observant and descriptive. That was the way we found to become self-taught in a world where there are no teachers. Science was then born as the attitude of seeking reality through the senses, which are no longer corrupted by sin. Phenomena cease to be deceptive appearances that hide reality and become what allows us to understand it.

The project of our knowledge then becomes the description of reality, and thus the rejection of absolute certainties is more than justified. Our knowledge ceases to be an attempt to explain and make sense of reality. In the quest for knowledge, all we have are notes about what we observe. We can rewrite them as much as we want and we will never achieve anything absolute, unless we laminate our notepads in the form of dogmas. The dream of an ideal explanation for existence still haunts us, but all we achieved with it was to invent countless imaginary worlds that say nothing about the one we're in.

As we can see, science will never give us absolute certainty, and repudiating it with absolute uncertainty means resurrecting the error for which it was a solution. We're ridiculous when we try to refute physics with metaphysical uncertainties. The knowledge achieved by observation can only be refuted by observation - that is why so many wait for miracles. We overcame our fundamental error by abandoning the religious concept of ideal certainty and embracing the human concept of real description. If, now, after so many advances in this direction, our sense of security tempts us to once again have faith in the possibility of definitive theories about the world, we know that this is unsustainable, because everything that seeks to idealize reality is unsustainable. With this, we are only trying to mitigate our insecurity in the face of the world through final scientific dogmas.

Science is true because it concerns what is real. We shouldn't confuse the fact that our theories work with the idea that the world is a scientific theory. It would be foolish to close ourselves off to the world, embracing our conclusions in a mirrored dome while declaring ourselves the measure of all things. In the absence of a heavenly father, we cannot simply declare ourselves to be the supreme owners of the truth. The world is something autonomous that precedes reason. It is not the description we make of it, but what we observe externally, that is the object of our descriptions. Something that is independent of us, in which we exist as a chance circumstance, not as an eternal essence.

Therefore, we will never find absolute certainties, because they do not exist. They are not just something that we are not capable of because of the incompetence of our mental faculties. Certainties are only important to those who need to have faith, not to those who need to know. Then, when we find certainties, it will only mean that we declare ourselves the ideal essence of the world, which has always been our secret metaphysical ambition.

The truth is not something ideal and rational, but real and irrational. Our knowledge of the world, therefore, cannot be anything other than the descriptive rationalization of a fundamentally irrational existence. In this situation, our only criterion of truth can only be reality—and our theories will be true as long as they are in accordance with the facts we observe. Of course, such correspondences, being human constructs, are conditional and relative in nature, and can never be found behind the world, *in* the abstract.

From this perspective, the only truth is reality, and the only thing we can know are the facts that we observe. The rest are errors, although we prefer to call them "personal truths" whose reality is only in our heads. There are no reasons to be discovered, just facts to be described. To date, this has been the only view that has proven to be objectively sustainable - and by that we mean *proven*, and not by theologians or other irrational animals.

If you are wondering what reality is, what could we answer? Now, if you want to know it, then let them help us find out, but in the right way, that is, with the eyes, not with the head. We don't want guesses or advice, or higher truths about a parallel dimension where sparkling corpses are floating. Those are the conditions. If they're not willing to help, then at least shut up, sink your eyes into your bibles, and leave us alone. We don't want theology to meddle again in what never concerned it.

In these circumstances, we know that our knowledge can only be relative and subjective, since it comes from the relationship between the subject and the object. Even what we observe in the objective world results from the activity of a subject. There is no absolute and impartial knowledge, regardless of a particular perspective, because we can only contact the world through private perspectives; there is no way to observe without an observer; it is impossible to be impersonal because we are people. Our knowledge cannot be objective in and of itself because it is not in the world, but only in our subjective understanding of it.

In order to resolve this impasse imposed by subjective relativity, we have developed methods to ensure that our knowledge is independent not of the subject, but of the particular circumstances of those subjects, so that it applies equally to everyone under any conditions. Completely impersonal knowledge cannot be our goal, because it would be incomprehensible to us, something inhuman: an indecipherable dogma that we do not know where it came from or what it means.

This relativity, as we see, is a real problem, not just a pretext for ignoring the facts. Every effort of science to constitute itself as a reliable method of investigating reality has as its fundamental goal to reduce this relativity to acceptable levels, so that embracing doubt becomes something less plausible than accepting the knowledge resulting from observations. In science, we never work with certainties, but with probabilities. When it's much more likely that we're almost right rather than completely wrong, we're on the right track. We may be wrong, but we don't see any problem with that: we will correct the error as soon as we find it.

What we call objective knowledge, therefore, is not something that exists without a subject, but that can be independently verified by any subject, as many times as they want, for as long as they deem necessary, always arriving at the same results. Unlike subjective and personal knowledge, which is mixed with mutable elements that exist only within our minds, objective knowledge is a methodical and accurate description of the reality that exists independently of us. With this, we are very close to understanding the world in itself, but without inserting ourselves into it. Rather, we brought it within us through observation.

＊ ＊ ＊

Only after looking at a long distance does it become possible to also look inside with the same clarity as those who observe themselves from the outside. We finally discovered that the ideal is only a tiny fraction of the real. This clear distinction between subjective and objective was only possible because we understood that we are also reality, that the subject is not a ghost that escapes the rules. Even the most delusional daydreams about a parallel reality objectively happen in the subject's head, and we can prove it experimentally. With this, we found the link that allows us to relate both spheres and understand them as a single reality, which can be viewed from two completely different perspectives - the subjective and the objective.

We know that our subjective world results from physical processes that occur objectively, creating a kind of subjective virtual reality, that is, what we call consciousness. Because arbitrary content is presented to our consciousness, without the necessary correspondence in external reality, it seems to exist in a "parallel dimension" to the material one. Its supposed independence from the physical world, however, is an illusion. *However, if it seems to us that the creation of a virtual subjective universe with an objective basis is an absurd hypothesis, based on radical and extreme materialism, it is enough to observe that computers essentially do the same using microchips.* The difference is that we use neurons.

Such discussions seem distant and irrelevant to us, but we reap the benefits of it all the time. Today, we know how to explain why we are rational and why we often become irrational. We know the reason for being born, for dying, for everything that happens in our bodies. We were able to understand why we became sick and also why we were cured. We discovered why birds fly, and we built machines that also fly, based on the same principles, and we used them to transport us around the world. We understand why we fell in love, why we were happy or sad. All of this can be explained and demonstrated in material and logical terms, including the behavior of those who refuse to accept such explanations. Anyone, faced with this, who affirms that our knowledge about the world is not real, probably has a notion of reality according to which the very world we are in is not something real.

We can affirm, therefore, that the world is not a subjective illusion, since even subjectivity can be explained in objective terms. The senses are not deceiving us, but informing us about the world. Senses that deceive their owners would never have allowed us to survive. If we can deal with the world through them, that means that they work, even if they were created for different purposes. We have to admit that, if not because we think that being eaten by a hungry beast is also not something real, that we are faced with the illusion of a fictitious animal that deceptively devours us, throwing supposedly red blood on all dubious sides of an uncertain world.

Faced with the rigorous, independent and experimental construction of knowledge so precise that it allows us to even understand why we were wrong, it is not admissible to doubt it without also doubting the existence of the world itself. Not that this isn't done, since many make hypotheses about other worlds with other rules just to demonstrate that we may be wrong. But even if that were the case, we wouldn't be wrong about *this* world. Furthermore, we would be very interested in observing this other world as well, if it existed. What we cannot do, however, is to physically demonstrate the non-existence of what does not exist. We can only observe and describe what we find - what we see exists, the rest does not, at least until the contrary is observed. Of course, we haven't found everything yet, but that's no reason to assert that we haven't found anything or that we should respect hypotheses that are hidden from observation in parallel worlds, accessible only through faith. If we are ignoring some reality so grandiose that, when studying physics, we are only wasting time, whoever knows it will do us the expensive favor of showing it. It's not inside us; we've already looked in that place, especially in the heart, and we haven't seen anything other than what appears in the anatomy books. We are open to the facts, we want to know the whole reality, without exception. What we don't want, however, is that they come to us with absolute truths, gods, or smiling pantheisms; we don't want to know the world like someone who prays to it.

✳ ✳ ✳

After so much discipline, we regret the restricted use given to scientific discoveries, which do not cover the so-called "important" issues. Reality is ignored in exchange for asynine beliefs about magical entities that come from heaven and commit suicide to save us from something that she herself created. They believe this nonsense and, however, when they have to print their holy books, they don't raise their hands to the heavens and ask for the pages to be multiplied. They use the advanced digital printing technologies developed by science. They buy rechargeable batteries of 100% earthly origin, place them on their wireless microphones designed by science, and transmit their metaphysical preaching at frequencies discovered by scientists, in which they discuss at length the nullity of the material world.

Nothing perplexes us more than to see objective truth being placed as a means to, it is said, "higher" ends. The truth cannot be used, since it is the ground that allows us to walk. There is no "for" for us to walk or "for" for us to achieve any goal. The world is not a red carpet created for our legs to walk happily. Objective truth is the world itself, and we exist within it, not the other way around. There is no way to "go beyond", "transcend" reality, whatever such meaningless expression means, and we are also not interested in consuming the hallucinogens that allow such transcendence.

Means and ends are things related to mammals that need to fill their bellies. The reality is what determines how all this happens - it is the emptiness of the belly, the one who feels hungry, the food, and everything else. Believing that we can feed on rocks will not nourish us. In a deck game, cards are reality: absurdity defines them, chance delivers them, and we play them among ourselves, in the game called life. All we can do is understand how things happen. We don't have a choice. Believing that we have any already shows that we don't understand anything about the world in which we live, that we are still stuck with notions of an ideal reality invented by ourselves, in which physical reality is an imperfect version of our beliefs. Being stardust, for example, is not something you choose, it's not something you believe in, it's not a state of mind for those who feel in union with matter — it's our only condition of existence.

Someone who believes more in money than in reality has probably forgotten that we invented paper money. Let them seek power, if that's what they want, but they won't be able to buy the truth, they can't get it into prostitution; no matter how many digits there are on the check with which they try to bribe gravity. The position of those who deny actual reality and place humanized or transcendental ones in its place is no less foolish. Personal beliefs and superstitions that reinvent the world make us blind, like those who have eyes only to see reality and then deliberately believe otherwise.

The truth will never be on our side, nor on the opposite side, because atoms are not attached to those who give them affectionate nicknames. It doesn't make sense to challenge it, deny it, or affirm it. It doesn't stand up against us, nor does it hide. He doesn't judge us, he doesn't care. You don't have to be defended, because you didn't commit any crime to need lawyers. We, as real beings, are part of the truth: it is our abode. When we defend the truth, we do so as someone who defends himself, as someone who protects his nose from a punch. We are curious because those who know the world know themselves. Pretending only works with other human beings. Matter cannot be fooled. The same brain that creates our subjective world works within the parameters of objective reality. Even when we lie, when we're wrong, it happens honestly and physically. We're not running away from anything with foolish beliefs. Daydreaming, the most abstract dream in an alternative reality, only happens after this one.

We can see that, in terms of knowledge, when we place reality as the ultimate value, as the ultimate truth, we are adopting the only stance that can have an objective criterion, which is independent of us. Thus, objective knowledge becomes the only legitimate currency, since there will always be a reality that corresponds to it and assures its value, whatever the circumstances. Facts without underlying realities, on the contrary, are like unbacked paper money, bottomless checks issued by human understanding—valid only to their owners.

From this point of view, nothing is more universal than science. Everyone has access to reality, although apprehending its rules requires research, reflection, and honesty. Research to see them, reflection to learn them, honesty to accept them. However, what's the point of studying the human brain scientifically if we don't guide our lives by what is discovered? We are wasting time studying without reaping the benefits, claiming that in practical life things are "not quite like that", as they are. Everything is like that.

When we stop separating ourselves from the world, when we recognize that we are not in reality, but that *we are* also reality, that physics does not stop where our consciousness begins, we are mature, ready to follow the thorny path of thinking for ourselves freely, without the danger of succumbing to the seductions of error. To illustrate this position, let's think about the following: how would we live if we needed to be honest as if our lives depended on it? We would be honest out of self-interest, we would always tell the truth so as not to suffer the consequences. That's exactly the case. Reality cannot be deceived, and when we are deceived, we will suffer the consequences of being ignorant. It's a sign of maturity to be honest, because our lives really depend on it.

Understanding that the value of knowledge lies in its reality, it is common to be fascinated by the search for truth, which means investigating the world. From then on, we did not admit that it must compete with lies in search of space and recognition. Because it's the only thing that exists, truth has already proven its worth, and we don't need to justify our disdain for error. Guided by this understanding, we began to seek the truth out of personal interest. Being honest becomes an indisputable starting point, and everything you lie about becomes an enemy. We became lucid, fully aware of our condition, and began to seek knowledge like someone who finally learned to use the brain for our own benefit. Everything begins to be interpreted according to objective reality, even our subjective desires, because your satisfaction must occur objectively. In that moment, we see that the ideal itself consciously becomes real. We see our subjective lives taking place within our minds as an objective fact. The result of this is honesty, the most profound honesty that we can conceive, which is to be guided, as a subjective being, by understanding the rules of the objective world. We glimpse the real perspective of everything we know theoretically. From that moment on, we admitted that we existed in the real world without reservations or pleasantries, and the idea of being wrong about this is repudiated as absurd, insanity, and imbecility.

✳ ✳ ✳

Man finally becomes an adult, abandons his metaphysical toys and sets foot in the real world. However, the fact that this process is painful does not make it worthy of any praise - because, if pain were a good criterion, all truths would be achieved by torture. It is a personal quest, like any other, even if we are looking for something that may be useful to everyone, since objective knowledge is universally valid. Any individual can make use of the knowledge of reality. This only requires that we be honest, that we see the world with our eyes, separated from our lives, values, and beliefs, without interpreting and falsifying it from a personal perspective.

Even so, we are necessarily honest only with ourselves, as social honesty is an entirely different issue. Integrity can only be valuable in a personal approach, insofar as it requires us to be absolutely honest with ourselves, making us more aware of reality. That same integrity, from a social point of view, would no longer apply. In society, being completely honest is equivalent to the most complete inconsequence, since the rules of the social game are different. Lying to others is inevitable. Lying to yourself is largely optional.

Obviously, being enlightened is not about kindness, because we are not lucid like those who give charity to the blind. We want to guide ourselves, not guide them. If we may help others, we must know and make it clear that this was not the original intention - by chance, this was an indirect and inevitable consequence of our activity. It is not up to us to demand gratitude, since this task stems from our personal need to walk with our feet on the ground. In this we find the direct advantage of not stumbling all the time, because we know well the terrain on which we are walking. We don't require others to follow in our footsteps, but if that happens, we will benefit indirectly. This fact will not help us in any way directly, however, by ceasing to be blind, the others will at least cease to be a wandering obstacle. They'll be more unlikely to bump into us for free.

We know that, in the end, we have no choice as to the path we follow. Some men are free to seek the truth, others are not. Integrity would be the undoing of those who rely on delusions. That would implode them. The man who suffers with the truth must lie instinctively, give it the names "evil" and "sin". Honesty becomes a vice and faith a virtue. We don't see this as a matter of choice. We can't live any other way either. We need to be honest, just like others have to be wrong. All the romantic daydreams about the spiritual greatness of those who seek the truth are naivety: to believe that, we would only be fawning over our personal vanity. We're honest for the same reason we scratch our heads with matches: because the other way around doesn't work.

Just as fingernails grow on our fingers, thoughts grow in our minds. Just like our nails are tough, we're honest. We deal with the world through intellectuality because we are naturally intellectuals. We rationalize the world because we are predominantly rational. This activity is part of our lives as second nature.

It never occurs to us to be compensated for our honesty, it never crosses our minds to ask for approval from others. This is as spontaneous and inevitable for us as breathing. It doesn't matter if our conclusions will be in accordance with the taste of the general public, with intellectual trends. It only matters that they are in accordance with reality. Our goal is not to gain public veneration - if this occurs, it will be by the simple chance that honesty is in evidence by some fleeting circumstance.

Since we do not cultivate knowledge with the purpose of pleasing others or convincing them of anything, it is certain that we could not compete with the fatty concepts and the sugary confections of charlatans who reduce philosophy and science to candies and fast food. Even if we try to unmask them, our calls for honesty won't be heard by the foolish, and the wise don't need to hear them. We can't just spit lucidity and expect them to thank us for the clarification; that doesn't work. For certain truths, one must be sufficiently mature.

Undoubtedly, the knowledge that they call "alternative" - which is a euphemism for unfounded - is much freer to invent itself and be attractive to individuals' personal vanities. It appeals much more directly to their intimate needs, since it was invented precisely to console those who suffer from reality. However, we can only recognize the creativity of those smart guys who profit from the ineptitude of others.

Of course, it may be said that those who can believe what they want are more "free" than those who limit themselves to what is likely to make sense. However, nothing causes us less envy than the complete freedom to *be wrong*. Like children, we do not judge the value of food by how much it pleases at first sight, but by the health of the bodies it builds. Similarly, we judge the value of an idea by the reality of the vision it creates, with lucidity being the distinctive sign of intellectual health.

Just as the lives of the blessed presuppose lies, ours presuppose the truth, and we cannot allow error to creep into our thoughts without this being our bankruptcy. Faced with the possibility of living up to reality, flirting with error is like exchanging gold for trinkets. No lie can be more valuable than the truth simply because it refers to something that doesn't exist. The placebo philosophy developed for motivational purposes doesn't interest us: a thought that sells itself doesn't even deserve our word; they're just toys, crutches for those who can't deal with reality.

* * *

To illustrate this position, let's imagine a fact. If we roll it up, we know that all possible outcomes are equally likely. It will be no use blowing them, uttering mantras, or invoking the "power of the mind" to influence the results. We can even rewrite the numbers printed on each side, multiply them by a thousand; it won't make any difference. In this situation, being superstitious consists of believing that being wrong about the real possibilities will make all the difference. To be honest, on the contrary, would simply be to admit that a die works like a die, guided by the understanding that the result will always be a chance of unpredictable circumstances, but always between one and six. If we want to influence the result, we know that the only way is to vitiate the data. This is the essential idea that we must incorporate into our lives in every sense, that is, guided by the understanding of what is actually happening, not by beliefs about what we would like to see happen.

In this sense, self-criticism and honesty with oneself work as a tool to extract from ourselves the full potential of lucidity, so that we have the courage to truly live according to what we know. It is up to us to cultivate the prudence to seek and accept the truth so that we do not have to learn it with the disastrous consequences of error, as do all animals and most men. There is a lot of intelligence in anticipating the exposure of our misconceptions through the fierce criticism of our own opinions; that is what theoretical knowledge is for, and not just for designing buildings and appliances.

Even if the truth is often painful, being denied by reality will be much more devastating, since, unlike us, the world is not delicate, it does not spare us from our mistakes out of compassion. It's too late to open our eyes when we're already in the abyss, and we can't avoid it without the vertigo of having known it. Truths cannot be discovered by approaching the world delicately, nor are they protected from reality. Like muscles, our intellects outperform themselves only under pressure, when forced to, and only then will we be able to reap the benefits. We cannot perceive ignorance in and of itself: we recognize it only after it has been overcome. Thus, when we protect ourselves from the weight of reality, we are condemning ourselves to incompetence, fleeing from what inescapably determines our lives. Given this, if we choose to close our eyes, that's fine, the choice is ours. However, we must continue walking, now guided only by chance. When we fall, we will see what is the result of embracing beliefs that place more value on calm than on gravity.

When we decide to be guided by reality, we must cultivate that kind of severe love for truth, which makes us indifferent to the conventional values that surround us. So instead of listening to "advice" from others about the right direction, we'll do better to look at the compass and draw our own conclusions, regardless of what is said about it. We went in that direction because it's the right one, because it will take us where we want to go, not because we "believe" in some metaphysical nonsense about the "meaning of life" or anything like that. If we don't give ourselves the duty to be honest, no one will.

After so much effort, study, and discipline dedicated to the purpose of becoming sober and enlightened, it would be rude to allow ourselves to be influenced by drunken and stupid opinions, which focus solely on your personal interests and do not see a foot in front of your nose. Unless they present themselves before us with facts, hearing them will only be a kindness that we will regret in a few minutes, like someone who hears a broken record that only knows how to repeat their beliefs.

It would be like a doctor asking his patients for advice when interpreting the results of a blood test so that the final diagnosis would deny any illness. The doctor's duty is to be right, regardless of what that means. Your patients' ignorance about themselves should not influence you. They may believe that their illness is due to some "evil spiritual influence", to the fact that they have sinned or lied; it doesn't matter. Your role is not to cure them of their stupidity but of their diseases. As an expert, your first commitment is to the truth, and that's just why we're willing to pay you very well for your opinions regarding our health; we wouldn't give a penny to those of a mechanic in this matter. We know that when our physical health is at stake, invoking relativism over the definitions of illness will not save our lives. We need to resort to the raw reality that our bodies are machines that sooner or later have defects. We have the right to be wrong, but we know that on decisive issues, only the truth works. In other areas, on the contrary, doctors can be as illogical as they want and, for that very reason, their opinions cease to be worth more than anyone else's.

Suppose, for example, that we have become crippled in a car accident. *Many raise their voices to the skies and shout why?!* Well, just because the impact injured the spine, which is responsible for the transmission of the nerve impulses that, among other things, control our muscles. Now we can't walk because the way the brain communicated with the legs was interrupted, just like a light bulb that went out because we cut the wiring. The collision, in turn,

105

occurred because the car collided with another object and, by the laws of physics, given the speed, direction and mass of the objects involved, the consequence could not have been different. It doesn't matter whose fault it was — if ours, if another driver's; the cripples are now us, and we will have to live with it, without any existential compensation. Too late to be honest about the purpose of seat belts and *airbags*, about the scientific studies that relate alcohol consumption and our reaction time. Lame excuses are useless: we pay the price of our thoughtlessness in sight.

In this way, if we want to discover the truth about something that we consider important, we will be foolish to blindly trust the opinions of others. If they are wrong, the responsibility will be theirs, but the consequences will be us who will suffer. Let us therefore take the responsibility into our own hands and discover the truth for ourselves, based on facts, reflection, and study. It is imperative that we be rigorous and honest about the facts involved, as well as scientists. Each fantasy eliminated will make us more enlightened about reality, more aware of what is involved in determining that particular phenomenon. We must then put into practice what we have learned, regardless of what is said in this regard, because we know that those who give the last word are not the opinions of others. And even if the search for a definitive truth is something utopian, since we can only build it slowly and provisionally, and only with our own hands, to stop searching for it and presenting any nonsense as a substitute is nonsense, like saying that it is better to eat garbage, since everything will end in the sewer. This stance only serves to solve problems that lie between truth and profit. We are explorers because of our eagerness to understand, and what can be received from others is therefore a problem that we leave to the merchants.

* * *

When we investigate the great questions of existence, we embark on a kind of grandiose adventure with no clear meaning, such as climbing an unknown Everest. We test our limits just to become more lucid. We may learn this or that in the process, but only as an indirect consequence. We will not discover specific facts about a certain subject, but we will be expanding the horizons of our global understanding of existence, which extends to all subjects. We achieved a more complete and cohesive view of reality, whose value can only be apprehended in view of the total set of our knowledge. From a panoramic perspective, everything starts to make more sense. We guess obscure relationships between distant and apparently disconnected facts, we better integrate our understanding of particular facts, we organize them with greater precision and more enlightened criteria. It is an exercise that makes us more intimate with our knowledge, better suited to your employment. In the end, there are no sudden changes or grandiose rewards. The world just becomes subtly clearer.

From this perspective, it is clear why those who think for themselves see so much value in the study, in the research. By studying, we rapidly expanded our understanding of reality without the need to personally research each particular subject, even because there wouldn't be time to do it ourselves. As long as we limit ourselves to modern and current science-based studies, we can be sure that the facts presented are reliable. They have been thoroughly investigated by experts who have no interest in ruining their reputations with baseless claims. Before publishing their findings, they themselves, and especially their opponents, did everything possible to refute them. The fact that they failed to do so is reason enough for us to consider them reasonably trustworthy.

Of course, in this sense, nothing would be more logical than taking part of our time to dialogue with the most eminent scholars who have dealt with the same subject that interests us at the moment - to hear their opinions and conclusions, their suspicions and criticisms. Through reading, we are in contact with the thinking of the most profound intellects that have ever existed on the planet, and their presence honors us. Individuals with intelligence recognize themselves readily and know when they are faced with someone worthy of consideration or, on the contrary, with a pedant, an impostor, whether in person or through books.

We feel as a gift the great effort made by those who came before us. If, today, we reflect and investigate on firm ground, if we are always building on the knowledge that was bequeathed to us, there is nothing fairer than recognizing the value of those who allowed us to get here in such a short time. For those who live immersed in the now, as if locked in the immediate present, limited to

107

their own time, we may seem lonely and distant. We are, however, in great company, as we share our lives with all those whose purpose was to raise human understanding. Without studies, we would overlook the most fantastic discoveries. With great luck, we would only reinvent the wheel for the thousandth time.

Of course, as we said, no one seeks such discoveries other than out of personal interest. However, we are united by our common interest in knowledge. We value ourselves because there are always few who bother to keep burning the torch that guides humanity over the centuries. Those who choose to enlighten themselves with personal truths may be comforted by the apparent brilliance that they now possess in front of others, but this creates an ephemeral perspective, which will be forgotten as quickly as themselves. Only those who illuminate the world commit themselves to a work that, although anonymous, will remain forever in the minds of those who seek to understand it. Even if we didn't discover anything during our lives, when seeking knowledge, the same lucidity that made us more enlightened also kept the world more enlightened, without this having cost any additional effort.

The reality is harsh, and few like it. Even so, we prefer the truth, whatever its price, because we couldn't see value in anything else. In our minds, we feel that it must reign alone, away from all coercion, away from all petty interest, away from all haste to become useful. Our understanding will be polished to reflect the world in the most precise and crystalline way possible, without fear of consequences. In it all facts will be safe from the hatred of the foolish, from the persecution of the stupid, and from the revenge of the resentful. The smallest fact will have a guaranteed right to be fed up with laughing at the grandest illusion. The most terrible truth can be presented without embarrassment, without fear of intolerance or prejudice; we will know how to accept it and recognize its due value. Everyone will be able to speak freely, big or small, and celebrate the victory over ignorance alone in a place that is all their own.

Alone with our thoughts, the only ones who can pass the leg on us are ourselves. That's why we never hesitate to let our guard down and be honest. We found the advantage precisely in remaining vulnerable to the world. Because only then, wounded by a truth, do we also become more true. We know that finding it to suffer from it is an astronomical fortune, the privilege of the few who were gifted by nature with exceptional intelligence and by circumstances with the rare opportunity to cultivate it.

UNTRUTH

The bottom line is that lies and truth are exactly the same thing—but only inside our heads. So, if we want to be right, and not just believe that, we need to see beyond that. To better understand the biased mechanics of our opinions and beliefs, it will be very useful to think not only about the veracity of the subject itself, but also about how our brain works, about the criteria it uses to process and weigh the relevance of each information. Perhaps this will also allow us to begin to understand the mechanics of the placebo effect, and how much we use it in our daily lives, even if unconsciously.

At the outset, let's think about the following: pain. Why can't we feel it voluntarily, simply thinking of pain anywhere in the body, as easily as we can move our muscles? Because we're not programmed to be like that. Of course, if we could choose pain, we would never choose it. However, since pain is necessary for us to survive, and since we don't like it, the only way out would be to take it out of our control—exactly what biological evolution did. We hate pain because it is a coercive mechanism through which the brain blackmails and subdues us, a system that has been slowly and carefully refined over countless generations with the sole purpose of being unbearable, and it doesn't matter if it makes sense: the meaning is pain.

We can't feel pain voluntarily, and thinking about doing something painful doesn't hurt either. In other words, intelligence cannot control our emotions. Emotions, in turn, can control but cannot understand intelligence. Let us then realize that pain does not have free access to the content of intelligence; our emotional brain does not understand it well enough to be able to "monitor" it — otherwise thinking about suicide would be extremely painful — but intelligence, even if indirectly, has access to pain through beliefs. In other words, intelligence cannot control emotions arbitrarily, but it can inform them. For example, when we receive a phone call and are told that a loved one has died, for us this is exactly as terrible as the sight of the corpse - as long as we believe that information, of course. So, if we don't believe it, we won't feel anything. But, if we believe it, we will. This means that whether our loved one really died or not matters little. Of course, it's a single reality, but in emotional terms, the important thing is what we believe—not because beliefs, in and of themselves, have any special importance, but simply because our emotional brain has no other way of informing itself about reality. This brain does not know how to think: its only way of having opinions is believing, and beliefs are nothing more than the obese, slow and stupid version of rational opinions, but created by the emotional brain.

We know that reality is one thing and that the idea we make of it is another, and also that both things do not always coincide. However, emotionally, reality is the idea we make of it in a much more radical and inflexible sense than rationally. This means that if we believe that our relative did not die, then he really did not die, and nothing will convince us otherwise. It's dead, it's decomposing, but it's not dead. Well it is. It may be absurd, but it's also the key to understanding the issue: believing works, and it has profound effects on how we experience reality. In affective terms, the difference between truth and lies is not in reality itself, but in the imperfect version of it that exists in our heads - and it is our heads that control our bodies: let us be careful to calmly ruminate the importance of this.

Far from being perfect, our knowledge is just a kind of bet we make about what reality probably is, and it just needs to be good enough to guide our actions. That is its original function. Of course, sometimes we make the wrong bets, because our opinions don't have time to be scientific, let alone our beliefs, but it's much more likely that we have erroneous beliefs than opinions, since the former are much more resistant to change. Thus, with the exception of controversial issues, most of individuals' opinions about reality are usually reasonably wise, but beliefs are often decidedly stupid. In general, we correct our opinions of our own free will, but in relation to our beliefs we want the corrections to magically come from a fantastic corrective intervention. Furthermore, we think that erroneous beliefs must have something psychologically different from the true ones, but they don't. Being wrong doesn't necessarily cause discomfort. We can feel good or bad depending on true or false

111

beliefs, because the belief that something is true and the very veracity of that conviction, as well as the resulting effects, are completely different issues that only tend to go hand in hand. In fact, for some issues, being wrong can be good - as if to motivate us. In others, no — such as about the voltage of electrical appliances. However, if we think that, within all this, there must be, in the end, some reliable criterion that guarantees that our beliefs must have at least some necessary relationship with reality, the answer is simple: there isn't. Let us remember that the meaning of life is to survive, not to understand.

Now let's consider the following: we have a rational brain and an emotional brain. One thinks, the other feels. So if we mix thought and feeling, what will we have? Belief — that is, a passionate dogma armed with philosophical reasons. Let us realize, then, that our beliefs constitute a kind of bridge between emotions and intelligence, and that is the reason why, once these connections are made, emotions begin to exercise exclusive control over such opinions, and reason no longer influences them, whether they are true or not. To illustrate, it is enough to think about what is called an ideology, that is, an opinion that appears to be rational on the surface, that even makes use of reason to defend itself, but that in fact was born and is at the service of emotions.

Our philosophical opinions, for example, are formulated by the rational brain, and they are malleable because they are emotionally neutral. We can discuss them, and we agree to change them without any difficulty. Beliefs, on the other hand, are emotional opinions, they are the equivalent of an opinion, but in our primitive brain, over which we have no control. Not only is this emotional brain out of our control, but it is also much older and more rudimentary, much more inefficient than the rational brain, and the number of interpretation errors and *bugs* that occur during trivial update processes is remarkable. The primitive brain doesn't work as well as the rational brain, and it didn't get that name by chance: it works really crude—it's limited, inflexible, and frequently errs on issues that, for the more modern rational brain, would be obvious. However, evolutionarily, it came first, and that means that its power over the fate of the organism is greater. That's why death, on the other side of the world, is a statistic; on our side, it's a tragedy, and we don't have the freedom to see things differently.

✳ ✳ ✳

In a sense, as we saw above, it makes no difference whether a certain belief corresponds to reality or not, and it also doesn't matter what we think - it matters what we believe. So, since beliefs involve both emotion and reason, this means that in these matters reason will always be obliterated by emotion— always. The reason will only be taken into account if it has emotionally relevant information. In other situations, it will simply be ignored. Thus, when discussing issues involving emotional beliefs—the belief in immortality, for example— we may believe that being wise and presenting concrete evidence that proves our point of view will suffice, but this is a mistake, because in fact we are not arguing with the individual's rational brain, but exchanging growls with their emotional brain, and that's literally. The emotional brain interprets contrary arguments as barks, not as words — and in this process, reason is busy counting how many teeth each one has. Not to reach the truth, they are arguing just to prove that they are right, to win, defeat the opponent, impress those who observe, and that's it.

Therefore, when discussing such issues, we are in dialogue with the individual's mammalian brain, and how stupid this is requires no comment. Whenever the issue is brought up, it is as if the reason were left with its hands tied while an impostor speaks on your behalf: an emotional kidnapping, pure and simple. And the distinctive sign of this emotional hijacking is that, even if the individual maintains his speech within a superbly rational style, he behaves like an ignorant beast — and, in the face of conflicting evidence, his reaction is to raise his voice. He may be the greatest doctor of philosophy: at that moment, his soul is that of a donkey. Of course, in other subjects, emotion retreats and gives space to reason, and that ignorant beast returns to being the kind bipedal we knew until we touched on the subject.

This explains a lot of things, but it explains the difference between science and religion exceptionally well. We have two brains, and those two areas represent our best efforts to talk to just one of them in isolation. That's why science is cold. That's why religion is emotive. That's why scientists are open to evidence and, religious, to revelations. Therefore, for science, truth is objective;

for religion, subjective. That's why science is able to update itself easily, but religion remains stuck in time. One deals with the rational brain, the other with the emotional brain - and that is also why it is possible for us to be scientists and religious at the same time. Thus, we may see scientists, but we will never see science claiming that everything, except man, is matter, because science uses techniques that protect us from this kind of emotional coercion that distorts our knowledge. Religion, in turn, does exactly the opposite: it seeks to protect us from reality.

We know that opinions are easy to correct: just let us know. However, erroneous beliefs, due to their emotional background, are extremely difficult to abandon, because in order to be subject to correction, it is not enough that they are erroneous, it is not enough that we know this, it is also necessary that we believe in this - and this is the biggest problem: how to inform and control the emotional brain rationally, if reason itself is under your control? We can't: beliefs shackle intelligence.

Thus, on the one hand, the emotional brain has no way of knowing whether a belief is true or false and, on the other hand, intelligence is not capable of exercising direct control over it: the result is that there is no way to change them directly and voluntarily, through the use of reason. Maybe we know that's wrong, but we feel it's right, so for all intents and purposes it's right, period. Emotional beliefs only change for emotional reasons, and that's a well-known fact. So, if we want to influence our emotions, how do we do it? We know that we cannot control our emotions directly, but indirectly, yes, and the recipe is simple: just say what they want to hear in a language they can understand - and they listen, because beliefs are not our enemies, they are just dumb. We can then use the rational brain to create a kind of theater in which there will be emotionally relevant situations that will lead us to believe what we want according to any objective. In other words: brainwashing.

Of course, when thinking of brainwashing, we immediately imagine brainwashed religious people or prisoners of war under torture, but that is a narrow-minded view. Let us think about the following: what characterizes religious conversion? Personal experiences — of which faith is a consequence, not the cause. The same is true for physical torture: it changes the way we see the world after we have been subjected to that traumatic experience for a sufficiently long period. That is why religion is not discussed: it is practiced. That's why torture is not discussed: it's inserted under the fingernails. Only through action can we achieve emotionally significant results.

To understand how vast the scope of this idea is, it is enough to go to a field further away from these crazy things - for example, the medical field focused on mental health - and observe that they are guided by exactly the same principles in the treatment of phobias: putting it into practice. We know that talking rationally with fear is useless, so to overcome it, we expose ourselves controllably to the situation that causes us fear as often as necessary, until the emotional brain is convinced of this, and allows us to be rational in that matter again. This is also brainwashing, but for constructive purposes, and let's realize that none of this is too far from our daily lives. If we pay some attention, we will see how common and easy to find examples of the application of these ideas are: in churches with their holy contradictions, in companies with their motivational techniques, in self-help books with their headless optimism, in psychological therapies with their canned self-knowledge, in group activities with their coercive prejudices and the like - there are countless techniques that we develop to manipulate our emotions indirectly, and none of them are related to the truth. All are based on the same principle of brainwashing: the affective conditioning performed in order to alter our way of feeling reality and, therefore, the rational opinion we have of it. We know that such things are lies, but we like our emotional brain to believe them, so we use them. There are, of course, many interesting possibilities to be explored in emotional manipulation, including the possible advantages of believing in lies. However, everything has a price and, if we are not careful, the process can leave irreparable scars on our intelligence - which is the reason why God exists.

With that in mind, let's realize that the idea that "it's enough to believe" actually applies, at least in certain subjects. It is true that reality cannot be controlled by our beliefs, but our way of perceiving it can - and the detail is that, for us, it is the same. Beliefs, true or false, influence our consciousness, our emotions, our biology, and there's nothing magical about that — it's an obvious consequence of the fact that our bodies are managed by our brains, which can do whatever they want. However, we must bear in mind that this control is restricted to what is physiologically feasible, affecting only what is physically connected to our brains. Ignoring this limitation gives rise to several beliefs about the power of the mind - *e.g. the blunders promoted by parapsychology*. Our beliefs only control our idea of reality. The reality itself always remains the same. Therefore, when we think about this issue, we must limit ourselves to the universe created by ourselves, that is, to our representations of reality.

To better illustrate the mechanism behind this idea, suppose that we feel insignificant before society and want to change that situation. Since we cannot simply give ourselves that feeling through the use of intelligence, we will have to manipulate ourselves indirectly, and in this process there are two approaches: we can do everything possible to convince others that we are important, and then believe their testimony, or simply believe it on our own for reasons that only exist in our heads. In other words, we can play fair, as biology intended, that is, manipulating reality, becoming socially outstanding, gaining that importance indirectly, through a *status* reflected in public opinion, and as a result we believe ourselves to be important - or simply manipulate the mind, cultivating any erroneous beliefs that provide us with that same feeling. The result is identical: the belief that we are important and the net profit in pleasure.

Let's think more about it. What's the difference between being important and just believing in it? In terms of truth, none. However, in terms of society, the whole. If only we believe that we are important, that is a lie; if everyone believes that we are important, that is a truth. That is why in these matters lies and truth are exactly the same thing, since none of them corresponds to any objective reality, but only to collective judgments, which agree on the values that guide society as a whole. Such arbitrary beliefs — such as our personal value — are, strictly speaking, just delusions, but they can also be understood as games that appeared in us as a side effect of their reproductive utility. In other words, we compete because it works, not because it makes sense. Thus, let us bear in mind that such competitions orchestrated by biology are at the service of genetic perpetuation, and that our need to compete, in itself, is only an indirect consequence of the types of behaviors that are favorable to the reproduction of our genes. Of course, such competitions, in and of themselves, are empty, because the game is nothing more than a medium for competition, which in turn is nothing more than a means for perpetuation. However, it doesn't matter that those beliefs have no reality behind them, because in life, as in any game, the important thing is to compete.

From this point of view, it is obvious why we give much more importance to the opinion of others than to our own regarding our personal value, even though we know that, rationally, this does not make the slightest sense. The opinion we have of ourselves is emotionally irrelevant in this regard precisely because winning alone is worthless - for any belief to be biologically relevant, everyone must believe in it. So, since the value of these conventional games can only be understood if we consider the implications of competition in genetic eternity, it makes perfect sense that the belief that we are important is pleasurable, and it also makes perfect sense that we cannot believe this voluntarily, because we are dealing with the representation of importance, not with the importance itself. It's vital that it be difficult to fake.

Of course, within that, our personal motives, our explanations and rationalizations of our actions are just verborrhagic dreams. What really counts is our behavior. In other words, it doesn't matter the reasons why we think we compete, but only that we compete according to publicly recognized criteria. Our tendency to use public recognition as a value reference reflects only behavior that was favorable to genetic perpetuation. This, on the one hand, reveals the gratuity of our competitions, but also the reason why we do not welcome those who have beliefs that do not correspond to reality. This is because, for competition to be biologically relevant, it is important that our beliefs are honest indicators of reality. That's why we don't envy those who feel pleasure without deserving it: even if they feel like a winner, those who win alone can only be a lunatic. These are things like that we think of those who try to defraud emotional brain games. Although, in the end, there is no difference between one thing and another, we insist on believing that there is, and we use such pretexts to feel justified.

✶ ✶ ✶

So far, we've investigated why it's difficult to control our beliefs, and why it's important to do so. We also understand that reality and our idea of reality are not necessarily corresponding—and also that much of our idea of reality is simply an invention within the game of life.

What is the relationship of all this with our daily lives? All of it. Such biological *nonsenses* are what drives us. If we don't admit it, it's just because we don't like to touch on a subject that will inevitably arouse the fury of our inner quadruped. However, the fact is that we are an evolutionary workaround, and even if this idea is uncomfortable, it allows us to understand why this virtual reality called consciousness is programmed - and the emotions that guide it - and thus finally we understand a little better why we are so contradictory and so complicately incoherent.

At first, the idea that we live in a reality invented by ourselves may seem absurd, but in truth it is too obvious: we are talking about what is known as *culture*, which is a kind of expansion package for biology. The interesting thing about arriving at the notion of culture through the idea of an invented reality is that this allows us to understand it from another perspective — as if we were almost outside of it — providing us with a very clear idea of the point at which biology and culture intersect. So, if we want to discern between culture and biology, it is enough to realize that biology is based on physical reality, and that culture is an arbitrary continuation of the physical mechanisms of the functioning of life, invented by ourselves: we build a contingent relationship between biology and physics based on learned emotional behaviors. In other words, the cultural portion of reality is equivalent to a physical reality whose need is guaranteed by our beliefs.

In this way, just as the reality that we learn through the senses is a representation, so is culture. The difference is that the representation created by culture does not have an objective reality behind it - it is simply a phantasmagoria that we believe in for emotional reasons. It should be noted then that biology has its own existence, but culture does not. In this sense, if biology were a house, it would be a real house, with real rooms, and culture would be composed of representations of rooms - such as doors painted on walls, arbitrary internal subdivisions, and the like. However, in practice, we live as if both types of rooms, biological and cultural, were equally real, for the simple fact that we emotionally believe in them.

Biology, therefore, is reality in itself, and culture is based on our idea of reality. This view offers us a good criterion for discerning between objective facts and subjective beliefs: facts do not need to be defended, since they can be observed and proven. Beliefs, in turn, can only be defended, since there is no way to observe or prove them, since we invented them ourselves. To illustrate, let's think of a child. An objective fact would be this: children are the pups of *Homo sapiens.* If we saw her born a short time ago from an adult, that means that she is a puppy. It doesn't matter if we like her or not, whether we sympathize with her parents or not. Whether we love or hate that child, it is a developing physical organism, its existence is a fact, and it doesn't matter what opinion we have about it.

Facts are the kind of issues for which there are never two sides - they are something that is not discussed because we will never find anyone who disagrees with us. On the other hand, a cultural issue would be this: children should not work. On this issue, there are those who defend that it is right and those that are wrong, but we are not trying to find out who has the best rhetoric, but who is right. But where could we look for physical evidence of this? We cannot, because such an idea does not correspond to a physical reality, just to a custom, a belief. Culture isn't based on evidence. This means that both are wrong, or at least that neither is right, since the fact is that there are no moral realities. Then, whatever our opinion is, there will be no way to prove it objectively.

So, on subjective issues, no matter how much we discuss, we will never arrive at the truth, because there are no subjective truths — we will reach, at most, a consensus. In turn, on objective issues, it doesn't even occur to us to discuss, because objective facts, because they are impartial in themselves, are also impersonal and emotionally neutral. In other words, relativity is not in reality, but in our very creative beliefs about it. What reality is in itself not only independent from one perspective, but it also does not admit any perspective:

there is no way to have personal opinions and views about whether potassium atoms exist or not. On the other hand, the truths that enable optics are also reduced to them: inventions of monkeys vying for metaphysical bananas. So it doesn't matter what we think about one thing or another, because, in one case, it won't change anything and, in the other, neither will it.

The distinction drawn above allows us to understand the following: the fact that children are human pups is knowledge; the fact that children should or should not work is a judgment. Thus, in general, all the issues for which it is not enough to understand, but also to experience, take sides, and be personally involved in order for us to perceive their supposed truth, are contained in the portion of reality created by ourselves. This means that political, religious, social, moral beliefs, etc. — that is, everything that we scream but unable to prove — are our personal ways of flourishing and distorting reality based on those blind emotional beliefs that are right, period. The characteristic sign of knowledge, on the contrary, is the fact that we don't have to believe anything to recognize its validity: it is self-evident and needs no introduction or optics. Objective knowledge simply ignores our imaginary separations, our cultural beliefs, crossing them as what they are: nothing. Of course, knowledge, alone, generally seems cold, limited, and unsatisfactory to us, as if it needed to be interpreted for it to gain meaning, but it doesn't have to. We just have no interest in defending something that does not admit a partial perspective, which we cannot distort in our favor, and that makes it an emotionally useless issue, but it does not diminish its true value in any way. The problem is just that we don't love the opinions that don't love us back.

Since all of these arbitrariness that we fight for are essentially emotional, which one we believe in, and on which side we fight, depends only on the type of brainwashing that we receive throughout our lives, and especially during childhood - implying that none of this is chosen. So, whatever the conviction, if we feel inflated and start fighting to defend it, that's what matters. This is because, since such realities are our own creation, being right doesn't matter — nor is it possible — because the important thing is just to be convinced that it is worth fighting to defend them, even if there is absolutely nothing to be gained by doing so.

The general case of these beliefs can be put as follows: we insist on being right in a question invented by ourselves — and we are willing to fight to prove it — while our enemies are wrong because they did exactly the same thing, but they didn't invent the same conclusion as us. The dispute begins; however, since both are arguing about which fantasy is more real, facts cannot decide anything: it will be certain who wins the fight. Religion, sports, and politics are crystal clear examples of this.

Let us also note the following: we can only cultivate rationality in spaces that emotion does not occupy. So, if, on any issue, we want to remain rational, the only possibility would be to try to remain calm and emotionally neutral. This is because, in relation to rational opinions, emotions are like a jellyfish: they are petrified when they see it - and they will never change again for the rest of our lives. Thus, if we want to become freethinkers capable of independent reflection, we must resort to study and books, not to debates, militancy, and heated disputes, and do everything possible to distance ourselves from emotional situations involving the subject, dissociating it from our interests and vanity. It is wise to proceed in this way because, when we are personally involved with any issue, it is inevitable that we will become biased. Whenever we can choose an issue in which we are involved, we will choose partially - it is a temptation that we cannot resist, and the only alternative is not to have a side to choose from. Then, once we manage to achieve this perspective of distance, we will finally understand that, for whatever reason, socialism is correct, and so is capitalism - depending on the myopia that hooked us.

In these imaginary disputes, we like to believe that we're the only ones with reason on our side, but we're just short-sighted monkeys blabbering about their absurdities. Whatever it is, the choice we are left with, despite feeling inclined to praise it, will depend only on our personality - and our personalities are just a personal accident, a miscellany of inherited and learned prejudices, without there being anything worthy of respect in the opinions that they inspire, because all the truths that need to be defended are lies - especially those that, right now, we are looking for a pretext to classify as an exception. Within that, the way in which each one governs their life is merely a matter of style, and as much as we disagree with that statement, it only reveals our partiality, our inability to look at ourselves with the same contempt that we dispense with the opinions of others simply because they do not correspond to ours.

To illustrate this rather inelegant phenomenon of hating individuals for free just because they don't agree with us, let's think of the classic dispute between those who delude themselves and those who are disappointed, between those who love lies and those who destroy them in the name of truth, keeping in mind that our passions enslave us. Which is better: living in the name of happiness, even if it involves being wrong, or living in the name of truth, even if it involves being disgraced? The answer is simple: whatever. However, if we look at the issue more closely, we will also see the following: those who love lies and despise the truth will be slaves to lies, but those who love the truth and hate lies will be slaves to both - they will be certain, but they will be forever enslaved to it, as fanatics of truth, emotionally submissive to an impersonal reality and arch-enemies of a clumsy lie. In practical terms, the burden of the former seems lighter. However, if we like to be certain, whatever the cost, that's fine, but that doesn't make us superior to those who like to delude themselves, because they are guided by other criteria, and with good reason they view us with the same contempt with which we view them. The fact is that there is no reason to be proud of choosing the most enlightened way of returning to non-existence. Whatever side we take, if we can't choose it now, that means we never could. So if we don't have a side yet, maybe the best we can do is to continue like this.

* * *

Let us now return to the issue of religious belief and continue on this subject a little more from the perspective that we have outlined so far. Some people are religious, others are not. However, those who don't believe in gods are generally amazed that so many are able to believe so firmly in something for which there is no evidence. In general, believing in lies is not a good *idea—e.g.* going on a trip based on the mere belief that there is plenty of gas in the tank. We do everything possible to be right, but we can't always choose. Sometimes we close our eyes, but sometimes our eyes close by themselves. Therein lies the key issue. Let's take a closer look at this mechanism.

Theists are wrong. We know that. But why can't we convince them of this through reason? For the same reason that we couldn't, through reason, convince a man to have sex with his sister. Even if we demonstrated scientifically that there would be no problem with that, such evidence would simply be ignored. In other words, in certain matters, we are not willing to be rational. We couldn't. The parallel allows us to understand that discussing religion is exactly like arguing against sexual taboos. That kind of opinion cannot be chosen - it is called *belief, conviction*, or *faith*.

Since beliefs cannot be freely chosen, beliefs cannot be acquired, abandoned, or corrected through reason. So, in and of itself, the content of the belief is irrelevant. Its intellectual value is nil. The only thing that's really important in our beliefs lies in the fact that we own them. Naturally, since we cannot control them, they control us, they force us to act as their mouthpieces — we are emotionally coerced into embracing them, meaning that every faith involves some level of enslavement of thought. In this way, it doesn't matter if we have faith in gods or in sexual taboos: we will continue to have that faith, probably forever. And not only that: we will continue to have that faith, even if science proves us wrong. That is the reason why discussions involving such issues are useless, since we would be rationally arguing about an opinion that we would not be able to abandon, even if it were refuted.

We all have meaningless prejudices, we all believe in things that we know are rationally unjustifiable. That's inevitable. It's part of who we are. However, when we are not aware of this as an exclusively personal phenomenon, we are one step away from idealism - and the other from intolerance. To know if we are dogmatic on any subject, it is enough to imagine in which situations we would be inclined to rethink the opinions we have about it. In this sense, a clear sign of dogmatism would be that we could not conceive of a situation in which we would abandon such opinions. Let's start with something simple: *we don't want to eat because there isn't the food we like*. So if there were, would we eat? If the answer is *yes*, that's fine; the argument was legitimate. However, if *not*, problems are in sight. To understand what these problems are, it is enough to replace this emotionally neutral phrase with something that involves our taboos, and we will see that many times we would not be able to change our minds, no matter how much we were shown to the contrary. For example: *why don't we kill?* Let's say the answer was: *because killing causes suffering.* That's fine, but what if it didn't? The answer could be: *because we will be arrested.* A reasonable idea, but what if we weren't? Perhaps the answer would be: *because no one wants to die.* But that person wants to. We would end up saying something trivial like: *because it would make* a mess. But if it didn't, would we kill that person in cold blood? Not either — and so on, indefinitely. In these matters, reason never seems to us to be a very convincing argument. We don't take it seriously.

Now let's mentally do the exercise of asking ourselves this kind of almost impertinent question, but involving the following subjects: cannibalism, religion, incest, pedophilia, zoophilia, zoophilia, polygamy, homosexuality, torture, war, slavery, drugs, orgies, violence, murder, abortion, robbery, suicide, betrayal, lies. At least in some of them, the idea of reconsidering our personal opinions will never be allowed, even if all of our reasons are refuted one by one by the process exemplified above. Thus, if, even with great reasons to do so, we still feel disgruntled at the idea of changing our opinions, this indicates a clear incapacity to be purely rational in the matter.

That's believing in something. There's always that metaphysical climate in our beliefs. *It can be said that, from the point of view of intelligence, the typical sign that we are under the control of emotions is the clear impression that there is something more inexplicable surrounding the subject, something inaccessible to reason — as if, after removing all physical reality, that something else would still remain.* That is the origin of our metaphysical delusions. From this perspective, metaphysics is situated in a kind of intersection between a blind spot of intelligence and our emotional prejudices. That's why it's so problematic, because it's an open door for our anthropocentric fantasies to infiltrate our knowledge without going through any critical analysis. To illustrate, let's think of a person with whom we are or have been in love: they never seem like any other person to us. The same goes for our families, friends, etc. — we have the impression that there *is* something more involved. That's *what* our delusions are. Loved ones don't seem like just matter to us, just like money doesn't seem just paper to us, but we know that they are. The fact is that emotions always color and control our thoughts, often without us realizing it, but each time without us having a choice.

This means that our most beloved opinions, exactly because we love them, are not rational — they are beliefs, emotional prejudices. Truths that only we defend are not true. The whole world isn't conspiring to hide the realities that only we see. We really are wrong in every opinion that only applies to us, and feeling that we are right doesn't change anything. However, only those who do not love their own opinions are free to correct themselves, otherwise they will control us. So to be rational is to be cold.

By the way, maybe that's why the idea that atheists "don't believe in anything" is so frightening to religious people, because the impression one gets is that, if they don't believe in God, they wouldn't admit anything that would be justified by the same process — that is, morals. In fact, it doesn't matter if God exists — scientific discussions are something else. We're dealing with beliefs. The fact is that those who have the courage to face a taboo involving God could easily face another, involving murder. Why not? Those who are cold enough to kill could easily be cold enough to steal. The connection makes sense. The reasoning isn't bad at all. It just doesn't match the facts. Atheists believe in a lot of meaningless things, God just isn't one of them. Even so, by not believing in God, we are saying something that, emotionally, is equivalent to saying *I don't believe in laws* — so *I would kill to buy cigarettes*. At their emotional root, the belief that killing is wrong and that God exists are deeply related. If we understand why killing is wrong, we will also understand why we believe in God, because the process by which we are made to believe in both things is the same — emotional conditioning.

So, as you can see, beliefs are meant to control us, not to make sense. Believing makes us emotionally submissive. That is why, in practice, when we declare ourselves atheists, we begin to be seen as someone who does not respect morals, exactly as an incestuous or a pedophile. Of course, this doesn't make sense, but that's how our emotional brain sees the issue, and little can be done about it.

We can conclude that, insofar as they are impartial, men tend to agree with each other - and science is a great example of this. However, in these emotional issues, we are guided by personal prejudices that control us. Thus, instead of reasoning, of evaluating the facts, we are left looking for pretexts to justify our short-sightedness, which are never really questioned. To fight for what one believes is to arm oneself with an endless series of pretexts to continue believing - be it belief in God, or belief in morals, whatever. It doesn't matter. Men are differentiated by the mistakes they believe in.

* * *

It was a bit of a long digression, but quite valid. Now let's return to the central issue. On a daily basis, the distinction between facts and personal judgments is always obscured by our interests, and we don't realize how much this blinds us. However, since being certain fills us with pride, we make a point of mixing truth and vanity. What's more: for us, being right is usually just a specific way, among many others, of winning - because of this imaginary competitive world that only exists in our heads. The result is that there are many opinions that we insist on stating that they are founded, although we know that they have none, and we are unable to abandon such emotional judgments, because it is because of these prejudices that we live. Therefore, since we can only pay attention to our own interests, let's try to understand how interesting the ability to distinguish between our fantasies and reality itself can be for us.

In theory, every belief should correspond to reality; in theory, the meaning of life and pleasure should coincide, but they don't necessarily coincide, and that's our problem. Thus, knowing that we cannot control emotions, our only way out is to respect their space, cultivating thought in the spaces that remain. Similarly, since we will never be able to be perfectly indifferent to reality, it remains for us to learn to discern between knowledge and judgment, because then we can continue to judge as we see fit, but aware that this is a judgment, which is not mixed with knowledge.

Thus, recognizing that judgments relate to the way in which we personally experience reality, and that objective facts relate only to what reality is in itself, and that one thing does not diminish the other, there will no longer be such a tense conflict between the two. Obviously, we will not stop having personal prejudices, but at least we will know what they are, and this will improve our chances of satisfying both sides, our emotions and our intelligence, allowing each one to walk more freely within our understanding of reality, without requiring that one must necessarily agree with the other because of some metaphysical perfectionism.

The clearest symptom that we have reached this state of emotional neutrality in relation to any subject is the fact that we do not change the idea that we have in that subject when our emotions change. This is because, if we want our opinions to be based on facts, we should only change them in the face of evidence, not in the face of life lessons or mystical feelings of enlightenment. Let us think, for example, of the meaning of life when we are sad; then let us think of the meaning of life when we are euphoric; when we are irritated, sleepy, anxious, calm, drunk, and so on. It must always be the same. The meaning of life cannot be happiness one day, genetic perpetuation the next. If we want our opinions about what reality is in fact to relate to reality itself, and not to our mood, it is simply unacceptable that our idea of the world should fluctuate according to our momentary disposition. The world doesn't change according to our feelings. So if our opinions change, they're simply wrong.

In general, we're good at seeing others objectively, but never ourselves. We don't judge ourselves by the same criteria — generally under the pretext that doing so would make life uninteresting. For example, our beloved, who is not just any person, but a very special person. It's not merely a female that we fell in love with by chance. Is there, however, any plausible reason to consider it special, other than the fact that we like it in person? No. We live convinced that we love her for various reasons that have nothing to do with sexual instincts, even if we have no idea what those reasons are - and in addition, we are the only ones who believe that. Let's think about how well this applies to so many other subjects. Our parents, who are not just any parents. Everyone else is but ours. Our family, which is not just any family. Our beliefs, which are not simply personal myopia. The human being, who is not merely an animal. Our planet, which isn't just a pale blue dot. Life, which is not just a physical process. The list could be expanded very easily, and all of these judgments illustrate how much personal involvement misrepresents our ability to be objective. For practical purposes, there's nothing wrong with being biased — we all have beliefs that set us apart from reality. However, for knowledge purposes, this partiality is the exact definition of what should be avoided.

Thus, if we want to cultivate unbiased knowledge, it must be unrelated to personal judgments. Our judgments can — and should — fluctuate according to our mood, but our knowledge cannot. We have to be cold about knowledge, and that is essential. Of course, it won't be a problem if we want to be passionate about reality, as long as we have enough mental clarity to realize that this is a personal judgment, not an objective fact external to us. So, regarding our personal impressions on any subject, we can freely think whatever we want, but it is important to bear in mind that others will do exactly the same as us, and for equally free reasons that only concern their personal feelings in the face of that situation - and, if they do not agree with us, it is for the same reason that we do not agree with them; if our case seems to us to be the only exception, let us know that this illusion also embraces them. Knowing this, it is likely that we will become more tolerant of other people's imbecilities, as well as our own, but, for the most part, individuals are not very clearly aware of this distinction.

With the passage of time, and cultivating the habit of paying attention to such distinctions, we will slowly learn to separate knowledge and judgment, reason and emotion, so that it will become increasingly easier to identify what is real and what is personal, and increasingly difficult for an emotional judgment to infiltrate our knowledge without being noticed. Until, finally, in a kind of mental ambidexterity, we are able to sense reality and understand it simultaneously, visualizing with perfect clarity the difference between reality and our judgments, so that, when we see a bird singing, we can differentiate our pleasure from the beauty of the bird that sings — which is in our head — and the material bird that sings outside of it according to impersonal biological programming, also understanding that the displeasure of a second observer does not conflict with our pleasure, this will open the way for us to reflect impartially on almost any subject, including ourselves.

III

ON LIFE IN SOCIETY

A SIMPLE POLYGRAPH
WOULD DESTROY ANY FRIENDSHIP

SELFISHNESS

Selfishness is a reality. Selfless altruism is a myth. If men are living beings, it follows that all human actions are selfish. All of them. What drives us is interest, and every interest is always our own. There are no selfless actions like there is no dehydrated water. Those who deny the above statements are simply unaware of their own nature or, because they are committed to delusions, have become unable to admit the obvious.

In everyday life, we judge selfishness to be bad because we tend to have a frivolous view of the issue. We see it on the surface, inserted in a relative moral context. In our minds, selfishness is opposed to altruism as good is opposed to evil. However, when we analyzed the issue with a little more attention, we found that there is no such opposition. We realize that selfishness, alone, is the central element of life.

This derives from the fact that life is selfish in itself, objectively and solitarily selfish, and it is evident that, since we do not speak of selfishness in a moral sense, there is nothing that contradicts that reality. At that level, for the same reason that there is no way to conceive the opposite of life, there is no way to conceive the opposite of selfishness.

Life is something that exists and works only according to itself. It is not inserted in a broader context aimed at some kind of balance. Thus, if life is enclosed in itself, without any objective other than itself, being alive has no context, it has no relativity: life is its own value and its own measure. Life is only about itself, and there is nothing outside of it that is positively or negatively opposed to it.

Even so, it will be almost automatic for us to think of non-living matter as its opposite. Inanimate matter, however, is not opposed to life. It can only be understood as something that lacks life. From this perspective, if life were represented by the number 1, inanimate matter would be equivalent to 0. In physical reality, there is no counterpart to life, what would be equivalent to -1. There isn't an antilife made of altruistic antigens. Death itself is nothing more than the return of matter to 0.

Thus, we should not understand the selfishness of life in a moral sense, as the opposite of charitable giving, of philanthropy. It's not about ignoring or helping others. All of these are moral issues related to life in society. We are not referring to interest on a subjective level, but to the objective interest of life for itself, to the physical selfishness that genes manifest when building bodies that will work to perpetuate them.

As far as the selfishness of life itself is concerned, it would be illogical to insert altruism into the equation. Logically, it also seems strange to talk about selfishness on an objective level. However, we speak of selfishness only metaphorically, because, in itself, life is pure indifference, like the rest of the universe, like any fact.

Therefore, even if we are not discussing virtues and vices, when analyzing the mechanics of life, the behavior of the robots it creates, we see that it exhibits a selfish profile. We make this statement in the same sense that computer viruses can be interpreted as selfish in their infectious and self-replicating behavior. We're not insulting genes by calling them selfish. We do it as someone who describes how they work, not as someone who qualifies them.

Of course, if such genes were altruistic, we would designate them as altruistic genes, but how would that be possible? The idea will become clearer if we observe that there is no way to conceive an altruistic life in and of itself. What are altruistic genes? What would be your priorities? Help inanimate matter to be increasingly dead? Help chance to become more and more random? Are they antigenes of antilife, philanthropic molecules concerned with making selfish genes less interested in their own perpetuation? But in favor of what? Perhaps to fight for the abolition of carbon chains? To try to find a family for hydrogen? It seems evident that life itself would have nothing to sacrifice for - how could we be selfless if we were the only person, the only organism existing on the face of the Earth? It would be impossible. Life cannot be selfless because there is no context outside of itself that makes this possible. Therefore, we are not talking about virtues, we are talking about facts, about amoral facts.

We use the term egoism only to designate the behavioral profile of a specific type of material phenomenon called life. We do this because, when we open a dictionary, we see that this term perfectly describes the idea that we want to transmit - that of something that only thinks of itself. If that were not the case, we would invent another better word, something that science knows how to do very well, but there simply was no such need. We are being insistent on this point so that we can place the selfishness of life as a physical reality, as an objective operating principle, as a fact that can be demonstrated experimentally.

∗ ∗ ∗

Considered in its global behavior, selfishness is equivalent to the structural ethics of life - understood as a mechanical system programmed for self-perpetuation. It is because of this that it defines what is right or wrong for life itself - in the sense of whether or not it serves its purposes. From this point of view, selfishness is the supreme genetic value, something that crosses life from end to end, making it what it is. Selfishness runs through the veins of life. Your heart beats out of self-interest and for him alone. Selfishness, self-love, guides and keeps life running. That is its principle, its driving spring, its only possible sense.

Without half-words, the meaning of life is to continue existing. However, in making such a statement, we speak of material facts, not of deliberate intentions. Life doesn't have an existential purpose, it just behaves as if it had, because *DNA* is programmed to propagate. It is a purely inertial sense, made self-sustaining because the information encoded in such molecules programs organisms according to their own perpetuation.

Because life is based on self-replicating information, it can be understood as a kind of virus of matter. This virus reproduces because it works, and that's why we exist. It is a machine designed to reproduce itself, and there is no meaning beyond that, nor could there be: its meaning is self-sustaining precisely because it is circular. Life reproduces to continue reproducing because it is programmed that way, and any other programming would cause its extinction. Obviously, nothing would prevent a type of life that was not programmed in such a way, but the fact is that it would cease to exist quickly, leaving only those aimed at eternity.

It is a fairly simple sieve, but it works very well, creating machines that are increasingly specialized and efficient in the task of perpetuating themselves over generations. Of course, if all currently living organisms stopped behaving as a function of perpetuation, there would be nothing wrong with that, but life would be extinct in a short time, as the *continuum* that began 3.5 billion years ago would be interrupted. Once dead, we would become part of the planet's landscape, as there wouldn't even be bacteria to decompose us.

Life, therefore, will only continue to exist as long as it remains selfish in its goal of eternalizing itself. Those who deviate from that path, who cease to be selfish, will cease to exist in a single generation. This makes it clear that there are no options: selfishness is imperative to the maintenance of life.

In practice, life expresses its selfishness by playing on existence, and against each other, organisms that will fulfill their self-perpetuating designs. The food chain, in its impassive mechanics, reflects life's absolute interest in itself. Notice that, in this scheme, the emphasis is on genes, not on individuals — individual bodies are nothing more than a toy, a medium that genes use to launch themselves into eternity. We must see organisms not as ends in themselves, but as means, as the end result of the strategies that genes have developed over time to perpetuate themselves.

* * *

Now let's look at the issue from another perspective. Considering that life is a material process, its behavior seems rather unusual in relation to non-living matter. Because its meaning is circular, life has the aspect of a megalomanic and autistic phenomenon, alien to the rest of the universe. It always remains closed in the system that it created itself, and it does not even allow the existence of what is outside. The death of a star, for example, doesn't pity us. Why? Because stars don't have *DNA*. If inanimate matter were, so to speak, starving, life wouldn't give a damn, because it only has eyes for itself, for animate matter. This is for the simple reason that life is programmed to give importance only to itself, to have as its ultimate purpose.

That is the reason why, in addition to being selfish, life is also the best possible example of egocentrism. To understand it, it is sufficient to observe that, when matter takes the form of living beings, that same matter, formerly inanimate, is considered something different, as if the rest of the material world were the ground on which it steps: matter became life, the measure of all things. In all forms of life, this egocentrism remains absolute, and we are no exception. Because we are human beings, we also consider ourselves something other than inanimate matter, and our only reason for that is to be heirs to that biological tradition. Human beings are important because they're programmed to feel important, and that's it. This is not about metaphysical importance, but about genetic preprogramming.

Because genes are selfish, driven by their own interests and nothing else, it is inevitable that the bodies they build are also egocentric and selfish. However, that doesn't mean that all organisms are hermits, solitary robots, and misanthropes. We know that we, in life in society, for selfish reasons, sometimes manifest altruistic behaviors, that is, of self-sacrifice. Why? Because it works. Genes are selfish, but the bodies they build can be selfless as long as that works.

Genes alone are inherently selfish. The bodies they build, being programmed according to the interests of the genes, can be individualistic or collectivist, solitary or gregarious. Only the end, the perpetuation, is predetermined. The means can be any means.

Therefore, as long as this results in some benefit to genetic perpetuation, organisms can behave as if they were not selfish, and this in fact happens. Turning our eyes to nature, it is obvious that, under certain circumstances, the strategy of building organisms capable of helping each other in the process of survival is interesting to life as a whole. On an individual level, the priority is not to be selfish, but to survive and reproduce. Selfishness is only a priority when it comes to genetic perpetuation.

In this way, whatever the circumstances, the selfishness of life itself remains absolute, and the relativity of that egoism only begins to exist from the moment we consider life from the perspective of the particular organisms. In this sense, since basic selfishness lags behind individual life, determining only the essential objective, but not the means of achieving it, nothing prevents individuals from helping and sacrificing themselves for each other in practice - just as nothing prevents us from having three eyes, from dedicating ourselves to useless tasks from an evolutionary point of view. We can be optimists or pessimists, erudite or ignorant, restrained or spontaneous. That's irrelevant. Genes don't matter as long as we keep reproducing them.

✶ ✶ ✶

Once the objective selfishness regarding the mechanics of life has been clarified, we can now approach the issue from a social point of view, even if there are no significant differences. This is because, considering society as a whole, we see that it also exhibits selfish and closed behavior, similar to that of life at the genetic level, that is, society's priority is to ensure its own existence for no reason other than to continue existing. Therefore, even when it comes to life in society, there is still no contrast between selfishness and altruism.

Where, after all, is the altruism? Within selfishness. Selfishness relates to satisfying the interests of individuals. Altruism, in turn, relates to a particular strategy aimed at satisfying those same interests when inserted in a context of group life, whether in societies, families, tribes, that is, the sacrifices that we are willing to make for each other, not out of love for others, but out of self-love.

In addition, altruism, sacrificing oneself for others, is something that we see quite frequently in nature. It's not exclusive to humans. We didn't invent it. Altruism exists because it is a strategy that produces results at the genetic level, and the fact that we sacrifice ourselves for each other in life in society is nothing more than a repercussion of this at the level of particular organisms. Even if we don't admit it, it's also out of self-interest that, in our society, we encourage altruism. We do so in the hope of taming and limiting individualistic and egocentric behavior that, in excess, would destabilize it. Society encourages altruism with the selfish purpose of ensuring its own existence, which in turn ensures the existence of genes, which orchestrate everything by remote control.

There seems to be a great mystical aura surrounding altruism, but this is only due to religious propaganda that misrepresented it with its daydreams. In a broad sense, the essence of altruism is simple, and it boils down to what we know as social conscience. Through it, individuals become aware that, by harming society, the environment in which they live, they are spitting on the plate on which they eat. They become aware that, by sacrificing themselves for it, they are helping themselves indirectly.

Altruism can therefore be seen as the relativization of a particular egoism in favor of a collective egoism. As it is an approach that seeks an indirect benefit, and without guarantees of return, it must be used with great discretion, or we may not reap the benefits we expect. Altruism is not something to be employed for free, but only in situations where reciprocity is likely to produce better results.

Sometimes we think of altruism as something disinterested just because, because it is an indirect investment, it is common for us to lose sight of the interests implicitly aimed at, but they are always there.

* * *

In life in society, individuals sometimes act selfishly because they are unable to see things in perspective or in the long term. However, in most cases, we are aware of all this, but we are simply more interested in our immediate satisfaction, which is guaranteed, even if this occurs at the expense of others. If, for example, we light a cigarette in the middle of the street, we know that we are polluting society's air, but we also know that this will not bring us any noteworthy consequences. If, on the other hand, we are in a closed room, this pollution will affect us directly, and it will be in our immediate interest to avoid it. We could, of course, do it by giving up the addiction, but since that would be very costly, we preferred to be practical: we left the window open. The same is true for our behavior in relation to those around us: we sacrifice as little as possible, always prioritizing our immediate interest.

Now let's think about garbage. Normally we don't see any problem with throwing garbage on the street. However, when everyone starts to do the same, garbage begins to appear on our sidewalks, and this becomes our problem. Since we are selfish and immediate, it is inevitable that we only worry about this type of thing when it affects us, when we cannot dump our garbage in the neighbor's backyard without the same happening to us. Thus, when remaining selfish becomes an unsustainable strategy, we relativize our interests and begin to take into account the interests and well-being of others, because we are also the neighbor of another who is as selfish as we are.

In this situation, we become altruistic, we begin to worry about the whole, not out of charity, but because we are also part of that whole. Altruism, as we see, is just the name we give to selfish, socially strategic behavior in which the well-being of others is taken into account because it benefits us indirectly. Then, not as an end in itself, altruistic behavior begins to exist only as a very particular appendix, as a sophistication of selfishness.

Let us try to clarify this process of relativizing immediate interests. An individual may, for example, be very rich, absolutely rich. Suppose you have in your hands all the riches of the world, and that you don't want to share them with anyone. This makes the rest of them absolutely poor. Money, however, cannot be eaten, and an individual, alone, is unable to provide himself with everything he needs to survive in society. Some of the absolutely poor individuals, farmers, for example, will be unable to buy seeds, fertilizers, and other elements needed to cultivate crops and provide food to society. In this situation, if the rich are not selfless, everyone will starve. Then, in view of his well-being, he sacrifices himself, takes from his own pocket the amount necessary for farmers to have the means to keep society supplied with food.

In this situation, due to their common interest in surviving, both worked together: the rich were willing to pay, the farmers were willing to plant — that is, there was a negotiation between both parties, who decided to cooperate, relativizing their immediate interests based on their long-term well-being. Of course, individuals towards whom the rich behave selflessly are a means to their selfish ends, through which their bellies remain full. It takes into account the interests of others because it depends on them to satisfy its own. The same is true for farmers, who work to ensure their livelihood — not because they love to feed humanity. There was, of course, more sacrifice on the part of the rich, but he simply didn't have a choice.

Selfishness, as we see, is not a problem, but the essence of life. Altruism, on the other hand, is not the solution to all problems, but merely a strategy to solve a particular type of problem, and is only useful in moderate doses. Exclusive altruism is not a socially or evolutionarily stable strategy. To exemplify, suppose that the entire society had become exclusively altruistic. What would happen? Just an outsourcing of the problems. We would solve other people's problems and they would solve ours. However, at some point, someone would have the brilliant idea of becoming selfish and not solving any problems while others solve theirs. Thus, feeling fooled, altruists would stop solving the problems of selfish individuals. In this situation, since reciprocity was broken, seeing their problems only accumulating, the altruists would also have to become selfish and solve their problems themselves, since blindly trusting others ceased to be a stable strategy capable of ensuring their existence. The altruistic system would collapse. The result would be the same if the altruists continued to solve the problems of the egoists: all the altruists would die and, as a consequence, the selfish parasites that were supported by them. This explains why purely altruistic systems are highly unstable. Furthermore, we can also see that it is out of self-interest that we turn our backs on those who do not return our favors. Dumping free philanthropy on those who will not return anything, whether for us or for society, may seem virtuous, but it will only contribute to the decay of the social system.

In a broader perspective, the following illustration will suffice to understand more clearly the humble role of altruism compared to that of selfishness. Suppose that life were a building. What would your structure be? Pure selfishness, from foundation to top. Altruism would only concern, for example, the proper use of elevators. Located within this mega-structure, the selfishness that we refer to in everyday life as the opposite of altruism is reduced to an insignificant detail, an itch, a banality that we only attach importance to because it causes us personal inconvenience. It would amount, for example, to the selfishness of those who push all the buttons on an elevator to annoy their neighbors, or of those who push the emergency button just to be able to satisfy their sexual fantasies.

In that building, of course, we would also have those souls guided by high values of charity. Entities that, in a material world, who knows how, live detached from materialism. They consider themselves virtuous when using the stairs, as this allows others to use the elevators more effectively, or they secretly lubricate the system's gears in the middle of the night. They always insist that such facts be kept confidential, because anonymous virtues are much better seen in the eyes of a clear conscience. However, since such individuals are only concerned with being virtuous, not with being useful, it is common for them to use the stairs even when the elevator is unoccupied. Thus, in their paranoid mission to become the best philanthropists in the building, they end up losing contact with reality, and the entire existence, the essence of the building as a whole, is then reduced to the non-use of elevators.

For our purposes, selfishness is sufficiently well explained. We realize that selfishness is intrinsic to life, something within which altruism is situated only as a particularity, an arm of that same selfishness. Altruism is only a sociable and well-mannered selfishness that knows how to recognize voluntarily when it is appropriate to relativize immediate satisfaction according to long-term interests. Thus, just as selfishness is not related to vice, altruism is not related to virtue. In practice, what we mean by selfishness in a vulgar sense is just social ineptitude.

∗ ∗ ∗

Finally, let us make some comments about the so-called pure altruism that is now in the fashion of spiritual virtues. If, on the one hand, selfishness is a reality, on the other hand, altruism, when viewed as an exercise in charity, of love for others, is never more than a pastime for unemployed and needy moralists. Masters of the unnecessary, such individuals are freely charitable because this is *fashion* in the eyes of the good Lord, something that may bring them better living conditions in the afterlife.

We have nothing against altruism, but its value is far too exaggerated. We admit that cooperation, that mutual assistance, is appropriate under certain circumstances. We even grant that charity can be pleasurable because of the sense of superiority it provides. But it's unthinkable that there should be what they call disinterested altruism. What exists is selfish interest in others, even if for charitable ends, something very different from disinterest. The pleasure that some find in goodness, others find in malice. The means change, but the end is exactly the same selfish pleasure, the same personal satisfaction.

If, for example, when helping people, we felt the same pleasure as when having sex, isn't it obvious that we would help them? Wouldn't we help them madly without expecting rewards? That's exactly the case. Kindness is as selfish as badness. We turn a blind eye to an idea as incoherent, as rude as selfless selflessness because, of course, we would love to be gifted, to receive favors in the name of free kindness. We sympathize with those who want to help us. It is something that we consider good because we expect to be benefited, not because it makes sense.

Some may even think that absolute disinterest is impossible, but we can easily demonstrate the opposite with our absolute disinterest in the explanations through which they try to show us that there is no selfishness in the fact that they are interested in what interests them, as long as this occurs charitably. We will only pay attention to what they say when they start doing favors for what really doesn't interest them, such as rocks, for example. When we find someone donating blood to a tree, that will seem disinterested altruism to us. However, if the transcendental philanthropists, motivated by stupid metaphysical beliefs, want to declare that the truth is inside their heads so that they never have to open their eyes to the most basic facts, amen to that: they must deny themselves until they become one with ignorance.

Let's also note the following. It is very common among spiritualists to say that charity is an end in itself, that the compensation for virtue is virtue itself. If so, great: that they bring the presents. That's what they say, it's what they'd like us to think about you, but things aren't that simple. There are unconfessed reasons. The militants of selfless altruism are not snipers, they do not profess blind philanthropy that occurs without more or less. This is not unrestricted goodness: there are criteria, conditions, strategies. For example, although they claim to be disinterested, it is common that, in exchange for concrete favors, these benevolent beings have the right to rent our ears to propagate their ideologies of effeminate rickets.

Furthermore, they consider themselves distinct and require that all charities be treated with distinction for what they do. They may not ask for rewards in the same currency, but they won't admit that their virtuosity is disdained. They want to give *status* to their virtue so that it benefits them indirectly. Therein lies the key to understanding your secret interest. Your selflessness puts a card up your sleeves. Thus, the first time it is convenient, they will play this joker in the face of others - or even in their own face - to apologize for their addictions or to obtain any benefits. As far as we can see, it is obvious that these spiritual altruists are seeking moral immunity and recognition, and to that end charity is the most well accepted medium in modern times. Through it, they gain the good opinion of others or, alternatively, give themselves a good opinion about themselves as a gift.

So when someone says that selfishness is bad and that altruism is good, that's someone who just doesn't know what they're talking about. You're probably just trying to compliment yourself because you set aside a few hours a week to distribute soup to beggars. We did not listen to this nonsense, because it is equivalent to forgetting the ocean of our lives in order to prioritize a miserable straw that was completely lost in order to be able to praise itself in secret.

Selfishness exists by itself, but altruism doesn't — it emerged only as something subordinate to selfishness, not as its opposite. Even in a moral sense, the usefulness of altruism is evident, but that of selfishness is infinitely greater. It is ridiculous that, as spokespersons for altruism, we feel entitled to approach selfishness with disdain, since this amounts to an intestinal flora that is considered to be more important than the organism that hosts it. It doesn't matter if we sympathize with charity, with philanthropy: this concerns a small detail within a context created solely by selfishness. We are absurd in arguing against selfishness, because we argue against ourselves, against evident facts, becoming entangled in ridiculous incoherences.

Mondays, Wednesdays, Thursdays, and Fridays: intentions. Saturdays and Sundays: interests. Selfishness is never on vacation. We are all selfish because selfishness created the meaning of life. We will cease to be so only when we kick our boots and return to being the runway on which life parades.

HYPOCRISY

Despite the almost desperate appeal made to honesty as the only possible salvation for humanity, we lie all the time, throughout our lives. Denying it would only add another reason to laugh at ourselves. Abandoning lying is not only impossible but also undesirable. Even if it's hard for us to admit it, pretense and concealment are also basic pillars of life in society, not only because lying is useful, but because it is an integral part of the social façade scheme that we have incorporated since our birth.

Society is a representation of our humanity, an indirect and often false representation of our intentions. That is why those who learn to distinguish between real and social needs are good. We can define social needs as a representation, in an encrypted and twisted language that, in general terms, translates the real ones objectively, but not with the innocent inefficiency of an automatic translator, but with the malice of an old lawyer who must earn a living. Distinguishing between needs and appearances, between realities and theaters, is a skill that relates to our immediate well-being, to our real condition - which is for our social condition as our intimate satisfaction is for our identity card. Therefore, compared to the first, lying has a definitely pernicious effect, and hardly anyone reaches the degree of foolishness of actually dismissing their real needs in favor of mere conventions.

The functioning of this social system is something that can only be learned by oneself through experience and reflection — it is not immediately accessible to us. We always hide what we really experienced; we never say what we actually think. Everything is under the covers. The real and authentic facts of life, as each one feels and conceives them in their heart, are a kind of taboo. They should not be brought to light publicly. They are hidden in favor of appearances, which, however, everyone knows to be false, and that is why the embarrassing subject is avoided at all costs. For example, when some wise man stated that our savior was born of a virgin, that's not really what he meant. Your words should not be taken at face value. We know that an allegation of this kind is not an affront to common sense and biological science, but merely a polite way of saying let's *change* the subject.

It's hard to pinpoint the culprit for our need to lie. Perhaps the representatives of Christian idealisms who, upon attaining power, established impossible values as goals, are, in part, responsible for the aggravation of this phenomenon. Because, with that, honesty, that is, everything that concerns our true humanity, became not only a second minor reality, but a lie, something shameful, unworthy, which we must hide as if it were a crime, and this in favor of another reality that not only misrepresents our true needs, but in fact slanders them, denies them in favor of a fictional world. That's why the gods of Greco-Roman mythology, which reflect our intimate nature, are so preferred to the castrated ghost of Christianity. Let us think, for example, of how we were able to identify intimately with Dionysus, god of wine and orgy; Vênus, goddess of love and beauty; Mars, god of war and violence. This is because they relate to what actually moves us as living beings, what makes us what we are. They were designed to reflect and exalt human nature, not to falsify it. All Christian metaphysics, on the contrary, has its core in the denial of itself and in the worship of unhealthy characteristics that seek to root out our basic instincts and to deride our nature. They find their maximum expression in the cult of chastity and submission, in the resignation before the world and in the praise of suffering - so much so that their symbol is a shawl nailed to a *cross*.

Given this perspective, we could suppose that every doctor should be careful to warn his patients against the unhealthy practice of being a Christian. However, this is not even necessary, because few are foolish enough to actually try to live their principles. Not only because they would be miserably unhappy, and it is likely that they would end up in an asylum — or a convent — but mainly because they cannot feel such principles as something intimate and personal. That is why it remains, as it has always been, a cover religion, something that should not be practiced, but only staged.

However, even if we teach that ignoring reality is a good thing, it would be wrong to blame religion for our need to lie, first because no one really believes what it says; then, because it is likely that this is nothing more than a device invented to make lying, if not desirable, at least excusable. In this sense, let us realize that religions are not the cause but the effect of our lies — they serve as a scapegoat that carries a portion of the weight of our contradictions, hiding some of the skeletons that we have in our closet. The most likely hypothesis is that this makes us feel less guilty for deceiving others, and also less ashamed for allowing ourselves to be deceived, since we can ultimately push the responsibility beyond.

✶ ✶ ✶

A plausible explanation for the existence of this radical divide between what we are and what we appear to be can be found in our own nature, in the fact that it is not only inconvenient to be honest without reservation, but that the ideal of that honesty cannot be achieved, since it is impossible to make others apprehend our intimate, and vice versa. What flows so freely in our inner world cannot be represented except by conventional symbols that almost completely empty what is being communicated. Thus, even with the most frank honesty about something we feel, in the minds of others our explanation is for a bad photograph as the feeling itself is for the original landscape, which, however, cannot be visited. They will never be able to see with their own eyes, and so they will have to trust our word. We can see, at the outset, how problematic the situation is.

Since we are inescapably tied to the fate of living in our own skin, and since we are unable to apprehend the intimate of another human being in the same way that we feel ourselves as subjective beings, this is the first division of reality: the self as a subjective entity and the other as an objective entity. It is true that we are capable of some alterity, that is, of placing ourselves, *in the abstract, in* the situation of another individual as being subjective like ourselves, but this, in addition to requiring some intellectual effort, is hardly used except for our own benefit, since it is very rare to really worry about other people's issues beyond what seems desirable in terms of courtesy.

Thus, in an interpersonal interaction, the following situation is more or less designed. We have two individuals, and both are subjective beings well aware of their true opinions and intimate motives regarding everything that interests them. In their relationship, however, they are only able to reach the most superficial layer of each other, that is, what is objectively presented before their eyes. Since every human being is uniquely and exclusively selfish, everyone will seek their own satisfaction through games that explore this abyss of the uncommunicable and the uncommunicated, without ever allowing their intentions to be revealed in an open way. In this theater, you calculate very well what you say, but especially what you shut up. This is also because our inner self is made up of such petty and vile elements that it is difficult for another individual to disguise the disgust if we showed ourselves as such.

Examples of this type of game can be found everywhere. When we go out on the weekends, we find countless individuals who are extremely well dressed, flaunting expensive possessions and qualities under the pretext of recreation. They spend hours walking, talking, and drinking apparently at the same time. They crush into human clusters for no clear reason. In other words, they are socializing, which is the human version of the struggle for *status* and the mating ritual. When, for example, they talk publicly about difficult topics, they never speak softly. On the contrary, they unnecessarily increase the volume of their voices in the hope that someone will notice their intellectual gifts, their erudition, because they want to be admired. None of them would admit the real reason that led them to wander around the streets; but if anything is certain, it's that it's not mere fun.

Let's suppose that a man and a woman went out in search of a partner. The man wants a short-term relationship and the woman wants a long-term relationship. When they meet, both will talk about various seemingly trivial topics, such as personal tastes, music, work, art, events, etc. But in this process, the conversations, dinner, drinks are just a pretext, and what is actually tried is to decode the other's words, extract from their statements and subtleties of their behavior some data that will be useful for them to guess what are the true interests and conditions at stake, because only then will they discover if their objectives are compatible, if there is anything useful to be found in that relationship.

Thus, in the initial approach movement, something like the following will happen. The man observes the woman and thinks: "she's pretty, but a bit dumb;

she has a big nose and crooked teeth; at least she has money, although she has a flaccid body; with all these faults, and still few friends, she probably has low self-esteem, and is likely to be able to keep her submissive and still continue with other lovers". It sounds like a scoundrel, but a woman's cynicism is second to that of a man. She will think something similar, but depending on her long-term interests - for example "even though he's handsome, I don't like him very much, and the sex is terrible, but the important thing is that he has a good job, important friends, and social prestige; so, if I have a son, I will probably be able to marry him and, with that, I will be able to enjoy security for the rest of my life; when I need sex, it will be enough to look for a real man".

Let us then realize that, in the process of relating, both lie from beginning to end, and they keep their secrets very well to protect their interests, leaving on the surface only a childish romanticism, in which only idiots believe. Of course, once we decide that the person is worth it, we continue to lie. Instead of telling the truth — what we really think about during the decision-making process — we simply utter the classic sentence: I am in love. We use encrypted and indirect language, making ourselves naive so that this gives the partner some sense of security, so that we are never forced to confess the mysterious "motives of the heart".

The investigation of each other happens in this way because opening up our interests does not work well, since we are extremely perfidious beings, and it would not be long before someone would find a way to take advantage of our frankness. Let's see what would happen if, let's say, both were direct and honest about what they want. The woman would say: "I want someone who has enough money to support me and who provides me with security; in exchange, I can offer beauty, affection, sex, and descendants; that's why I put on silicone implants, waxed, cut my hair, bought dresses, did exercises, and used makeup; would anyone buy me?"

A man interested in a short-term relationship, faced with such a statement, will immediately be tempted to lie. However, if you tell the truth, revealing that your interest is just casual sex, you will probably get slapped, and that's it. However, if you decide to put your interests first, you will make promises of eternal love, you will say that you are able to satisfy all your desires, you will agree to all the conditions. He will inflate the woman's vanity with any compliments and lies, until he manages to take her to the motel. The next morning, however, the conversation will be quite different.

No wonder the woman will feel deceived, but that was the fault of her overly naive strategy. A more efficient approach is to demand proof of commitment, not just promises — and this generally takes the form of a long courtship, which means lots of presents, lots of public displays of affection, monogamous agreements, marriages, and partners. If a woman wishes to be bought, not just used, nothing more logical than refusing to sell herself yarn. Admittedly, in this matter, neither men nor women will ever open the game, but that is something that we should not regret.

Let's use another everyday situation to illustrate our motives. Imagine that we left a certain person with whom we had a stable relationship. We spent some time feeling a bit lonely. However, soon another person appears with whom we live much better. In this situation, it would never occur to us to think that we made a mistake in leaving the first one, which is quickly forgotten. However, if we didn't find anyone, or if the second person were even worse, we would begin to believe that we made a mistake, and then we would regret having abandoned them, because the malaise quickly convinces us that we loved them.

This seems to indicate that love is nothing more than an emotional memory involving the usefulness of certain people in promoting our well-being, manifested as a well-being in the face of those who are likely to be able to satisfy our needs. Thus, in practice, we meet several people, we test them in a process of trial and error, and we are left with those that make us feel good; we will begin to love those with whom we accumulate a certain number of pleasant memories. The detail is that, just as we only think of food when we are hungry, these memories will only be evoked in moments of discomfort, meaning that all love denotes some lack. Nobody loves out of kindness. To love is to need help, and to remember those who have already given us alms.

As can be seen, we do well to keep a respectable distance from one another's intimate, and this applies not only to sexual relations, but to human relations as a whole. If we get too close, socializing will be made impossible by disgust. Like our bodies, our personalities may be beautiful on the outside. However, inside, we are all human. There are certain things that we think of each other that we would only confess under torture—and even then only after days of torture. Before that, we would categorically deny everything, and even feign indignation to be more convincing. Still, on big issues, it would be easy to be heroically honest, but telling the truth in small, everyday matters would just mess up our existence. As everyone is like that, there's nothing to be done. It remains to be accepted, albeit for purely aesthetic reasons.

Another case of social theater is commerce. We see an individual on each side of the counter and we already have a very good idea of what is likely to happen. A seller, trying to earn a living from the profit derived from his merchandise, tries to convince an individual to buy a certain thing. The customer knows that the merchant's only true interest, in the end, is to see the money go from the buyer's pocket to the cash register; that's why their initial stance is already quite defensive and skeptical about everything the merchant says in order to praise their products. The seller, for his part, knows that if he is honest, he will be beaten by the competition, who is willing to lie. Then look for ways not to inform the buyer about the product - because to do so it would be enough for him to deliver the instruction manual - but to seduce him, convince him that he needs such an object. Try to demonstrate why, by buying it from him and not from the competitor, you will be getting the best deal, even if it is exactly the same product with a higher price. The customer's strategy is to try to dismantle the seller's devices to arrive at the truth, and the seller's strategy is to deceive them, leading them to believe anything that overvalues their merchandise. The practical result of this is what we know as negotiation. When they bargain, the two are actually in a kind of dispute, in a nervous war, in which the objective is to unmask the true intentions of the adversary. No matter how much one tries to alleviate the climate of hostility present in confrontations of this species with smiles, cups of coffee, gifts, and attendants with full breasts, there is no way to disguise the discomfort and exhaustion involved in the art of exploring others without being exploited.

* * *

These general principles also apply to friendship, which basically consists of a network of mutual help, in which individuals are committed to each other's well-being. Of course, interests can be deeply affective or strictly material, but if that were not the case, there wouldn't be the famous saying that we only discover who our true friends are in times of difficulty. Those who don't admit something so basic must have a lot to hide, especially from themselves. Raising dust curtains over relatively simple concepts is always suspicious behavior.

This resistance, however, can be justified by the fact that most human relationships would not survive honesty. We have to deceive, and often also deceive ourselves, for the sake of self-defense. The fact is that, if our objective were to think, we would read books. Friendships happen for reasons unrelated to the truth, inhabiting a parallel world whose rules are determined by our personal needs. It turns out that, on some issues, we do not have the freedom to speak and think honestly, with impartiality, because our well-being presupposes lying. Hence the discomfort we feel when raising objections to the incoherences that make us human. To be sociable means to see some things in a hopelessly distorted way, to lie almost on principle.

This explains why, in certain subjects, this blindness occurs naturally. It seems strange that we, possessors of such keen reasoning, allow ourselves to be deceived by lies as palpable as sincere friendships between exclusively selfish mammals. But this fact occurs only because we are committed to an outlook that forces us to act like idiots. In this situation, as gentlemen, we are polite to leave uncomfortable details aside, and we expect others to do the same. The reality is in the background so that we can feel comfortable in the theater, so that we can maintain spontaneity, that is, improvise without satisfying anyone. This kind of calculated childishness is what we call enjoying life. To be an off-duty actor.

On the one hand, assuming the vocation of actors without guilt is important so that we do not feel our nature as a burden, but this, on the other hand, makes us naive, easy prey in a world of civilized predators. The truth, while protecting us from delusions, also prevents us from living without prevention. We want to lead life lightly, but we know that we are in a minefield. That tension wears us out. The anxiety of constant mistrust keeps us too awake for life to be pleasant. We sleep with our eyes open, we are ungrudgingly warriors, because there are no declared enemies, just opportunists waiting for the easiest victims.

So we're constantly looking for the chance to put the weapons away. We want to rest from the weight of our social masks. The price of rest, however, is becoming vulnerable, and we only feel free to let our guard down when we are sure that our friends will look out for us—that's why we don't find the same rest in solitude. So, as we can see, friends are not dear to us because they allow us to be true — whatever that means — but because they represent our only rest from life. Our trust in them allows us to be naive without fearing the immediate consequences of this. Friendships are like agreements between night guards: they keep an eye on each other during the weekends so that everyone can sleep without being fired — we are not, as is normally supposed, interested in hearing each other's snore.

The bottom line is that friendship rests on loyalty, not honesty. That is, friendships are not sincere, just useful. That's the only reason we cultivate them. It would be impossible for us to be completely honest with our friends; a simple polygraph would destroy any friendship. Friends are committed not to the truth, but to each other's well-being, and that's exactly why they can't be honest, they can't say much of what they really think about us. That's the reason why the compliments we receive from our friends aren't usually worth anything. They avoid criticizing us at all costs, and when they do, they just say harmless platitudes. Their criticisms are almost always evasive, superficial, and full of ridiculous euphemisms. Friends lie and omit because their main concern is to preserve the friendship. Even when our friends ask us to be completely honest, we lie, because telling the truth would be too risky, it could easily undermine our social investment.

The criticisms of our enemies, on the other hand, are often very trustworthy. They can be, and generally are, very honest in what they say about us, because they have nothing to lose—they are free to be honest. Your point of view is not committed to the interests aimed at maintaining friendship. Therefore, since friendships are supported not by truth but by mutual interest, we should ask for the opinion of our enemies on the most important issues.

Their criticisms may be acidic and disturbing, but they're generally sincere and unbiased.

Given the situation, it seems inevitable that this game of interests called friendship is quite fickle. For example, when, and only while, someone is our friend, we flatter them, praise them, praise them. We do everything possible to please you. We repeatedly affirm to our friends how important, virtuous, and priceless they are. As a rule, this is all outright lies. We say such things just to delude them with a greasy sense of importance so that they remain on our side.

Friendships require that we lie all the time, and there are not a few situations in which we are forced to defend our friends against accusations that we know to be true. If we don't lie in your defense, we'll lose your friendship. On the other hand, to protect the relationship, we are silent about many of the faults we see, about much of what we really think about our friends. In general, we will only discover the truth about what was thought about us after a certain individual, perhaps due to a personal disagreement, ceases to be our friend. Before that, all we had were two individuals who lied to each other out of interest. Only after the friendship has ended can honesty truly come to the surface without prevention. The individual is free to say what, in secret, he has always thought about us. Many times his words shock us, because perhaps we thought that, simply because he was our friend, everything that the individual said about us was sincere. *O sancta simplicitas!* Let's at least admit that when a friend betrays us, he's not being hypocritical, just disloyal. As friends, both were always hypocritical. That's inevitable; it's part of the game. The truly regrettable fact is that we do everything possible to deny the obvious. It's unfortunate that we consider it a virtue to be completely naive towards our friends until they betray us.

This may all sound sad, maybe even repulsive, but it's a fact. If we believe that we are exceptions within this scheme, if we think that such facts do not apply to us, dumb ours. We know that's how the world works, because we see examples of this on a daily basis. If we want to make misunderstandings in the name of childish romanticism just because it calms us down, that's fine, but we would achieve that same calm with wine, and it will only be a matter of time before we see our delusions shattered by reality.

151

In this scheme, we are no exception, because there are no exceptions — the idea of maintaining any relationship based on honesty is worthy of an immortal laugh. We should be satisfied with the fact that thinking doesn't make noise: if only we were able to think out loud, we would probably never have friends.

✶ ✶ ✶

As we saw in the examples above, only after living with such a conventional system of hypocrisy for some time did we become able to infer its rules, and this always in an indirect way. Intuitively, we outlined the boundaries between both things, between the real and the conventional. Everyone is aware of this theatrical nature of society, and they gladly limit themselves to playing with external appearances as a kind of made-up and vague language that saves us from directly manipulating the viscera of our nature. Perhaps this will also help us to be able to endure life in society without souring our stomachs with each conversation.

Let's look at another practical case that illustrates the phenomenon of conventional hypocrisy:

An individual wakes up to the sound of the vagabond and infernal alarm clock that he got from a friend, even though at the time he had said that he loved the gift with a smile that both perceived to be false and, out of politeness, kept silent. He goes to the bathroom, brushes his teeth, not because he feels amazed by the refreshing sensation of toothpaste, but because he knows he has terrible breath, and this has often caused him embarrassment. Shave, comb your hair, apply gel, deodorant, etc. Defect anonymously while reading interesting events in the newspaper so that you have something to talk about if you meet someone you know with whom you have nothing in common. Put on your work uniform and walk to the bus stop. While waiting, an old colleague drives by and offers him a ride to work, but he refuses and says that he has unfortunately already agreed to take the bus with a friend, and in fact he just can't stand the company of that individual, and he said the first thing that came to his mind to avoid half an hour of incredibly boring and vulgar conversations about his personal difficulties and about how much he is suffering because he has been abandoned by his wife. Since he had already invented dozens of lame excuses for the same purpose, the acquaintance says "okay, partner, stay until the next time", and continues driving while thinking "that imbecile is too proud to accept even a ride". He answers "bye, and thank you again" as he looks around pretending to look for his friend who would take the bus with him, until the car left his sight. He sighs relieved that he had circumvented the inconvenience of renting his ear with nonsense that didn't matter to him, and then he sees the waiting bus arrive. She gets up, climbs the steps, sits down in a chair and disappears on her way to another predictable day in which she will have to endure the demands of her boss in silence. The stranger who sat next to him while this was happening seemed inattentive, but to alleviate the boredom, he followed everything that happened and, seeing that no friend arrived to accompany him, he thought to himself: "wasted time listening to these disgusting people! If only they had discussed it, it would have been more interesting!"

This type of banal and ordinary event is something that we would not even consider hypocritical if we were the person in question. Since it causes no harm, we don't see this as a true lie, but only as a way of avoiding inconveniences by the law of least effort. The fact is that, if we were forced to tell the truth in the face of each uncomfortable situation, we would probably live in a perpetual war motivated by banalities that, perhaps, for us, are truly insignificant things, but which, for others, may represent a profound offense to personal vanity, something that they will certainly try to avenge. It's not socially intelligent to risk our physical integrity for the sake of the truth that the hairstyle of the individual we talk to is ridiculous. So for all intents and purposes, we've never seen *such a modern* cut.

As can be seen, we lie or reveal the truth that is partially or completely accurate to the extent of our interests. For this reason, unless we are concerned with cultivating a certain social image, we should not take too seriously what others think about us. Whether it's a compliment or an insult, the truth behind the statement always hides some interest that is not immediately accessible to us. It will be up to us to try to discover it if we don't want to be carried away by appearances, since they are always designed to lead us to think something that, first of all, will be beneficial to those who forged them. Thus, to take advantage of others, we carefully design appearances, sometimes with varying levels of perfidy, so that they do not have access to the truth that we should hide, and we lead them to believe in lies like someone who, in fencing, plays a feint. Whether we like it or not, we always have the shadow of personal interest behind everything related to life in society. Becoming malicious represents the essence of human socialization.

Then, when faced with something that is said about us, we will never know how much is truly honest. Even so, even if what was said were totally sincere, no one has direct access to the object to which the observation refers, except for ourselves - if we have already begun *to know yourself*. If we know from experience that we are not good drivers, what can we infer about someone who considers us to be excellent drivers? Either the individual is wrong, or is trying to manipulate us through praise. It would be rude of us to throw out the window all the knowledge we have on the subject just to allow ourselves to be massaged by a palpable lie.

Honest truth about us may be desirable, but it will almost never come from someone else. In addition, others will never get to know us better than ourselves, and it's good to keep that in mind when they say something that contradicts, in a positive or negative way, the opinions we have about us, because they are generally wrong. Suffice it to note that others often have secret opinions about us, and often the sincerest confession of those opinions shocks us completely, not because of their truth, but because of how completely wrong the target is. This shows how difficult it is to achieve a reasonably clear notion of what is inside each one, especially if we are not the person in question, or if we have the terrible habit of lying to ourselves.

Such misconceptions are frequent because, when we are unable to understand a certain person, it is common to simply invent what that person is. We declare that this fanciful imagination is the purest truth, believing that the individual really boils down to the opinion we have about him. This gives us a sense of security, but fatally results in erroneous beliefs. Such a phenomenon occurs quite often among those who, out of love, idealize a certain person. In the eyes of the one who loves, the beloved object becomes not the person itself, but what he invented about him. As we deny reality and replace it with our fantasies, it turns out that few are loved for what they really are - if at all.

* * *

Armor may be good, but we also have some tools for discovering truths. The most efficient way to get someone to tell the truth is, without a doubt, physical torture. It works wonderfully well, but it's illegal and inconvenient. There are also various forms of psychological torture, very efficient blackmail techniques, but they are methods that will make others start to hate us because we are violating the rules of the game. There are more intelligent and less invasive devices to be able to extract the truth we want without leaving room for such obvious counterattacks.

The first is praise, through which we disarm our opponent by posing as his allies. When well applied, praise reduces an extremely perceptive and well-articulated individual to a mouthpiece with a bovine expression that allows himself to be inflated by the most idiotic comments. Once placed in this situation, we can freely manipulate the individual's beliefs, since their critical sense is temporarily suppressed by the inflated ego. With the feeling that we have ceased to be their enemies, the individual will not only stop protecting the truth, but will also make a point of saying it in an attempt to create a bond of trust with the one who made him feel so important. Now we have an originally wise man turned into an idiot who is at our service simply because he was unable to protect himself from praise.

Another device to extract the truth from a certain individual is to enrage them through insults until they get out of control and use everything they think of as a weapon - and no weapon is more powerful, more incisive than the truth. Adding that, when furious, the individual will not be mentally able to organize elaborate attacks, we have another very efficient way of making him stupid and reckless in our favor. In this state of animality, all you can do is throw at your opponent the most poignant, low, and degrading truths you know.

Thus, if we maintain our composure, we can guide its chaotic flow of ideas as we see fit, taking the discussion to the subject that interests us, seeing the most hidden truths sprouting in profusion from that sparkling mouth. Combined with this, there will only be a few automatic insults and vague innuendos, which can be easily identified and discarded, since if he knew something in fact he would make a point of proving it, not being limited to mere insinuations. With this, we now know what our opponent's weapons are, and it will be easier to exploit their weaknesses, since we are aware of the type of threat it may pose.

Insulting is a very interesting maneuver from a strategic point of view, provided that we have already become accustomed to absolute honesty with ourselves, so that a truth told about us, even if uncomfortable, cannot infuriate us equally and cause us to lose the advantage. Because if something is true, there's no need to raise protests against the truth, and if something is false, there's no need to bother with something that doesn't apply to us. In this we see an example of the importance of discerning between truth and appearance.

The example above also reveals that the reason why honesty is valued is actually strategic: it's always easier to defeat an enemy that we know well. So, in stating that honesty is a virtue, what we really hope is that others will become transparent to our intentions. It is a trick even more subtle than praise and more efficient than insult, demonstrating that, ultimately, we like honest people for the same reason that we like dogs.

✳ ✳ ✳

The fact that we need to carry a bunch of keys to enter and leave our homes already reveals perfectly well what we think of each other, and should reduce the possibility of being honest to a joke. But we're reluctant to admit anything so visceral.

Of course, not all of them are chronic deceivers waiting for the first opportunity to stab us - although they are rarely very far from it - but the fact is that everyone lies because honesty — always telling only the truth without taking our interests into consideration — is a gross strategic error, an intangible naivety inspired by insipid idealisms. Being honest is an approach that simply doesn't work, as we need to protect ourselves from each other's intentions. In this sense, the virtues that we trumpet do not actually correspond to what drives us. On the contrary, they are largely a way of disorienting fools. Living involves competing, and competing involves playing dirty. From this comes the need to lie, at least to protect oneself. Besides, being honest is never more than a handout.

Let us realize, then, that people are not difficult to understand: the fact is that they don't want to be understood, because being understood involves revealing secrets, something that would leave them vulnerable. Thus, in the process of hiding sensitive information, countless false information is born, which is indistinguishable from the true, and this very intentional confusion of versions is what makes people apparently incomprehensible. From this was born the myth that there is something sphingic in people, when there isn't. Understanding people is easy: it's hard to get them to tell the truth. At best, we *wish we could* be honest, but we simply can't — for the same reason we can't reveal the password to our bank accounts.

✳ ✳ ✳

Realizing how hollow, misleading, and low there is in all relationships between individuals, we realized how harmful it is to our well-being to cultivate an erroneous notion about human nature and relationships between men. It's common to imagine that we ourselves are, so to speak, outside the theater, especially when it comes to our most intimate relationships. But this is the type of illusion that we do best to extirpate ourselves, taking care to harm ourselves as little as possible, otherwise it will eventually be debunked by a misfortune that devastates us mercilessly.

We must know that it is always a real possibility to find ourselves betrayed by those we trust the most. Adopting the naive stance that being honest is enough to make us immune to the tricks of life in society will only ensure that we become even easier victims. Considering that we are social beings, it is a matter of intelligence that we never forget the basic rules of the vile game called coexistence.

Undoubtedly, cultivating idealized notions about the integrity and honesty of individuals who are dear to us is one of the best ways to be disappointed. The most we can hopefully hope to find is a fair balance in exploring one another, i.e. a healthy relationship. It is also important that we never close our eyes romantically under the pretext of trust, because the temptation to pass the leg on others has proven to be numerous times more decisive than loyalty - in the real world, the goose that lays the golden eggs often actually carries a beautiful amount of this precious metal within it.

We should not, therefore, suppose that we would find in the depths of individuals the same as what they exhibit outside. With that, we would get used to taking for real facades that are mere theatrical realities. We would be adopting completely conventional notions as desirable that, with good reason, would make us feel different, displaced, lonely, suffering because we never found honesty in a world driven by interests, impostures, betrayals, and untruths.

Thus, when judging the issue, when trying to discern between the authentic and the affected, it is prudent to take the big difference between what we are and what we display to others as a reference, since it is likely that they will do the same, and with the same malice - even though this stance disgusts us for throwing away all our poetic and delicate ideas about sincere friendship, according to which everyone is idiot and only we have the right to think one thing and say another.

MORALITY

We are used to understanding morals as a "spiritual" issue. If we were dis-embodied souls, that's fine. It would even make sense. We don't see how incoherent it is for humans to propose spiritual solutions to material problems. In the spiritual realm, we consider it logical to leave matter aside — we never wonder if spirits are entitled to retirement. However, in the material sphere, we consider it absurd to leave the spirit aside. We believe that following ideal values will make us good, but it will only make us blind. It turns out that, instead of considering idealized values a fantasy, we consider ourselves unworthy of them. We began to believe that the values are better than us, the immoral, the weak, the sinners, those who strayed from the path that no one can follow.

Evidently, it is not possible to approach the issue from a spiritual point of view simply because we have no spirit. So, delusions aside, we are material beings living in a material world. When, after that, we say that our morals must be materialistic, we have to understand that this is not extremism, but the only possible starting point so that we can reach true conclusions that relate to reality.

What escapes most people about what they call materialism is that, by re-jecting it, they are not only missing the opportunity to understand the world and make sarcastic jokes, but of — woe to us! — live according to reality. So let us allow ourselves at least a brief moment of honesty to illustrate what exactly is at stake. Then, each one draws their own conclusions.

Humanity has always behaved, by all definitions, inhumanely. Isn't it per-haps time to reevaluate our concepts of what a man is, instead of insisting on carrying forward a vision that is evidently based on erroneous notions about our nature? Good or bad, constructive or destructive, a human being will never stop being human. Being inhuman is a thing of rocks and bottle caps. Isn't it enough that we were born in a world like this, full of free miseries, is it not enough. Do we still need to bear the burden of living as blind volunteers in the name of what is considered morally correct? It's not enough to honestly assert our impotence. Do we still need to embrace spurious theories that console us by implying that the problem is fleeting? Because, if there is anything within reach of our eyes, it is that we have no reason to believe that reality will change from water to wine. On the contrary, we are moving more and more towards vinegar. Within this, not even the most optimistic perspective has the courage to point out a tangible solution, and it limits itself to vaguely pointing to a remote future in which we will be different by some grace of fate.

Whether we like it or not, we are essentially shaved monkeys that, with the accumulation of technological advances, now have too much power and less reason. Our remarkable capacity to make mistakes increasingly equals the risk of death. We have more immediate force with a finger on the trigger than with any other weapon that biological evolution has provided us. This is for the simple reason that evolution would never equip us with any device without first making sure that it will not allow us to be constant victims of our own stupidity.

For example, what can an angry monkey do? At most, go out screaming and gesturing like crazy, biting and assaulting those who are nearby. Is it a monkey out of its mind? Same thing, except maybe you'll jump off a cliff or something. That was the limit imposed by evolution as a preventive measure. But a monkey shaved out of its mind can do much more with all the power it has in its hands due to technology. You can blow up entire cities with the push of one button, or completely incinerate them by pressing another.

It turns out that, now, the world is a much more dangerous place to live in, since not only do we need to protect ourselves from our own stupidity, but especially from that of others, and for that it is necessary that we have a clear and lucid view of reality. Deceiving ourselves with ideals of unrealizable peacefulness is an extremely effective way of becoming victims of our own naivety.

The possibility of universal peace is nothing more than a misunderstanding. *Humans kill because life has been killing to live ever since it appeared — that's the meaning of life, the eternal struggle for power, anything goes with DNA.* A bunch of platitudes invented by autistic theologians won't protect us from this reality. Nothing is more strange to us than seeing pacifist individuals — whose evolution basically consisted of tearing the heads off wild beasts — claiming that they did not understand the motives of violence in society. We have the impression of being faced with another species, such as innocence. To those spiritual beings who have just arrived on planet Earth, we recommend vacations in the real world. Maybe this will clear your eyes.

If we want to seek useful foundations for our ideals of human morality, we would do well to look to the side, not to the sky. We will do even better to forget the concept of ideal and embrace the concept of real. This will put our feet back on the ground, and we will begin to see morals as a means of solving the problems of the reality in which we are. Let us forget the idealized perfection of the world in which we would like to be: the ideal is a dream, and to dream is to close our eyes.

Our situation is as follows: we are civilized beings who can't stand civilization. Malaise crosses life in society. We live in a perpetual war because our most basic interests are conflicting. We cannot live together in peace because the satisfaction of our desires involves fighting against each other. Let us understand, therefore, that the problem is not in society itself, but in us. Society will never be perfect because it is made up of human beings. We're not peaceful — we never were and we never will be.

To solve this problem, or at least alleviate it, two solutions were proposed: police and religion. The religion's approach consists of rendering a man harmless by trapping his mind. The police, in turn, renders the man harmless by trapping his body. The difference is that religion can be legally employed as a preventive measure, ensuring that individuals never cease to feel constantly being watched by the Grand Policeman. It is something analogous to a photographic radar that does not take photographs. We know that it doesn't work very well, but at least it reduces total costs, and it's justified for that.

In general, we think of religion as the true guardian of human morality, without which society would disintegrate. It is believed that without God, everything is allowed. Why do we think that way? Because memorizing platitudes is easier than thinking. It is easy to demonstrate that religion, in moral terms, is virtually useless and has, in practice, only a marginal value.

At first, let us realize that the moral values espoused by this or that religion make sense. The fact, however, is that by taking them forward, we never achieved the promised results. Why? Because they are based on false assumptions. Because it idealizes man, the moral principles that religion elaborates are something impossible to put into practice, since they relate to something that does not exist. There's no way to expect values made for spirits to work for primates. What sincerely could we expect from the morality of a monkey that believes it has an eternal soul to be judged by an immortal superchimpanzee that lives in the stratosphere?

Furthermore, in the development of such principles, it not only systematically misses the mark, but also never demonstrates a positive approach. Religion does not seek to solve problems, but to prevent them from arising through the denial of our nature. It seeks to cower us before the world and before ourselves, diverting our eyes from the present and encouraging a passive myopia that will be rewarded in the afterlife.

Let's look at the issue as follows: the function of morals is to manage the social problems resulting from human beings. What is the religious solution? *To dehumanize the human being, that is, to deny it, to castrate it, to make it sick, i.e. to spiritualize it.* Its value, therefore, is merely negative. Its principles are not respected because they are useful, but because they have the support of the creator of the heavens and the earth, providing some sense of security to those who need this type of crutch. That is the only use of religion in the moral sphere. It is an indirect contribution, a pretext for acting morally - even so, not like men, but as servants to ghosts.

Let's analyze the issue a bit more. We know that a considerable portion of the world's population is religious and believes in moralistic deities. Doesn't it seem strange, however, that we see as extremists those who actually follow the principles of their religion? In practice, those who govern their lives according to such principles are considered alienated fanatics, mentally ill. However, if religion were something truly true, isn't that exactly what we should do? But we don't. Religious or not, we are human, and our practical intuition tells us that there is something very wrong with religious moral values. Hardly anyone in real life takes such principles seriously. How can this be explained?

Let's see: why do we consider it inadmissible to place God above the law? Exactly because we don't treat God as something real — not literally — but as something that one chooses, similar to a soccer team or a political party. So, at the end of the day, we treat God for what he is: a belief.

This means that, as a rule, one does not literally believe in God, one believes in believing in God. They claim to believe in God but act as if he didn't exist. Let's use the creation myth to exemplify it. Does anyone really believe that the world was created in six days? We know that this is an obvious lie — not just something unlikely, but absolutely ridiculous, that even Christians can't take seriously. So why do we respect such beliefs? For the sake of good manners. For the same reason that we don't tell obese people that they're obese, paraplegics that they're paraplegics, and so on. We know the truth, but we don't tell it simply so as not to hurt them, not to hurt their feelings, because living is hard enough, and we don't have to throw their limitations, defects, and ineptities in the face of individuals simply because that is true.

Like any addict, someone who needs religious beliefs to be able to be moral probably has problems dealing with reality. We don't mock your beliefs, not because they inspire us any respect, but simply to spare them so as not to make your life even more difficult. We just have to imagine what our life would be like if we depended on lies to live in peace, if we had to defend them as if they were true, even if we knew perfectly well that they were lies, and that will give us an idea of how believing in nonsense must be difficult. For example, if we needed to believe that a three-in-one suicide hologram lives in heaven; if we needed to believe that our loved ones are immortal vertebrates. How can we continue to believe when reality shows that we are clearly wrong?

Our only viable alternative, in this case, would be to not think too much about it - and that's exactly what we do. That's because, for any polite individual, it must be quite disturbing to have to believe such crazy things. So we suppose that if you believe in something so foolish, you must have good reasons for it - and since those reasons are invariably shameful, we have the good manners to leave them alone with their dementias. The fact is that no one needs God because he doesn't exist. However, many need the belief in God, and that is the only reason why we respect such beliefs.

Let us illustrate this perspective with a practical case. Almost everyone knows the saying that there are no atheists on a crashing plane. However, in emergency situations, the last thing we think of resorting to are metaphysical superstitions. We can be certain that, in a crashing plane, no one will start praying until all physical possibilities to place the aircraft on the ground safely have been exhausted. When everything fails, not to say that we give up, we launch one *is in the hands of God*, which is the Christian way of saying that we are alone and are probably going to die. The fact is that no one prays as a first option - and that reveals a lot about who we are.

Of course, at our wakes, they will say that we went to a better place. The question remains as to why they themselves won't go either, since for that we do not need the Lord's permission, but only a faulty plane. Even if you invent as many explanations as necessary to justify your self-deception, you can never take seriously an individual claiming that their loved one went to a better place while remaining in tears instead of shouting joy - which is exactly what they would do if their relative had actually won a ticket to a better place, such as that dream promotion to a company abroad.

This makes it sufficiently clear why, when it comes to morals, religion is a distraction from the promotion of our well-being. There's nothing constructive about walking around blindly in exchange for peace of soul. At best, it's just a well-intentioned waste of time — although it seems more like a pretext for negligence.

＊ ＊ ＊

Such considerations illustrate that we should not be concerned with right or wrong from the point of view of morality itself, since such a stance places morality as something idealized and closed in itself, which does not concern the world in which we actually are, and this locks us out of the equation that we ourselves created. Moral rule systems based on idealisms are something that teaches us that ignoring reality is a good thing, and that being blind will make us virtuous - but only in that parallel universe in which no one is. Its message is as follows: *between a moral rule and reality, let's stick with morals.* Needless to say why this delusional stance should be ignored.

So how should we proceed? We must, when crossing the road, be concerned with what is right or wrong from the real point of view. That's because, after being run over, it won't make any difference what unfortunate belief crossed our minds when we concluded that we could ignore physics and let ourselves be guided by moral abstractions. That is the only sensible stance to be adopted with regard to morals.

Thus, before thinking of morals as a solution to social problems, we need to grasp reality itself quite clearly — understand it amorally. It doesn't matter that, when faced with any problem, we have the best intentions. Intentions don't solve anything. If we don't know what we're talking about, any judgment we make will be nothing more than nonsense. Cultivating a hollow moral based on rhetoric, instead of solving problems, only makes us ignore them, calling on everyone to look in the wrong direction in the name of some idea that pleases our imagination. Let's understand that there's nothing admirable about handing out beautiful advice that no one can follow; that's silly, a disservice.

So let's leave rhetoric aside and look at the issue from the point of view of reality. Society must impose certain restrictions on individuals to make it sustainable. Whatever society we are a part of, there are rules that guide it, and we really have no choice as to whether to abide by them or not. We know that unbalanced human impulses must be restrained in order for life in society to be possible, otherwise nothing would stop us from assaulting an old couple to buy chewing gum. But the detail is as follows: nothing prevents us. It's entirely possible to rob them, put the money in the pocket, look for a bar and buy gum there — not a stone will fall on our heads. In physical terms, there is no impediment. So, when it comes to morals, the question is the reasons why we consider ourselves impeded.

What are those reasons? In the first case, the reason is that we have a strait-jacket installed in our brains. In a second case, the reason is to be aware of our long-term interests. There are obviously more advantages to this second approach, but it requires more effort on our part. Such a stance requires the ability to exercise such restrictions ourselves, but with the advantage that they will be much less invasive, since each decision will be taken taking into account specifically our case.

Even if only in general terms, this sums up the issue fairly well. No matter how much we dream, morality only concerns life in society. The purpose is to allow us to live without disturbing each other. If we cross the limits, full of faith or unbelieving, guided by transcendental or mundane principles, the consequences will be the same.

Beyond that, morality has no specific objective worthy of consideration. To live is to walk in circles, and to be moral is not to step on the feet of others. By taking only the sensible precaution of not being arrested, everyone can act as they please. There's not much more that can be said. The rest are theories used to convince us that we have no freedom to transgress the law. What we don't have, in fact, is the legal right to do so, but to say that we're not free to do so is foolish. We have complete freedom, so much so that transgressions are a daily occurrence. The freedom we don't have is to transgress reality and jump to the Moon and return for lunch. Let us bear in mind that, in and of itself, living has no rules, only societies.

It is no accident, therefore, that the issue of individual freedom torments so many moralistic minds, as the implications of this are potentially terrible. However, we can know all this, all this arbitrariness, without feeling the least bit inclined to a life of crime. This is an issue related much more to our personal nature, to our character, than to our philosophical opinions.

In any case, when it comes to morals, society doesn't bother to monitor our motives for one thing or another. Your interest consists solely in delimiting our actions. We can think what we want, but not act as we want, and within that our motives don't matter. Then, as long as we don't cause a nuisance — or that we don't get discovered — we won't be punished.

Faced with this very clear perspective, it would be negligent to refrain from making our own choices out of respect for moral abstractions. We would be exchanging our freedom for a handful of dogmas that will ensure that we always act the same way, regardless of the circumstances. If there's one important thing to stress, it's that being stupid just in case isn't the smartest choice.

* * *

To be moral, we don't need the intermediary of some transcendental theory that tries to guarantee that our brain will never become part of the equation. So, as long as we're willing to think, there are much more interesting alternatives. We can, for example, find much more life wisdom in modern science than in any moral theory ever devised - with the advantage that we won't have to mortgage our intelligence. Then, quickly going through some controversial topics, we will see more clearly the advantages of inferring our rules based on facts and circumstances, not according to the rules themselves. We will see what benefits there are in first seeing reality in itself, and only then worrying about superseding that basic reality with another, composed of rules that delimit our actions.

Let's see what can be said in objective and scientific terms about drugs, legal or not. The definition is simple: substances that we use to intervene in the body's physiological processes. With the countless drugs already exhaustively catalogued and studied, we have no essential question about what they do. We know how they work, where they work, their duration, and the side effects, and we know that there's nothing wrong with them. It is absurd to point to a group of molecules under a microscope and say that they are bad and wrong substances because they produce a certain effect when administered to living beings. That stance borders on ridicule. Drugs are just substances that alter our physiology, and their value in promoting our well-being has been more than proven. Thus, before stating that drugs are bad indistinctly, we must consider what the drug in question is, for what purpose it will be used, who will be the user, what the dosage and for how long it will be administered. That's what matters in terms of pros and cons. The fact that some individuals use them in a self-destructive way is not an objection to drugs, but to self-destruction itself, since the same substance can be used to save lives. So if we don't want people to destroy themselves, for whatever reason, let's at least admit that that is the point, and that this, in turn, has nothing to do with the substances themselves, but with the purpose for which they are used. Furthermore, no drug flows into the veins of addicts. When they inject them into themselves, they lose the right to blame them, to consider themselves victims whose lives were destroyed by drugs. The addiction is not in the substance, but in the addict and their stupid behavior. So in material terms, someone taking headache medicine or someone else injecting heroin are doing exactly the same thing, that is, altering their physiology artificially to promote their well-being, just as we can alter it naturally through sleep deprivation, fasting, or exercise. It seems little, but that's all there is to be said about the essence of drugs. The rest are rules that we invented to regulate their use, and do not add or subtract anything from the basic mechanism of action. In this sense, when it comes to right and wrong, the only real classification that we can establish is that there are bad drugs and good drugs, that is, drugs that work well and others that work poorly. In and of itself, the use of drugs is not wrong for the same reason that it is also not right, that is, because it has no meaning, just as there is no meaning in putting oil in a car's engine. A bull enlightens us much more about this universe than any discourse by moralists.

About races and genders there are also some words to be said. The idea that there are no races among humans, only between dogs, has become common. We must classify ourselves into ethnicities. That may sound politically correct, but biologically it doesn't make much sense—after all, dogs are also virtually identical to each other. Changing words and definitions doesn't change reality. We know that there are physical differences between individuals of different races, and this is something that science has already proven very well. There are also physical differences between men and women, and they have already been very well established. We know that blacks are more prone to high blood pressure; that Orientals are shorter in stature; that men are more prone to baldness and, women, to cellulitis. We know all this because we saw it with our own eyes. It's proven by overwhelming statistics, and only someone who forgot to do their homework on scientific subjects would think that such statements are prejudices. Men and women are different from each other, and the races are different as well. This, of course, is no pretext for establishing a hierarchy of perfection, but to claim that we are all the same is simply a lie. On the contrary, we are all different, and we must take this into account when buying *shampoos*. The only exception to this rule, of course, is intelligence. That's because an individual may be a genius, an absolutely brilliant mind capable of bringing immeasurable progress to human knowledge, but he is still as intelligent as an ignorant drunkard with mental retardation. In this regard, no matter how much there is evidence to the contrary, we should simply ignore them, because everyone is equally intelligent, and always will be.

When we analyze the issue of sexuality, it is also not easy to understand where so many misunderstandings and absurd implications originate. Sexual desire is something extremely simple and easy to satisfy. In fact, wouldn't it be great if we could satisfy hunger simply by stroking the belly? But we love to complicate things. The issue can basically be boiled down to the fact that on Earth there are billions of individuals eager for the pleasure of intercourse. They are basically divided into men, who have penises, and women, who have vaginas. The genitalia must be stimulated in order to achieve the much sought after orgasm, and this can be done as, with which and as many partners as they please. The closest thing to wrong we could conceive sexually would be to try to get aroused by using things that don't work, such as masturbating with hammers. Wrong sex is one that doesn't give us pleasure, not one that violates taboos. Therefore, if the objective is to obtain pleasure by stimulating a certain set of cells in our body, we must understand what are the real, biological options before us, because the rest are secondary issues such as monogamy, fidelity, marriage, safety, feelings, venereal diseases, or unwanted pregnancy, all revolving around taboos and social interests. There is only one very simple equation whose main components are known to everyone: penis and vagina, glans and clitoris. It doesn't matter who uses what on whom nor how: man and woman, man and man, woman and woman, man and inflatable doll, or woman and vibrator, all of these combinations work. Furthermore, despite all the horror involved in the issue of pedophilia, the fact is that against it the only objection that applies is the same as that applied to zoophilia, that is, the possible physical incompatibility between the genitals. Against incest, there's no way to imagine any immediate physical objection. Whatever our personal preferences are, it doesn't matter what one says in the sense of approving certain behaviors or disapproving others, because biology ignores our taboos. Thus, since in terms of physical possibility the impediments are few and easily circumvented, it all boils down to a practical issue, not a moral one.

Finally, we can kill whoever we want. To do this, it is enough to have the physical means. If we can stop another individual's body from working, that means we can kill them. There is no need to involve such a fact in notions of right or wrong, or in considerations about the value of human life. The fact is simply that you can kill, and you do. We just waste time discussing whether there is a possibility of taking someone else's life. We know there are. The whole discussion boils down to whether the reasons for doing so are good or not, and that, in turn, is a completely different discussion. The most important issue brought to light when looking at the matter from this perspective is that no one needs just reasons to kill us. We can be murdered for reasons that we agree or disagree with. A gunshot between the eyes can be a just self-defense, an unjust personal revenge: it makes no difference what we think, it makes no difference if we recognize the moral right of the bullet that explodes our brains. Physically, the result is the same. So if we really want to grasp the crux of the matter, we must understand that murder is a physical act, not a moral one.

These are classic examples of how we can see the facts behind the moral issues raised by life in society from a purely material and objective perspective, free from prejudices. Thus, to be moral individuals, it is not necessary to believe, just to think. There's no need for unquestioned moral imperatives. We don't need to predefine virtue and vice, right and wrong, since such things depend on our judgment, not on reality. The only requirement for us to be able to guide our lives by intellectualized morality is to constantly use the brain to define our own judgments, values, and limits.

* * *

Such coldness is unusual in discussions about morals because, for most individuals, it is important that there be a "passion" linked to each moral value, so that we follow such or such principles because we feel they are correct. However, confronting the theory behind this criterion with the practical results, we see that it is not very reliable. On the one hand, nurturing values of this kind can make individuals more predictable, which is desirable for those who wish to predict and manipulate them. However, on the other hand, it does not guarantee an intelligent adaptation of your actions, since they will all be guided by passionate beliefs that do not accept thought as a parallel component.

The only difference between moral principles of an intellectual nature and others of an affective nature consists in the fact that only in the latter are punishments guaranteed. Feeling guilty when transgressing a moral principle is, by definition, what makes it efficient, that is, coercive. When a transgression is not immediately accompanied by punishment, whether internal, in the form of guilt or remorse, or external, in the form of reprimands, fines, or imprisonment, the principle is therefore no longer feared and, therefore, not respected. However, consider that, when this occurs, it is generally because the amount in question was useless. Because if it were a truly useful value, we would continue to follow it of our own free will, even though we knew that we would not be punished for transgressing it.

In any case, guilt is not a good foundation for moral values. Furthermore, our duty, as individuals, is not to punish ourselves, but to behave according to our interests, in view of the limits that society imposes on us. Our personal values can be any values. Before society, our only duty is to respect limits - punishing is the duty of the law.

Of course, the possibility of being purely rational in this matter bothers those who see morals as a second law, because they feel that it is necessary to follow one more rule and do not allow others to ignore it. However, this can be reduced to the rancor of individuals who cage themselves in prejudices and spend their lives hating those who are free. The fact is that, as rational individuals, we are as trustworthy as everyone else. Perhaps even more so, because our values are logical and based on facts, not on dogmas, beliefs, and fear. Our morals, from a purely rational point of view, may seem arbitrary, but our interests are not - and that is the important detail in this question. In both cases, the objectives are the same. The difference is that we took superstition out of the equation.

Strangely enough, most individuals do not choose the path of freedom, of rationalized morals. They commonly opt for emotional moral prejudices, that is, fear. They simply don't think why a given principle should not be transgressed. They only think that, when transgressing it, they will feel guilty or will suffer punishment, and that is equivalent to not thinking. In this situation, we spend most of our lives following rules that we never thought of. We never seek to understand why a society in which people are guided by such rules is more desirable. Sooner or later, however, we are confronted by situations in which we are forced to think, and it is only regrettable that an extreme situation is necessary to lead us to make independent choices. The rest of the time, that is, most of our lives, we limit ourselves to following principles instead of making decisions. We end up letting the whole life slip out of our hands through a consensual passivity, from which we only awaken when there are great things at stake, and our principles are visibly unable to deal with the situation satisfactorily.

Thus, if we are faced with a red light and, seeing an assailant approach, we still have any doubts about what is the best way out, this only shows that we never ponder the difference between physical principles and conventional principles. We can believe that we are right if, by not taking any action, we feel justified by the belief that "we have the right to live in peace", but there will be plenty of time to ruminate the matter when, after being robbed, we have to return to our homes on foot because, instead of wisdom, we choose a clear conscience. Such is the anguish we feel when confronted by freedom that, as a rule, we simply choose not to think. We prefer to keep a clear conscience at all costs, even if it costs us our lives. By the time we realize the degree of foolishness of this stance, it is generally too late, and now we play the role of honest victims. Those who give up thinking for themselves, believing that they will be safe simply because they are not breaking any rules, will soon find themselves constantly in the position of the victim of the world. He will be an innocent virtuoso constantly victimized by his silent stance of thoughtlessness, passivity, and cowardice.

Reality comes before law and justice, and this can easily be illustrated by someone who dies in a burning movie theater because, having paid for the ticket, insists on the right to watch the entire movie. He died in the name of his right. Ignoring reality in favor of the moral right may seem an absurd stance, but it is not uncommon to feel somewhat proud to be obedient, following meaningless rules even when there are no witnesses. We cultivate slave virtues in exchange for peace in the soul, for a clear conscience, but that is no guarantee of anything, other than that we stop thinking to prioritize obedience - as befits those who govern us.

＊ ＊ ＊

When we put morals into this perspective, we soon realize that what we follow are beliefs and conventions, not realities. Right and wrong are reduced to a false opposition that we have been led to believe. Thus, when proceeding with these questions, we may seem to be "disrespecting" good morals, but all we are doing is reflecting on why we should follow certain values and not others - or none of them. We are reflecting on your purposes and the value of those purposes. For example, in our society, for the most part, individuals maintain that killing is wrong. Well, if they believe that, they must have their motives. Then we turn to one of them and ask the obvious question: *why can't you kill?* However, instead of responding, the individual is merely indignant. We soon realized that those who react with indignation to questions of this kind are only disguising the fact that they have no answers; with their indignation, they are just trying to escape the embarrassment of admitting that they believe in social dogmas. In this situation, the individual does not know how to explain or justify their values - but, even so, they want to be rationally respected for their irrational belief.

If we want to distance ourselves from this dogmatic stance, we must learn to dissociate our behavior from the notions of right and wrong, good and evil, and begin to associate it with facts, reasoning, motives, reasons. If we want to have access to our own values, our morals cannot be a set of absolute commandments, without any context in which we can assess their justifications. When, for example, we think of murder, we should not think that it is wrong, but that it is the act of intentional taking the life of another person. Then we must think, in the context of a life in society, what are the implications of taking the life of another person, as well as the situations in which this might or might not be valid.

In this process, the conclusion itself matters least. This is because, whatever

173

reasoning leads to the conclusion that killing is right or wrong, we will see that, in each case, there are always a series of intermediate steps composed of reasons and reasons to accept that conclusion, and that is what really matters: thinking. Understand what led us to that conclusion. We should not simply be content to know it, because the most important thing is to be aware of the reasons that support that conclusion, so that when we are thinking about related issues, in order to make other decisions, we have access to the reasons for all our values, not just to its conclusions. In this sense, the conclusions only have a practical value, and that value is subject to the reasons that led us to them.

As we can see, reflecting on our personal values is equivalent to doing reverse engineering, seeking the reasons that caused them to be born. Let us try to illustrate. In our everyday lives, we follow several rules. Now let's think about one of them, no matter what: if we cannot answer, immediately and without hesitation, why we should or should not obey such a rule, it means that we never think about it. We simply let someone else think for us.

Only understanding will place us in the position of agreeing or disagreeing with the final conclusion - and there is no way to do so if we are not aware of the reasons behind it. This is clear if we think of obvious rules such as "it is wrong to drink seawater" or "we must wash food before eating it". We were able to deduce the raison d'être from these rules because they are clearly related to reality, and so it must be with all our judgments about the world: they must be intelligible and justifiable. When we stop thinking about the basis of the rules, we end up harboring foolish doubts, such as the possibility of drinking seawater after it has been distilled, since its "intimate essence" would remain maritime - and perhaps it would still remain pernicious in and of itself. In this situation, we became superstitious about seawater because we lost sight of the fact that underpinned the prohibition.

Thus, when dealing with reality, we must think in terms of real limitations, that is, facts, forces, atoms, actions, and reactions. Understand what facts we're dealing with in raw, physical terms. Only after that come the social or moral limitations, which are merely to regulate our collective behavior on this particular issue.

In this sense, the customs of a certain society are nothing more than conventional advice. Thus, no matter how much one praises this or that principle, no matter how transgressing it puts us in jail: it will never be more than advice that we can agree with or not. In logic, as in morals, they must be seen as fallacious appeals to popularity or seniority. Not just the conclusions, we also want to have access to the premises, because only then can we verify that the entire reasoning is valid.

So when it comes to morality, morality comes last. First comes the reality, then the reasons and, finally, the conclusions. We should only use the conclusions directly when the situation does not allow us time to think. Then, however, we must review the appropriateness of what we use without prior consideration. In the process of structuring a coherent view of reality, all the superfluous notions that we attach without a clear understanding of their function will only make us incompetent in the task of thinking for ourselves — of making our judgments, from beginning to end, in the first person.

Before closing, let us also add that morality has nothing to do with the concept of "virtue", which in turn is a completely empty concept. This automatic link that we see between one thing and another is just a rancidity of theology that still imbues us with metaphysical confusion.

Morality is a practical issue, it is what stands between us and our objectives, and it concerns the best means of satisfying our interests in the social context. The value of moral judgment lies in its capacity to deal with physical problems satisfactorily, without going beyond the limits established by social conventions.

As we explained, the application of morals in our lives can be done passively, through moral prejudices, or actively, through intelligence. Both approaches work, but only one allows us to know why. One accepts ready-made results, the other does its own calculations.

We made the choice to remain with our intelligence awake because it seems senseless to us to sleep in control of our lives, in a kind of moral somnambulism. We don't believe in the rules we follow, only in the interests that justify them. We have abandoned all the superstitions that make reasoning lethargic and obtuse. We don't believe in morals, we believe in physics, and we know that, in physical terms, the only thing that can be wrong in murder is shooting.

IV

ON THE HUMAN CONDITION

SUFFERING

Life isn't worth its cost in pain. If we consider happiness as the goal of human existence, we must admit that we are decidedly on the path to failure. It would be much easier to defend the idea that suffering is the true goal, since we have many more sources of illness than of pleasure. On a relative scale, our sensitivity to pain is several times greater than to pleasure. There are many more ways to be unhappy than the other way around. Our greatest pains are always more intense and lasting than our greatest joys. Finally, we don't need to cultivate our intellect, reflect on the world, or strive in any way to achieve suffering: it is available at any time. To suffer, it is enough to live.

Pain is like the essential element in which we are immersed, and happiness is just the moments in which we manage to reach the surface and fill our lungs with air and then be plunged back into the depths. This may sound unpleasant, but if we were to make a decisive bet worth eternal happiness, we would certainly place our trust in the ultimate victory of pain over pleasure. Faced with such an important bet, it is certain that we would quickly regain our lucidity and almost instantly reconsider our foolish opinions regarding the dreams of personal happiness that we cultivate on a daily basis.

From this perspective, all we can do is take the necessary steps to protect ourselves from suffering. When someone seeks or, even more so, demands happiness from a world like this, miserable as it is, this already shows quite clearly how much they are ignorant of their own nature. An individual who was aware of their true condition would be much more modest in their claims to happiness.

We have to understand that life, in essence, is a virus. We have come this far thanks to self-replicating molecules whose selection criterion is the reproductive efficiency of the bodies they build. This mechanical criterion doesn't even come close to touching on things that are almost metaphysical, such as dreams of personal happiness. With or without happiness, life will continue to roll down the mountain in the headless becoming of existence. Furthermore, considering that satisfaction, in general, makes us reckless and lazy, it makes perfect sense that nature has restricted its duration to short moments, followed by long periods of suffering that impel us to action, aimed at satisfying our needs.

This view seems to paint chance as something mean and cruel, but it is a superficial impression. If we want to think about the impersonal perspective of life as a mechanical system, we only need to imagine how we would build a living being if our only interest were its perpetuation. To do so, we can place in your own intimate constitution elements that aim to deceive you, deceive you, fill your horizon with false landscapes, all in the name of efficiency. Let's add that we will never be forced to keep our word. It all boils down to ensuring that the system works, albeit with large doses of suffering. In a short time, we would arrive at something very close to the robots that nature created through biological evolution.

Our situation is not much different from that of a donkey that has a carrot hanging in front of it. Our carrot is called happiness. Pursuing it, we run in search of something that we will never achieve. We have the impression that we were born to be happy, but only because we are tied to the internal logic of our

178

biological nature. The condition of being alive imposes pleasure and suffering on us as supreme references. However, pleasure is just a psychological mechanism designed to influence our behavior, not a reality that we are moving towards. This will be clear if we consider the fact that, when we achieve the satisfaction of a desire, we will only have a few moments of pleasure as a reward, and then new needs that will make us restless begin to bother us. It will not be long before we take action again, in a cycle of dissatisfaction that will only end with the death of the individual or with the acquisition of a grain of common sense.

Realizing that the search for happiness is a trap, we could have the wise idea of crossing our arms and remaining inert. It seems that this would solve all the problems related to suffering, since they arise, directly or indirectly, from all the things we want in order to achieve the fullness that we learned was possible in kindergarten. We imagine a certain dream and suppose that, once fulfilled, we will be satisfied. However, over time, we see that this does not happen. It will never happen. Then it would make sense to consider inaction, the absence of desire, as a solution. *However, those who bet on this idea will soon notice the obvious, lightheaded and unavoidable inconvenience called boredom.* A life steeped in this element is so unbearable that it makes us immediately return to action, even if we know that this is an investment with no future.

If, on the one hand, to desire is to suffer, on the other hand, not to desire is impossible. Therefore, whether through the illusion of happiness or through the tortures of boredom, we are forced to remain active, and thereby expose ourselves to suffering. In this process, reason can refute biology as much as it wants: it is spitting on the plate it eats and, sooner or later, it will suffer reprisals for trying to put aside our instinctive needs. The brain is full of mechanisms that detect attempts to circumvent the rules of this game called life.

In this game, we can believe that there is some chance of winning. Like in a casino, everything is designed to lead us to believe that we really have some chance of success. Let us remember, however, the main premise: the house always wins. It was nature that made the rules, not us - and since our most primitive instincts prevent us from giving up gambling, the fate that awaits us is certain bankruptcy.

The fact that we understand the mechanism that leads us to such an impasse does little to change it. Like chronic addicts, understanding our dependency situation is equivalent to illuminating the cogs of what controls us - just making our freedom an even more distant dream. We know why we are like that, but that understanding does not allow us to escape our condition. In this situation, all we can do is play within the rules as intelligently as possible, in order to minimize the suffering of which we are constant victims.

When we reject the idea of happiness as the ultimate objective of existence, we must also reject, for the same reasons, all the notions supported by that kind of reasoning - that is, everything that in our lives is related to meaning or purpose, all the anthropomorphisms that we insert into the world. Therefore, human life has no meaning, it is not part of a greater reality; a stumble has as much meaning as a death; a broken heart is as logical as a flat tire. There is no educational purpose behind what happens to us - except for the lessons that we ourselves draw from those experiences. It will be good to make this perfectly clear to ourselves if we want to abandon the naive stance of those who wait for opportunities that, it is said, will always arrive at the mysterious and invisible right moment.

For example, when faced with some misfortune, it is useless to rant, hurling insults and whines into the sky. Instead of looking away with meaningless revolts, it would be wiser to reason, to look at ourselves, if we want to find answers that are relevant to our purposes. We are tired of hearing the contrary, but we know that misfortunes occur for free, without any reason and without any compensation, as well as indifferent or positive things. The very fact that we did not seek punishments to balance the situations in which we were lucky already demonstrates our natural tendency to self-deception.

There is no justice, there is no balance: it's all chance. We normally think that this does not apply to human beings, but only to earthquakes, storms, and other natural calamities. However, if we adopt a vision that is broad enough to realize that life is also a natural phenomenon over which we have no control, which has arisen and is governed by the same circumstances as the inanimate world, this will convince us that life, in its heart, carries the same indifference as natural phenomena. Nobody, for example, is to blame for being born with a perverse character, nor do we have any merit if we have any special talent. We can be sick in a healthy majority - or *vice versa*. None of this means anything. If believing that we were born for some special reason is already absurd, what about those who believe that they were born sick for some reason? This is all just harmless lies that we tell ourselves.

As children, we imagine that deep down, deep down, nature cares about us, and just pretends to be impassive to discipline us. Whatever happens, we will never stop feeling like the most important thing in the universe. Many even consider this feeling as "proof" that the world has plans for our lives. It's not exactly clear how someone in their right mind can believe that kind of thing. However, if we have difficulty distancing ourselves from that hope through intelligence, we can achieve the same effect assuming that the envious universe will never give up its arm.

Thus, nothing prevents our lives from going on in their entirety without a single happy moment. It doesn't matter if we feel "deserving" of such joy. We're the only ones who care about that. Nature never promised us happiness. In case someone had promised it to us, they simply didn't know what they were talking about. So, if we don't receive the compensation we think we deserve in life, going through life feeling wronged will not make us a priority in the existential row of favorable accidents. We will die as dissatisfied as we live, and revolting against it shows only a regrettable attitude of thoughtlessness.

* * *

Philosophically, life is everything that we could consider undesirable: banal, hollow, useless, meaningless, as everyone knows. However, we cannot say that this, in and of itself, will entail a miserable existence. While we can be sure that most individuals will lead an almost indigent life, this is not due to the mean-inglessness of life or the nature of objective reality. Perhaps it seems the opposite because such elements are totally indifferent, and total indifference, in subjective terms, is something that we generally consider negative. The fact is that the subjective sphere of reality, created by individual life, has rules that define, in their own terms, the meaning of external reality. So, in this aspect, everything revolves around how we interpret the world and feel it personally, not really matters what the world is in itself.

In an analogy with a computer, we could understand objectivity as hardware and subjectivity as software. The physical rules of our existence would be determined by electronic components, which are fixed. However, despite this fixity, we can design countless *software* that, based on the same *hardware*, behave in completely different ways.

Any two individuals, placed in the same objective situation, can experience life completely differently from one another. The same stimulus can represent pain for one and pleasure for the other. For a hungry individual, a meal is a pleasure; for another who has just feasted, it is an endless martyrdom. Thus, it is not objective reality that defines the qualitative nature of subjective existence. Our knowledge about objective reality only explains *what* and *how* something happens, but the meaning of this will depend on the interpretation of the subject. Therefore, what happens to us subjectively is a completely separate issue, in which the brain determines the rules, which creates a kind of virtual reality in which we exist as the first person, as pilots of our bodies.

It follows that the reality created by our brains has no definite limits or criteria. However, as it was polished by the criterion of efficiency in dealing with reality, naturally our representation of the world became extremely faithful. Such is the uniformity of our sensory experience of the world that most individuals use psychoactive substances precisely to start seeing the world from another perspective for a few moments, in the hope of escaping boredom. We may think that this "excessive uniformity" is bad, but we will be convinced otherwise if we visit an asylum, that is, the place where human machines with defects in the virtualization system of reality are isolated. As a rule, this makes them even more miserable, since in their minds there is a world very different from the outside reality. Thus, they stumble not only on the pains of the world, but also on their own imaginary pains.

Of course, if nothing prevents us from suffering, nothing would prevent us from being exclusively happy beings either, except for the fact that we would never survive under natural conditions. We would be so happy that we would not protect ourselves from the dangers of existence. We would walk around like drunks smiling everywhere, oblivious to anything that could hurt us. We would fall into a hole laughing. Internal bleeding would make us scream with joy. Instead of calling an ambulance, we would be playing with open fractures. In short, we would be lunatics. It is still an attractive perspective, although it is not feasible - at least until there are more consistent advances in the area of genetic engineering and, thus, we can finally play God with more satisfactory results.

* * *

We can then be happy or sad with the same objective reality, and that will depend only on our perspective, that is, on the interpretation of the facts made by our brains. Because boredom, for example, is not a reality in itself, but a state of mind among many others. A certain book may be boring for one person or interesting for another, and it may be interesting or boring for the same person, depending on their mental state. Depending on how a person slept, whether or not they were well nourished, or a simple coffee, their attitude towards existence may be completely different. This is due solely and exclusively to the changes that occur in the physiology of our brains, since the external, objective reality always remains the same.

A balanced and healthy brain and a disease-free body, that is, a healthy mind in body, are the fundamental elements, the most important factors in determining the degree of our satisfaction or dissatisfaction with existence. Being healthy is much more relevant than, for example, material goods, fame, prestige, etc. Not that such things are unnecessary, but they occupy a much less decisive position. It is true that health, by itself, does not guarantee anything, but its absence, in turn, guarantees that we will be disgraced, regardless of how favorable the circumstances in which we find ourselves.

By seeing ourselves as machines that, on the one hand, are physical structures and that, on the other, create their own reality through physicochemical processes, this allows us to access both sides of nothing. This view is more or less equivalent to that of a programmer. When observing *software*, we have the graphical interface, which would be the part corresponding to our consciousness. But behind it, we find codes that determine its functioning, its particular way of interacting with the *hardware*, that is, what, in our bodies, is equivalent to the physical organization of the structures that constitute our brains. Thus, when we use *software* to make calculations, we can explain the same phenomenon from its different perspectives. In one, the *software* displayed the number 10 because we entered 5+5; in the other, given an *input* 5+5, the result 10 is inevitable. On the one hand, we have the subjective perspective and, on the other, the objective view regarding the same phenomenon.

Our consciousness is for the graphical interface of a *software* just as the codes that constitute it are for the neural circuits of our brain. Even if both are determined by the physical laws of objective reality, it is the way in which they are organized to fulfill a function that causes them to behave according to their own logic. We are machines, and we can see how this, while denying free will, does not remove our freedom as subjects - because there are infinite ways in which we could program a machine within the terms imposed by physical reality. It should also be noted that, when stating that we are machines, this only seems like a limited view because we imagine ourselves as a crude system of gears similar to a clock. Adding that we are programmable machines, this provides us with a much more satisfactory perspective, since, based on the same biological structures, we can have different programs, and with them myriads of different behaviors.

In this way, we have our *DNA* as the instruction manual for building a machine with an on-board computer; the *software* installed on that computer, in turn, was programmed by natural selection; and we, who are the end users of that system, have consciousness as the graphic interface from which we control some functions of our bodies, and we also receive information, internal and external, that allows us to monitor the *status* of that system. In other words, the position of our conscience is equivalent, more or less, to an administrative position in the biological company that is our body - such as a general manager whose function is to inspect internal elements, such as health and the processes in progress in the system, and external ones, such as competition, raw material sources, and neighboring companies willing to negotiate casual partnerships.

Awareness, based on internal data, can detect a problem in our energy levels and intervene with food; or, based on external data, it can verify the presence of danger and intervene with aggression. Of course, there are far more components in our machines than those we are aware of, but unfortunately we are limited to the graphical interface programmed in us by evolution. However, the very fact that we are thinking about it already indicates that evolution has purposefully left an area of the program reserved for us to place our own buttons. By this, of course, we refer to learning, which can occur with or without consciousness. From this perspective, we would still be in the position of ordinary users. The most interesting component of human consciousness is, without a doubt, the capacity for reflection, since it allows us to place ourselves in the position of a programmer.

A blind programmer, however, because our only direct point of contact with the outside world remains the interface provided by the senses. The intellect can imagine many things about the world itself, but it will still need the senses to verify the correctness of those assumptions. If there is no such independent verification criterion, we will be threatened by the relativism imposed by our condition as subjects. So far, the best method we could devise to distinguish between real and false theories is that only the true ones work.

In any case, it is a very considerable advantage, as long as we know how to use it with competence. In this situation, consciousness, through abstract reflection, can detect problems and intervene in areas that are not immediately accessible to it. In other words, reflection is like an extended interface for advanced users. Those familiar with programming will notice that reflection resembles a *shell* inside a preconfigured graphic system. It allows us, to a certain extent, to program some new custom *plug-ins* on our own. Humans are, therefore, in addition to programmable machines that learn, the only ones capable of understanding the language of objective reality and programming themselves as subjective machines. Of course, we cannot alter the programming determined by biological evolution. *However, we can develop codes that update their behavior and, even more so, that correct their painful bugs.*

The area that provided us with the necessary training to act as technical assistants for ourselves is what we know as science. From this perspective, it is clear why it requires so much discipline. Through science, the purpose of man, of the few wise men given to rational thinking, consists of founding a public university that makes individuals competent to deal with objective reality based on subjective reality. It's not, as in tradition, about following ready-made tricks;

185

it's not, as in religion, about executing someone else's *script* in our lives. Science aims to be a programmer's manual, an invaluable resource source for those who wish to develop new technologies that allow us to interact more and more precisely and efficiently with the world.

The end result of all this is that, now, when consciousness detects an inconsistency in the system's overall anxiety level, it can intervene with a completely new resource - *diazepam*, that is, an anxiolytic that will solve the problem without delay. The potential benefits provided by a science-based worldview are incalculable. However, in this case, imagination is not the limit, but merely a source of inspiration. The real limits are imposed by technology, which, to our satisfaction, moves very fast.

✷ ✷ ✷

So let's limit our imagination to the subject that matters to us here, that is, the reduction of unnecessary suffering. The improvement in the quality of life provided by science is far greater than any benefits derived from the wisdom of life preached by philosophical, moral, or religious systems — even if all put together and piled up. It is a fact that nothing compares to its effectiveness. Thus, we can spare our ears the endless speeches about virtues and vices. We don't need explanatory metaphors or testimonies of life, because we can get straight to the point, to reality itself, without any obscure intermediaries. Knowledge is at our disposal.

Everyone wants to solve their personal problems effectively. However, in the position of passive consumers, we forget that, in order to solve our particular problems, we must have at least sufficient technical knowledge to identify, with some precision, the real cause of what bothers us. In this sense, it is highly recommended that we have the prudence to rely solely on ourselves in this endeavor; otherwise, we will need to hire the dubious services of human psychology professionals who, for the most part, believe that all our hardships of now are the indirect result of some metaphysical trauma cleverly hidden by mysterious unconscious mental activity.

We know that understanding our own mental processes scientifically requires a reasonable amount of investment in technical studies. It takes some time before we become familiar with the proper language of science, which at first sight is not very accessible. This initial approach may be a bit frustrating, but it is necessary as a basic education about ourselves, because if we are unable to specify, in technical terms, the particular cause of our unhappiness, we will not know where to look for appropriate solutions. We wouldn't even recognize them if we stumbled upon them by chance.

To do so, it is essential that we have a sober and unprejudiced view, that we are willing to study and research a lot, because we will need to reorganize many central ideas regarding reality. Only then will we be able to conceive the functioning of our bodies in physical terms - including in the most important, intimate, and abstract issues. However, as this process is difficult, many try to take shortcuts through mysticisms that promise magical solutions for physical organisms, such as fitting a square into a circle and finding this perfectly normal. In this sense, a doctrine that is quite close to our central idea is Buddhism. According to this view, living means suffering, and that is why we must find ways to detach ourselves from life and thus achieve what they call *nirvana*, which is the highest spiritual state that man can achieve. However, in the beginning, man has no spirit; ceasing to suffer will not make us more evolved, just less disgraced; the only way to detach ourselves from life is suicide. There are several inconsistencies.

Understanding Buddhism, then, is understanding an error — it distracts us from the essence of the matter. It doesn't matter that both perspectives arrive at the same result. We also want to know how and why this result is achieved, and Buddhism cannot do that, since it explains reality in terms of "reincarnations", "spiritual enlightenments" and the like. Adopting Buddhism is equivalent to installing on our systems a *plug-in* whose programming code is not accessible to us and, in addition, whose language regarding the world is not compatible with the reality we know. While our biological system says "neurotransmitter," Buddhism says "enlightenment." These languages are incompatible with each other, and can only be harmonized through the suspension of critical thinking — the famous faith. In the absence of a better term, we can designate faith as a workaround made by those who don't know how to program. It works, but it's not known why or how.

✶ ✶ ✶

There are different ways to approach pain, depending on its source. If it originates from objective and external factors, we will have to attack it with weapons of the same nature. If the discomfort is caused by lack of money, for example, it will be useless to adopt abstract positions of social alienation. We need to eat, and food has a price. There's no way around that kind of inconvenience. It will be necessary for us to take objective measures to eliminate a source of illness outside of us, that is, we will need to find a source of income, a job. In the event that the source of suffering is internal, that is, coming from our own organism, we must approach it as such, keeping in mind the functioning mechanism of our bodies. As we explained, we have two perspectives from which to investigate the same problem. We can approach it intuitively, through introspection, which is a subjective tool preprogrammed in us by biological evolution itself, and we can also approach it intellectually, employing scientific knowledge regarding the physical mechanisms of our bodies.

On their own, both approaches are insufficient for our purposes; they are somewhat lost in and of themselves. Only when we observe how each one affects the other do we become capable of efficient and controlled interventions on ourselves. To do this, we must, at all costs, avoid the separation between biological and psychological, between mental and material, since such meaningless division fatally ends in the creation of two realities, and then the only logical way out is to reduce one of them to a ghost. Then we will have to declare consciousness as a subjective phantom or materialism as an intellectual phantom. What we have, in fact, are different perspectives on the same thing, not independent overlapping realities. Of course, only the perspective of science is objective, but our condition of existence is subjectivity. Reducing man merely to an objective perspective is equivalent to forgetting ourselves - that we are, after all, the most painful part of the equation. We want the final result to have some subjective impact, even if through objective procedures.

We can therefore understand hunger subjectively, as the sensation that translates the need to eat, or objectively, as the lack of blood sugar. If, for example, we have the strange idea of injecting insulin into our bodies, it will make us hungry — we will have the impression that we haven't eaten in days. If, after that, we inject glucose, it will pass. Hunger, like suffering as a whole, only exists in our minds. However, declaring it a subjective ghost will not reduce our discomfort, just as denying its objective origin will not stop glucose from having an effect.

Our brain is programmed to translate reality into terms relevant to the subject; science seeks to describe reality in terms of itself, from an unbiased perspective. We therefore have a subjective and objective perspective on the same thing. One speaks in the first person, the other in the third; one is the subject, the other is the reason; one perspective is the fruit of biological evolution, the other we ourselves develop through reflection and research. Both perspectives use languages that do not speak very well to each other, since they were born based on different assumptions - the first is aimed at survival while the second is aimed at knowledge. Considering their original task, both work respectfully well. However, considering that there is only one reality, it is as if we had discovered what exists from what does not exist.

* * *

Only now have we arrived at the truly big question: *so what?* That's why it's important to understand the world in order to live in. Knowledge allows us to deal with the world more effectively. All of this has been explained to understand that, for example, when we are sad, even with good reasons, we must bear in mind that sadness can still be reduced to our brain chemistry, and that there is no reductionism in this. This fact can be experimentally demonstrated by the administration of some substance that acts on our neurotransmitters. With that, we can go from sad to euphoric, from melancholic to desperate, from suicidal to supermen. With the simple alteration of our brain chemistry, the affective content of our subjective view of reality also changes - and it would be strange if it didn't change.

To be convinced of this, let's take as an example the sadness resulting from what we call a broken heart. We loved someone, and that someone leaves us: oh cruel world. We suffer immensely, it's true, but we don't usually see anything chemical in it. We think it's some inexplicable metaphysical pain. However, if we take the commendable initiative to think about the matter objectively, we will see that the pain of a failed love is very similar to the abstinence situation experienced by drug addicts when trying to quit their addiction. In both situations, the pain is intense, prolonged, and distressing. The suffering, at first, is terrible and overwhelming, but it lessens over time. If we recover our object of desire, the discomfort immediately disappears.

If there are many similarities between both things, this happens for a very simple reason: in our brain, everything is chemical. Love is as chemical as cocaine, and just as addictive — it can make individuals reckless, lead them to perform acts as extreme as those motivated by the abusive use of any other psychoactive substance, and is responsible for the destruction of many lives. Potent drugs do this, whether they are endogenous or exogenous. Logically, it's uncomfortable to think of our brain as a drug dealer. When he addicted us to something, we prefer to be poetic, to say that we were hit by Cupid's arrow. However, when we prefer to be realistic, we see that to love someone is to be addicted to them. When we get used to using someone to satisfy our needs, we become dependent on them, just like an addict who uses drugs to satisfy himself.

Another similarity is that, when we use a drug for the first time, the effect is very strong. However, over time, we become resistant, and we need increasing doses to feel the same effect. With prolonged use, it is more difficult to give up the addiction, and a condition of dependency is created. With that in mind, let's look at the following facts. When we fall in love, the feeling is overwhelming, just like a first dose of narcotics. We are effectively numb, our personality changes completely. What other explanation could there be other than that we are doped, and by our own brain?

As would be expected, that same passion, being something chemical, ceases to be so intense after a while. As the years go by, everything cools down, and fatally we reach the point where that same person that we once loved madly becomes an object of indifference. It seems that we no longer feel anything, that we no longer need that person - and we continue with that impression until they decide to abandon us. Only then do we experience a stinging pain that causes us to desperately want it again. We think about it all day, every day, something that we commonly call "nostalgia", although it is nothing more than an abstinence exactly like that of an addict who can't afford the next dose of narcotics.

All of this, at first, seems bizarre and surreal; an absurd hypothesis. We even admit that such facts may apply to animals, to some people we hate, but never to us, because our feelings are so sublime that they transcend physics, chemistry, biology, and wisdom. We can invent as many explanations as we want to set ourselves apart from reality. The result will only be that we will remain ignorant about what really drives us.

When we explain the rainbow, it doesn't take away the beauty of its colors. Likewise, when we rationalize love, it doesn't mean that we'll stop feeling it. Reason and emotion are two relatively independent instances in our mental lives. Understanding feelings doesn't change anything about what we feel, only about what we know. We can take a painkiller rationally, knowing that it is chemical, but it will have the same effect. We will feel its repercussions intimately, just as we feel love. There is no justification for a position according to which love is true and sedation is false, because both effects are equally true, that is, real. Whether we like it or not, science has already demonstrated that this is how things work. If we want more details about these processes, it is enough to consult a book in the field. We will see everything very well explained, much to the dismay of the romantics.

Seeing the issue from this perspective, it becomes irrelevant whether a vice occurs naturally or artificially. The important thing is to realize that we can explain both things objectively, by the same mental mechanisms. Most individuals don't like objective descriptions of feelings because they seem to lack the most "essential" thing, that is, the feeling itself and its immeasurable importance. But that only happens because feelings only exist subjectively. Since, in an objective explanation, the subject is necessarily excluded, there could be no elements in it that only relate to the context of their minds, such as the feeling of sadness. However, this fact does not make the explanation unsatisfactory or incomplete, since what seems to us to be lacking in the objective explanation are precisely the subjective elements created by ourselves, which could never be present in an objective description of physical reality.

191

When we are objective, the subject leaves the equation. We came to see it as a fact, not as a human being. Evidently, there is no way to conceive sadness without a subject. A laboratory can analyze the brain of a depressed individual, but we don't feel sad when reading reports about their neurochemical patterns. However, when we are depressed, if we go to the same laboratory and submit to the same analysis, we will see that the results will be the same, or very similar, and this time we will probably understand the relationship that exists between one thing and another.

Despite the undeniable disenchantment that we experience, everything is more clear when we understand how sadness happens objectively in the subject's brain, when we understand the chemistry of this process. If we find masochistic guinea pigs, we can even reproduce this subjective experience through objective procedures, making it very unlikely that we are wrong in this understanding. We therefore have concrete facts before us, and this is sufficient for us to be able to understand the phenomenon in a satisfactory way. The poets tried, but it was only science that was finally able to define love.

* * *

As we can see, to the same extent that life is banal and meaningless, it is also more comprehensible than we commonly suppose. The specific details of how our bodies work aren't exactly simple, but overall, there's no mystery as to the mechanisms responsible for our lives, with all their pain and half-joys.

Our private views of life, and even the age-old wisdom of the ancients, can then be updated to benefit from modern technology, that fallen gift of human wisdom. We may be perfectly aware of the nullity of life, but that doesn't have to make us pose as victims of chance under the pretext of naturalness. We can handle our disposition towards the world through intelligence in order to minimize our exposure to free suffering. This will not open the doors of happiness for us. However, it can make life much calmer and more bearable.

Thus, our starting point for avoiding suffering is to guarantee the health of our bodies. Then, we will limit ourselves to locating the elements that bother us and seeking ways to neutralize them by whatever means we deem most appropriate. The more banal our pains are, the closer we are to the ideal of the absence of suffering. Until we reach the point where, virtually undisturbed, we only need distracting occupations to avoid boredom. That's the closest we can get to a full existence. Anyone who manages to achieve a state in which they are far from the unnecessary torments of life, almost all of which stem from our irrational desire for happiness, can now consider themselves an individual infinitely less miserable than most of humanity.

Happiness could, in this sense, be defined as a state of perfect satisfaction, a point whose value is equivalent to zero suffering. If we represent such a state by a point in space, any distance from that point will be felt constantly and positively as pain, and any decrease in distance, only during the approach movement, will be felt as pleasure. Then we will begin to perceive again only the pain caused by the distance that still exists between us and the ideal state. When close to that point, we will be safe, not happy, and we will still need to keep moving constantly through small occupations, such as insects around a lamp, in order to avoid boredom. In turn, boredom can be understood meta-phorically as the apprehension of the meaninglessness of life itself.

PESSIMISM

When we become very sober, it interferes with the practical aspect of life, and it won't be long before we're labeled pessimists. But this has nothing to do with the philosophy that the negative aspects of existence outweigh the positive aspects, but rather with our taste for pinning inflamed illusions and seeing them slip into the purest reality. Cows may be sacred in India, but here we eat them unapologetically. The delusions of others never inspire respect in us - except if we fear some very real retaliation.

So, considering how much we depend on delusions to live, it shouldn't be surprising that we were disapproved for acting so indiscreetly in relation to them. Crude reality is inconvenient most of the time, and throwing an accurate truth at someone can be as aggressive as punching them.

This explains why we are not called down-to-earth, but pessimistic when we adopt a dry and cynical realism as a stance. If we walk into a bank and, contemplating the long line of bored individuals, we begin to brazenly laugh at the beautiful job they gave to its existence by summarizing it to carrying papers like a turtle's pace, we shouldn't expect the manager to give us a warm smile. Realism hinders practical life simply because it necessarily involves illusions, which are not always easy to replace.

It is to be expected, then, that pessimism will be considered an irrational and distorted view of reality, according to which living is reduced to a series of misfortunes that culminate in a tragedy; or to a series of jokes that culminate in a comedy. However, let's see: what does this so-called distortion consist of? One answer could be this: in shifting the central point of the worldview beyond the reach of our personal interests. In that situation, what is left? A mere objective description of reality - a description in which we are as important as what doesn't matter to us; in which our own delusions, now seen from a great distance, become worthy of laughter, like those of others.

From this perspective, pessimism does not bother because of its falsehood, but because of its blind and useless integrity, because it takes us off our pedestal, makes our own navel relative and causes us to doubt the very high value that we attribute to ourselves and to our dreams, which, however, after being dissected, hardly reveal anything other than a preventive measure against boredom. The problem is that the pessimist praises the truth so much that he forgets himself and the importance of lies.

Be that as it may, it is evident that we are mistaken all the time, and that is something that embarrasses us when thrown in the face. Those of us who, after so much pretending, imagine being superheroes, are forced to publicly recognize that we cannot fly: we just wanted to feel a little special. It would be painful to admit, for example, that all the occupations we dedicate ourselves to are just a pastime to support life.

On a daily basis, we always need to cultivate horseback enthusiasm and delusions of all kinds to obtain the necessary motivation to keep life on track - in other words, to remain oblivious to the distressing emptiness of reality. In the end, it is certain that the expectations set are always above the actual result. That's why, from time to time, we try to hide our bewilderment through big celebrations in which our acquaintances take time to praise us, and this means that we don't feel ashamed for being wrong for the rest of the year.

What would a runner think about himself if, when winning the Olympics and setting the new world record, there were no celebrations? He's probably a perfect idiot. However, since everyone applauds him, he feels like an admirable idiot. We are based on expectations that are always unrealistic, and the higher the expectation, the greater the disappointment. And even when we cast our hopes beyond ourselves, this is nothing but a means of ensuring that we don't live long enough to witness our inevitable defeat.

In the end, there's no logic to that. We need to overvalue ourselves and all of our goals for the simple matter of self-preservation. Human motivation is based on this type of self-deception. Maybe that's not bad, it's just weird, because it forces us to act like we're idiots — even if that's not the case every time.

In this sense, the pessimist is nothing more than an individual who is deep-ly aware of this pathetic side of our humanity, of what we would like to forget about ourselves, and points it out without the slightest discretion, knowing that it cannot be refuted.

✳ ✳ ✳

Let us note that, when looking at things in this way, pessimism is not opposed to optimism if we also consider it in its ordinary sense, namely, that everything will work out simply because we exist, because the world mysteriously conspires for our success and that we are already born deserving of it. Our life, which is *half a glass, is not only half* full, but it will become more and more full until it overflows with joy.

Optimism, as can be seen, causes our vision of reality to be distorted by irrational positivity, and pessimism does not, because the vision it paints is not distorted by a commitment to be useful. For there to be real opposition between the two, a pessimism that would distort reality negatively would be necessary, such as saying that, if we roll a die, it will fall more often on one just because we are destined for the inevitable misfortune of *a* disgraced life. That's the kind of craziness that optimism has the right to profess without any censorship.

Optimism is a childish and superstitious perspective that sees everything partially: for him, the glass is *half* full. *Pessimism is lucid and indifferent, and sees things as they are: for him, the glass is not half empty, but half empty.* It should therefore be called realism, not pessimism.

From this point of view, true pessimism would be equivalent to the statement that the glass is *half empty*, but this is a position that, due to its palpable incoherence, we rarely see being defended in practical life, and is commonly used as a joke in *Murphy's famous Laws* - which, in fact, could be called pessimism in a sense opposite to optimism.

What is termed pessimism, then, on a daily basis, is not in fact pessimism, in the opposite sense of optimism, but merely a kind of impertinent realism, which is inserted into social situations simply to overwhelm them. Even so, strictly speaking, the pessimist is not wrong in what he says. However, since the truth is often untimely, being honest becomes a disservice, and pessimism seems bad to us, not because it harms us directly in any sense, but because it prevents us from making use of the partiality that often makes our lives easier.

∗ ∗ ∗

Since the universe of practice is considered the real world par excellence, it is understandable that the veracity, or rather, the value of perspectives, is more heavily evaluated by their positive consequences than by their evidence or logical basis. Thus, if the fact that we believe that "in the end, everything will work out" helps us in some way, say, reducing our anxiety about the future, we have good reason to judge lying as preferable in terms of positive end results.

When our purpose is motivation, lying about issues that will improve our performance becomes a very logical stance. Prayer is a great example of this. From the point of view of truth, a prayer is equivalent to a placebo procedure that consists of believing, imbued with intellectually indecent optimism, that everything will work out because a puerile projection of a parental beneficent providence will violate natural laws to help an insignificant mammal achieve its equally insignificant objectives. However, from a practical point of view, a prayer serves to improve our chances of success through a confident stance. It's justified because it's useful, not true.

In defense of optimism, many may claim that the worldview outlined by pessimism is only a reflection of a depressive and neurotic personality. Of course, it's still true. However, we are discussing facts, not quality of life, and the fact is that the interpretation of reality posed by pessimism is the only one compatible with the reality that we know through science, and this can be seen as proof independent of pessimistic intuition. Obviously, pessimism doesn't justify depression, but it's not invalidated by it either — or science would be too because of the gloomy implications of its findings. Pessimism has always had reality on its side. If, to endure this reality, we need optimism, that is already a separate issue.

In terms of truth, it is ridiculous to say that there is equivalence between the two views. Unlike pessimism, optimism is not backed by evidence. On the contrary, it is largely refuted by them. The pessimist says: *life has no meaning.* Science shrugs its shoulders: *there really isn't any* evidence for that. Optimism continues to blab: the *important thing is to be happy!* Well, who was arguing about happiness?

Over the centuries, the wise have always been pessimistic and have always said the same thing—and the foolish, the opposite. Why should we be surprised that only the former were right? We should have already guessed that there is some fairly profound relationship between pessimism and intelligence, as both things have always gone together. However, let's set that aside and return to the main subject.

* * *

As can be seen, there is a lot of irrationality surrounding this controversy between optimism and pessimism, since each side uses different weights and measures, never admitting that they only defend this or that because of some peculiarity that only concerns themselves. However, we can explore the issue rationally, without engaging with beliefs. We can investigate the function of pessimism and optimism and draw some interesting lessons from that. Let's see how this all works within our lives.

It is prudent, for example, to think that, before acting, we must lucidly consider what objectives we have and what motives justify them. Only after this phase will we be able to insert "motivational lies" into the equation without causing harm. These rational deliberations serve to decide what is the best strategy to be followed, to anticipate the probable drawbacks and their solutions. The reason must come first because, once launched into action, we will no longer have time to think.

Thus, at the planning stage, we have the opportunity to consider the matter almost impersonally, with great calm and wisdom. If, in this situation that is extremely conducive to reflection, our action plan has been determined, it will not be during its turbulent execution that we will have the opportunity to see things more clearly. Then, in this second moment, the optimism is justified in its childish superficiality because we have already fulfilled the role of adults, and there is nothing more to be thought of that could benefit us.

Thus, when the objective sought is the accomplishment of a task, the veracity does not matter, but the efficiency of what takes us from point a to point b. In the process, there's no time to rethink everything about the issue. The mind, immersed in an action-oriented circumstance, becomes unable to approach it intellectually. If, for example, we are willing to participate in a soccer match, it is assumed that, in its duration, we will limit ourselves to following the rules as if they were absolute truths. If we spend all the time trying to justify our actions by meditating on the ultimate foundations of arbitrary rules, this will make us inefficient in following them. The time to think about this is before the game starts. Likewise, no assembly line would have a future if its workers had to justify to themselves the reason for each screw they tighten.

The suspension of critical thinking is also necessary for us to be able to perform tasks that have their own logic, determined according to objectives other than our individual goals. Being aware of this alienation is important so that we don't lose sight of our own goals when fulfilling other people's goals.

Sometimes we're right not to think too much, limiting ourselves to playing our role, because it's common for process chains to be so wide that we can't even conceive an image of the whole; other times this vision makes us so small that we feel bothered by our almost zero importance.

In any case, when the circumstances in which we find ourselves require firm action from us, using intelligence to try to justify it is not always the right option. Getting someone to reflect on this situation is equivalent to talking to the one who is reading: we will change the focus of their attention, and this will fatally impair their performance, which in this particular situation is the most important.

From this point of view, optimism consists of assuming that, if we carry out the present task well, the rest will work out. True or not, this is something that is independent of us. When our vision does not reach far enough, it is considered reasonable to suppose that what we don't see will go as expected, otherwise the anxiety caused by the sight of everything that could go wrong will paralyze us. So, in general terms, the function of optimism is, once we have done our best, to suspend judgment about everything else, about everything that we cannot change, and that could go wrong.

Thus, from an enlightened perspective, optimism is nothing more than the practical result of accepting our limitations, leaving aside the anguish that this causes us. Because it seems obvious that, if our determination is established based on a judgment we made beforehand, anything that causes us to rethink it at an inappropriate moment will undermine our firmness. We must calm down with the thought that we have done everything possible to foresee and protect ourselves from adversity, as the rest is beyond our control. Prepared against the worst, we can only hope for the best.

Of course, that doesn't mean that optimism is as right as pessimism — it just means that lies and thoughtlessness also have their value. Optimism is a naivety that we must adopt for the sake of saving mental resources. Pessimism, in turn, takes the necessary measures to protect us from the foreseeable consequences of that naivety. Both are necessary. Pessimism leads us to place wise bets, while optimism prevents us from losing the pleasure of playing.

✷ ✷ ✷

It should also be noted that, in general, those who protest against pessimism are precisely those who are aware that they have not prepared themselves well enough - otherwise pessimism would not threaten them. Excessive optimism makes us vulnerable to what the sobriety of pessimism could easily have prevented.

So when we react with indignation to a cynical remark, it just shows that we weren't completely honest with ourselves. What irritates us, in truth, is being confronted with our own thoughtlessness. With that undeniable observation, we saw an obvious truth. We suddenly find ourselves exposed and vulnerable to an evident fact against which we do not protect ourselves due to our own naivety. We were outraged, but we couldn't deny that that brilliant sentence brightens our ears.

All this optimistic mischief is introduced into human life for several strange reasons that, in the end, boil down to the need for well-being at the cost of some simplification or even falsification. In a world where few think, anyone who dares to point out such falsifications will immediately be called pessimistic, not realistic. If you refute them, you will be seen as a criminal who robs men of peace of mind.

On the other hand, since the function of optimism is linked to well-being, it would not really make sense to try to abandon it completely. In fact, who could really raise objections to well-being without being hypocritical? Even the priests of reality, who love the truth more than themselves, making it an extension of their happiness, still need to be alive to be able to dedicate themselves to reflection. Even when immersed in the most profound readings, they must suspend judgment about the value of grammar. Nobody escapes this problem.

The question is not *whether* we need to deceive ourselves, but merely to take the precaution of properly deceiving ourselves, without crossing the line after which self-deception ceases to offer practical benefits. Calculated blindness may make us more efficient, but in turn it also makes us more naive. As a rule, it makes sense to see only what interests us, as long as we have good reasons to do so, as long as we know how to justify why we close our eyes. However, when we are afraid to open them, there are generally very good reasons to do so - because we would see ourselves as fools who make mistakes on even the most important issues, and then play victims when the consequences come to light.

✶ ✶ ✶

Human motivation, as can be seen, depends on a fine balance in this art of being contradictory, of knowing when it is appropriate to open or blindfold your eyes. It makes no sense to pierce them in the name of optimism, nor does it make sense to cut the eyelids in the name of pessimism.

Measuring the correct proportion between both elements is not an exact science, but a personal art that presupposes self-knowledge. As a rule, we should be more optimistic about what is far from our reach, and less about what is close. In this way, we will distance ourselves from the extremes: from the naivety of optimism and from the stagnation of pessimism, when poorly dosed.

Considering that most individuals, unfortunately or not, lean predominantly to one side or the other, just as some are left-handed and others are right-handed, we can conclude that pessimists will be better philosophers and optimists, better workers, since one is a master in the art of reflecting and the other in the art of practicing.

However, in addition to this, we can also see that there is no radical antagonism between the two if we consider that each one has different objectives and that, to achieve them, they adopt different means. Our objective in analyzing the issue rationally was to envision the real possibility of becoming ambidextrous, even knowing that we will not be able to use both hands simultaneously. Even if we don't sympathize with one side, it's always more advantageous to have two cards up our sleeves instead of just one.

✶ ✶ ✶

We can illustrate the practical distinction between pessimism and optimism as follows. To launch into battle, warriors must ignite themselves with all the determination, with every sense of power they can obtain. Since the objective is not to refute the enemy, but to dismember him, it doesn't matter where they get their reasons from, because the truth that decides is the sword's edge. To this end, they adopt optimism. On the other hand, the strategists, who draw up the attack plans and command the warriors, cannot abandon themselves to a megalomaniac frenzy, launching their army like a herd of buffaloes, because that would be suicide if the enemy forces were balanced and minimally intelligent. Therefore, they need not bravery, like their warriors, but circumspection and prudence, cunning and sharpness of mind to understand the real condition of their warriors, to manage and protect them from their own irrationality. To this end, they adopt pessimism. Naturally, they never confess to the warriors what they really think of them, as that would demotivate them.

It is clear that the two perspectives can coexist and take advantage of the other's specialty, but not in the same head and at the same time, because pessimism would refute optimism, and the latter would respond: first live, then philosophize. The conflict would be endless, with the predictable result of inaction, since both the understanding of reality and the action in reality are elements that must be alone to carry out their role masterfully.

Our pessimism is an apostle of the goddess Truth; our optimism follows the goddess Happiness. Both are jealous and can't stand the other's presence — they fight right away at first sight. We know that they will never understand each other, and that monotheism is not an option. The task then remains to become politicians of our own interests, developing strategies so that these quarrelling and territorial spiders coexist peacefully in our minds. This often means that, by invoking the presence of one, we must deny the existence of the other. Depending on the situation, to obtain specific benefits, it is up to us to flatter the one that will best serve our purposes. The wisdom lies in never letting the other person know about the heresy.

SOLITUDE

Solitude is a clear awareness of our isolation, of the insurmountable gulf between us and everything else. It is not, therefore, about the mere fact that we are alone, with no one with whom we can communicate. It's about something deeper, the understanding that not only are we, but we are alone.

Considering everything that an individual can be, he can only be so by himself, necessarily. There is no way to share your personal existence with others, no matter how wrong we may be in that regard. Even when living together, when sharing experiences, the personal experiences of two individuals always go in parallel, like two universes that, even close to each other, never merge. Like two opaque bubbles: you can see each other, you touch each other externally. However, inwardly, they remain alone; their contents never mix.

At the first contact with loneliness, it is normal to have the distinct impression that we are going to die without ever having effectively exchanged information with another human being — information in the subjective sense, not tabular data. This is because everything that is unique seems to be doomed to misunderstanding, and much is unique in each human being. On the other hand, everything that is arranged to allow communication is so sealed, registered, stamped, evaluated, labeled if you want to fly that, in the end, it does not communicate anything other than what is scattered between dictionary pages.

In essence, we can only faithfully communicate what was done to be communicated, which was born as a definition within conventional systems. The rest, if you want to be communicable, must be subject to the condition of being translated to its closest equivalent within such systems. Thus, an interpersonal conversation is much more like an exchange of expressions than an exchange of impressions. We exchanged symbols instead of realities, as if we were giving each other packaging without any content. Normally we notice the big difference between what we want and what we can actually say, thinking that the distortion ends there - but we would probably be amazed if we realized the enormous difference between what we want to say and the other individual finally understands. The original reality must cross so many barriers, so many simplifications and conversions that it reaches the recipient in an unrecognizably mutilated form.

Our situation can be illustrated in the form of two hermits who inhabit distant islands separated by an impassable sea, so that they can never meet in person, nor can they hear each other. To mediate communication between the two individuals, there is language, which can be imagined in the form of a third person, but this is an autistic navigator, absolutely unaware of any reality outside his own, who never gets close enough to the islands for individuals to board. This traveler has a large suitcase full of objects that represent the world. These objects were made by the inhabitants of the islands themselves, and the traveler merely receives and organizes them methodically. Thus, arriving at an island, ask the resident to choose those objects that represent the message he wishes to send to the other individual. Once this is done, the browser places the chosen objects in a package, forwards them to their recipient, delivers and leaves without further consideration. The receiver will have to be content with decoding what was meant by the chosen objects and their arrangement, without ever being able to personally verify what they represent. It may seem frustrating, but this makes it clear how, in a world where every human being is an island, language is a very precarious substitute for reality.

To better understand how much is lost in the communication process, let us propose a second (language-receiver) loss of information similar to the first (sender-language), in which we follow the entire process. Representing our consciousness, we have two individuals who will talk to each other, but with their backs to each other, and each one in front of a mirror. In other words, they can hear each other, but they only see themselves. In this situation, one of them will try to communicate what they feel, but not based on what they feel, but on what they can see of themselves in the mirror in front of them. The other person's role will be to try to understand what they are first feeling based on the self-description they have heard.

What will be the result? Something like: I'm seeing teeth, but not all of them; one eye is half open; one cheek is contracted; the lips are curved. And what do those descriptions mean? We can only imagine. In this process, we use intuition to try to recompose the complete picture based on what we see in our own mirror, and this is done on the assumption that we have already seen ourselves exhibit features similar to those described, and that therefore the feeling must be similar as well - but, if it really is, there is no way to know. The only hint is the fact that, to describe it, both used the same words independently. Of course, we can ask for as many details as we want, but communication will always take place in this truncated and indirect style, and the individual will never be able to see with their own eyes what we are trying to describe.

The example above gives us a more consistent idea of how fragile our communication is. We talk about ourselves as we see ourselves, as if the person who hears us is seeing us just as clearly, but isn't. She can only hear our words, and her only alternative is to look at herself and imagine herself doing what we described. So, if the descriptions don't communicate subjectivity, and if we can't see it for ourselves, where is the communication? It's largely in our imagination. There never are exchanges of ideas or feelings, only exchanges of words that describe them - words in which we find ourselves deceptively reflected. Maybe a good term for that would be double-blind communication.

✷ ✷ ✷

So when we say that there is no way to escape loneliness, we don't mean that this is difficult, but that it is completely impossible. What other people know about us is just our mouths moving before them, and the ideas they build from that. In their minds, this results in a vision of ourselves as distorted as the view we have of them, which seem to exist only on the outside - and make no mistake, we get that same impression. However, like them, we exist primarily on a private level, which is inaccessible, meaning that all contact will have to happen indirectly.

We can only suppose that direct contact with another individual would be pleasant, but this is something that we imagine through the verbs that we see coming from other mouths, which are similar to what we would mutter ourselves. Perhaps it would be pleasant to have direct contact with someone else's consciousness, and not just with their vocabulary, but that's impossible. In relation to each other's intimates, we are all foreigners living in personal exile. Everyone is locked in themselves, and we only know what others say about themselves, never themselves — just as we will never be known, just as we will never be known, only heard about what we say about ourselves. Thus, loneliness is the awareness that we live alone in our bodies, and we can only contact other individuals through gestures that our bodies perform - exactly as if each one lived alone in a house, and could only contact other individuals through letters, without ever knowing the interior of other homes.

The ability to conceive the existence of another human being completely outside our heads is extremely rare. The idea we make of the other, in general, is just a third person, invented by our imagination. Even so, in everyday conversations, we think we understand very well what others say they are feeling, but of course we don't, because for that we would have to be in the skin of that other individual. Understanding what others say is one thing, but understanding what they feel is quite another. In this situation, we merely interpret, decode the information we receive, and then try to relate it to our repertoire of personal experiences compatible with the description provided. Evidently, if we have never experienced similar experiences, the individual's words will be perfectly incomprehensible to us, since there will be no way to relate them to any known reality. For example, those who have never had episodes of depression will probably conclude that the depressed individual is just lazy - because this, in their mind, is the closest element that can be used to try to conceive, in the form of a sensation, what it is to experience a depressive condition. Analogously, an individual who has never smoked cannot conceive of the feeling of nicotine withdrawal. It would be useless to try to explain it with gestures and analogies. You will only understand that we are anxious, like someone who is late for work.

We can describe objective facts, but subjective facts can only be alluded to vaguely. To illustrate, let's consider the following: sharks can extract infor-mation from electrical impulses. Sure, we can understand how this works objectively, but it's not possible to conceive, in our minds, what it's like to be experiencing this. If sharks could talk, they could describe their sensation as much as they wanted, and yet they would not be able to give us a clear idea of what is going on in their brains. A similar situation would be to try to explain to someone else what it feels like to have a color that is completely different from all the others. *Let's call that color green. Verca* is neither green nor blue nor yellow: it is *verca*; another completely different color. If we were to state that we liked that color, what would that inform those who listen to us? Nothing. Even with the greatest effort, we couldn't even describe blue to someone who was born blind. We could talk at length about wavelengths, draw analogies with other senses, but we would only be understood if they could actually see a blue object.

That's our situation. Our personal experiences are incommunicable. We can only allude to them, assuming that others have also experienced those same experiences independently. As there is no way to intellectually overcome this type of barrier, we always give preference to those who have had experiences similar to ours when we want to be understood. In this sense, living together is the best way to ensure that individuals have, in their baggage of experiences, a greater number of points of contact, and thus be able to understand each other more easily. The greatest intimacy imaginable between two people, however, guarantees nothing more than practicality. They will forever remain inaccessible to each other in what they don't share, which is almost everything.

It should already be clear that our understanding of someone else's subjective description is always an approximation that we make based on our immense, vast self. The richest description will be useless to those who do not have a repertoire extensive enough to reconstitute it; a poor description, in turn, will be a pure and simple waste of time, since it would be like reading a bad translation and not having access to the original to verify the errors. So if someone claims that they're sad, what do we understand about that? In essence, nothing. We don't go to the person's soul and recover their feeling and transpose it to our brain, nor does it regurgitate it in words to our understanding. We just turn to our personal repertoire of memories and knowledge of what we mean by sadness and, based only on ourselves, on the experiences we had, we interpret what the person is probably trying to say. And that's all. *To the nittygritty of the soul, everyone is their own island, and we only really talk through clichés, systems, conventions, highways of anonymity.*

* * *

It doesn't matter our skills for poetry — verbal language is simply unable to communicate feelings faithfully. If we have doubts about this, just consult a dictionary. Almost everything is lost. Only very vague traces of what was meant remain, which will only be comprehensible if we know them beforehand. Thus, from the beginning, there must be a very fine harmony between the messenger and the receiver for the communication to be minimally decent. The situation is similar to that of someone trying to carry water with their hands: seeing that person in front of us with wet hands, we can assume that there was water there, but that is very different from saying that person shared water with us, and it is also obvious that this mere residue could never quench our thirst. Of course, if we've experienced water in the past, we can imagine something relatively close to what the person is trying to say, but this is done not based on what they say, but on what we ourselves would say if we were in their situation. In this case, as can be seen, our past experience involving water is the only key to decoding its message, without which everything would boil down to noise.

Of course, the words that make up a language must have a sufficiently generic character so that they can be applied to the most diverse specific cases. This overcomes the individual barrier and allows communication, but we end up being ourselves, as subjects, excluded from communication. What everyone understands, in the end, no one feels; what everyone feels, no one understands. Since particular feelings are lost when converted to generic language, an accurate description would only serve as a hint about the circumstances under which we would feel something similar. In other words, talking about feelings is like verbal mimicry: we try to understand them intuitively, like someone searching their own house in search of an object that fits the description provided. Therefore, although we are able to communicate, we must bear in mind that language is a bridge between our bodies, not between our minds.

From this perspective, poetry could be described as the art of stitching abysses with words, being so beautiful precisely because it seems to come as a bridge that communicates something indescribable. Even though we are aware of this impossibility, we are still enchanted by the subjective consolation it provides. This art consists of polishing, with words, a series of images in which there are strategically placed gaps, so that, when interpreting a poem, we subjectively insert ourselves into those spaces and feel identified, resulting in the feeling that we have escaped our loneliness. It's surprising how this illusion leads us through the nose to believe in nonsense just because poets know how to do grammatical tricks as well as magicians pull pigeons out of the top hat, because the fact is that poetry works by the same principle as astrology, that is, calculated vagueness. If poetry, instead of being subjective and vague, were accurate and clear, it simply wouldn't work. So, knowing that, we no longer have to bother to hide what's in our hearts. Nobody's going to find out, even if we want to.

Given the way in which we evolve, it seems natural that this should be so, since intimate sensations are things that are only of practical use to the individual themselves, serving as a source of information about what is happening in their body, that is, it is a kind of biological metalanguage. In terms of survival, it's not important that we can describe our subjective experience of hunger. The important thing is just to make another individual, hopefully supplied with food, understand that we want to eat. To this end, language is a resource that performs its function very well, since it manages to articulate an agile relationship between our private sensations and the public reality, in which other individuals are located. It's a great tool for social interactions, and that's all. We must abandon the hope that it will be able to directly transpose anything we feel.

* * *

Having explained why neither language nor coexistence can be seen as a means of overcoming loneliness, it remains for us to learn to exist as we are: alone and limited to ourselves. Furthermore, since our individuality is the only element that intimately and truly accompanies us throughout our lives, it is also the most reliable. Whatever happens, alone or accompanied, we will continue to be who we are. The rest you never know.

When, in our daily activities, we do not feel lonely, this indicates that we have completely lost contact with ourselves. In this situation, our lives are focused on the outside, on those around us: we dedicate all our time to them. We live because of something that, at the same time, is not us or others, insofar as they also do not contact us.

We are content to believe that everyone is what they appear to be, including us. We choose to believe in the outside world to deny the distance between us and the other, and also between them and themselves. However, in the attempt to contact the other, we also only become distant from ourselves. Since we can only contact the social façade of others, we also consider ourselves a façade.

Thus, even if we are our only true companion, we prefer to abandon it believing in language. We cease to exist to live alone, talking to no one, and with that we intend to escape loneliness. We're like phones talking to each other, with no people behind. This is the figure that best illustrates human socialization.

It turns out that we live outside of us, where no one is, and we find that very natural. The common distance between everything soothes us as if it frees us from the responsibility of admitting that we exist. We see ourselves as a kind of abstract and distant philosophical question. We ourselves are a subject that doesn't interest us: let's leave it to the scholars! Our concern is to live in the admirable hollow world, in the reality that happens above people, in cities, in bars, in newspapers. We want to exist backwards, in an ordinary outer life, where our interior is so unknown that we call it free will.

We are an inside addicted to the outside, and the reason for that is very simple: vanity. We don't see the point in cultivating what others can never admire. Solitude refutes our value due to lack of audience. We find it ridiculous to harbor virtues that no one will be able to witness, for which we will not be recognized. Without the hope of being valued, we have no motivation. We only feel important to the extent that we can be observed and considered important. Thus, locked inside ourselves, we spend the whole day hugging behind the window bars so that someone can see us exist. We knocked on our doors to show that we're alive, but we only believe that after hearing the testimony of others. We call that living together. We live in this fantasy of a social reality with the sole purpose of being able to be praised.

As we are conditioned to give value and attention only to what is outside, loneliness makes us feel abandoned, as if we had ceased to exist. The idea of spending a few lonely hours is sufficient to distress most individuals; a month of isolation would drive them insane. We felt as if we were incarcerated in ourselves. We run away from loneliness like someone who flees from the mirror. We don't like to see ourselves so clearly. That's why *knowing yourself is* impossible for almost everyone.

* * *

Whether we like it or not, isolation puts us in direct contact with ourselves. Alone, we began to see quite clearly the distinction between ourselves and the outside world. Thus, to discover if any activity that we are engaged in is truly original to our person, we can imagine how we would live if we were on a deserted island, with no person nearby, without any chance of meeting another individual for the rest of our lives.

In this situation, the pictures that we paint, why paint them when there is no one to see them? Why cultivate the beauty of our bodies if there will be no one to admire it? Why smile or cry when that doesn't prove anything? Would we cultivate gardens if flowers were for our eyes only? What is the value of great possessions when they don't allow us to be enviable?

Faced with these questions, we were perplexed and embarrassed. We feel like a diamond that is not precious because it will never be found. This illustrates that many of the efforts that we imagine to be exclusively personal are actually the internalization of other people's objectives, that is, efforts that are not self-sustainable, that we would not do if we were alone. The activities to which we would dedicate ourselves if we were condemned to live alone for the rest of our lives would be the expression of what we are by ourselves, our most original and independent side. But what activities would those be? We can't tell, and we hope we never find out.

Isolated, we don't know what purpose to give to our lives, because we never gave them to ourselves. Throughout our lives, we've persistently ignored each other. Now, alone, we don't even know who we are, we don't recognize in ourselves what we believe to be. Our alienation is such that, condemned to solitude, we would be forced to become practically another person.

It saddens us to realize that this anonymous individual within ourselves is what we really are. It seems almost surreal that we're able to ignore ourselves so completely, but that's where the horror of loneliness comes from. When we say that we are actors, it is not a mere figure of speech. We've always been running away from ourselves—and what's left when we're not acting is exactly what we insist on forgetting.

For whom, after all, do we have sophisticated and costly personal preferences? Even our tastes are unknown to us when we don't know who to prove our finesse to. The only distinction we achieved with this was that we also became distinct from ourselves. When we realize that we can't even define who we are when no one is looking, we have no words to express the amazement of having forgotten.

The painful feeling that we generally experience in the face of this perspective testifies in favor of our internal poverty and dependence on others. Although we can go abroad, interact with other individuals, none of this becomes part of us. On the contrary, it only feeds our expectations and our dependency, directing our resources more and more outside of ourselves.

✶ ✶ ✶

Even so, the fact that we are inherently lonely does not mean that we live in a desert, but only that our home can never be visited by anyone else. Our private island can be a sumptuous palace or a garbage dump, and that will depend only on our commitment to cultivate in ourselves a world pleasant enough for us to feel at home alone.

A precarious inner world will make us victims of the boredom of being, ourselves, dry and insipid. It will make us use every possible resource to forget about ourselves, our misery, our abandonment, and from this a desperate need for socialization will arise. For this reason, the most vulgar individuals tend to be the most sociable. The lack caused by the poverty of their individualities makes them extremely dependent on external resources, so that their only pleasure in existence consists in running away from themselves.

Crude individuals are more sociable because the only pleasures we can cultivate alone, without pain involved, are those of an intellectual nature — meaning that our capacity to enjoy them will be determined by the greatness of our intelligence. Unlike physical pleasures, whose satisfaction is always mixed with pain, intellectual pleasures are realized without any suffering. An eminent mind is, in itself, an inexhaustible source of pleasure.

However, those who do not have considerable intellectual skills cannot find pleasure in activities that involve the use of intelligence, because, as they lack capacity, they cannot experience such activities as a personal interest, just as an out of shape individual cannot find pleasure in physical activities. The only drawback of high intelligence is the fact that, with the general increase in sensitivity, we become capable of great pleasures, but we are also exposed to a greater degree to the pains of the world. Intelligence increases the breadth and intensity of our personal experiences, and this means that the higher a man's intelligence, the more he suffers - but to the same degree, the more capacity he has to find pleasure and consolation in himself.

Thus, the greater your intelligence, the more interesting the content of your imagination will be, the more fantastic the trips of your thought. A well-exercised intelligence can find distraction in the objects of your thought just as if they were before your eyes, just like someone who, seeking distraction, instead of reading a book, writes it in thought, experiencing first-hand all the emotions and subtleties of the story, or all the depth and brilliance of the reflections. However, it is evident that, if we do not have gifts in this regard, paying attention to our imagination while trying to exercise qualities that we do not have will just be a silent way of achieving boredom.

Men with brute minds, on the other hand, are insensitive to abstract pleasures: a poem doesn't move them; a theory doesn't fascinate them; philosophy doesn't instigate them; science doesn't instruct them; art doesn't touch them; music doesn't inspire them. Your intellect has no tact, your imagination has no wings. The only use of their brains is to react to external stimuli. The environment completely conditions their activity, so much so that they can't even laugh when they are alone: they have to observe concrete scenes because their imaginative capacity chains them to the immediate present.

Thus, annoyed by not finding anything interesting inside, they turn to the outside, to distractions and to the joys of the senses: parties, sex, games, betting, competitions, etc. They seek socialization to escape from themselves, and they unite by their common purpose of not thinking; they get bored as a group. It is common that the highest meaning of their lives is to accumulate money and gain social prestige. However, once they have been achieved, they do not know how to use them. They become ends in themselves, and their lives boil down to the accumulation of wealth and public recognition. They work tirelessly and, during their leisure periods, they socialize. They are not free to explore other activities.

Rejecting loneliness, therefore, is nothing more than an indirect way of admitting that we cannot bear our own company, that we are an uninhabited island. Despite all the qualities that we think we possess, which we constantly brag about, we are often the last person we would like to live with alone. Others may believe in our everyday scenarios, but we know ourselves much better to believe in these impostures.

Of course, if we live to promote an image that does not reflect what we are, of course, alone, we will feel that living is meaningless - but the fact is that the absence of an audience only bothers actors. Loneliness only robs of someone whose life is reduced to what others think about them. Those who, on the other hand, seek solitude, are the ones who do not need others. When the value of our riches does not depend on the testimony of others, we will never care much about displaying them. Only those who think they are rich without actually being rich need others, because they must pretend to be rich - and their pleasure begins to consist of the idea of wealth that they cultivate in the minds of others, which is the reason why loneliness reduces them to indigent.

Such considerations illustrate that the fact that someone loves or hates loneliness is an excellent indicator of the richness or poverty of their individuality, since only alone are we in contact with what we really are. Those who are internally rich need fewer external elements to live, and that means being less subject to the changes of a destiny that is always willing to beat us up. The less we depend on external sources of pleasure, which are extremely uncertain, the easier it will be for our lives to go on without great turbulence and misfortune. That is why there is a lot of wisdom in focusing on ourselves what we need,

215

because that is where we are, where everything that is most important occurs - our lives, our thoughts, our pleasures and pains.

If we put in cells two formerly rich individuals, one vulgar and stupid, the other cultured and intelligent, with just enough to survive, there is no doubt which one will be more disgraced. One of them will continue as it always was, just without some of the comforts that it is used to, because its greatest wealth consists in what it is in itself. Even if locked in a miserable cell, he will be able to conceive the most profound theories, meditate on philosophical issues, dedicate himself to art, write masterpieces, and so on. You will find many ways to entertain yourself without the help of external elements. Even alone, you'll be in great company. The other will also feel what they truly are, but this, on the contrary, will not please them one bit, since their life has always been focused on the outside and, now, reduced to their own resources, they have become indigent. It is likely that you will limit yourself all the time to playing with all the objects that fall at hand, attentive to everything that happens in your surroundings, anxious to find someone to talk to, in a constant effort to forget yourself because of the terrible boredom caused by having a completely insipid mind in an also insipid environment. He has always preferred to buy securities rather than deserve them: now he despises himself because, having never invested in himself, he cannot even give himself alms, he cannot see anything useful in the fact that he is himself. You get bored because your mind is unable to move itself—like a weather vane, it only works when external circumstances induce its activity. The individual succumbs as a victim of their own uselessness.

* * *

This makes clear the importance of considering ourselves the essential undertaking of our existence. When we are the parent company, we manage our resources so that our investments actually return benefits to us, not mere representations of benefits in the idea of others about us. Since we are only publicly recognized for our facades, that is, for what is outside of us, it is not in them that we should invest our efforts. Any branches that we establish outside of ourselves will be certain losses, because even your profits will only be social representations of profits. Evidently, facades are necessary, but they should be seen only as small social investments, strategies that ensure the conditions that allow us to enjoy our true treasure, from which we can never be subtracted.

When we decided to live for ourselves, we saved the gold to adorn our lives, not our clothes. We don't want it in bars, to exchange for money: we want it for the works of art that we will never tire of contemplating. Thus, instead of being rich, we became priceless. At any time or circumstance, we always find in ourselves the reason for our satisfaction, because we are what we live for. *Wherever your treasure is, your heart will also be* — as they say, and so do we. We feel that the meaning of our lives is to become ourselves, more and more.

We want a willingness to enjoy our intellect and leisure so that we can work freely. Good mood depends on our health, while leisure depends on our wealth. Both are necessary for us to reap the benefits of intelligence. It should be noted, then, that money is only partially useful within our lives. The importance of wealth is undeniable, but it can only provide us with the least important half of what we need. When we are rich, we have at our disposal not all the happiness, but as much time as we want. That's why we don't need a lot of wealth, but just enough so that we have the freedom to choose the activity to which we will dedicate ourselves.

Naturally, we do not seek leisure because we hate work, but because we want to work only on what interests us. Even the most strenuous tasks, when done of one's own free will, are not felt as a nuisance. But that requires that we let our nature dictate them, not social circumstances. In this situation, by giving ourselves completely, we make our lives conspire in favor of the achievement of our objectives. Because we have good will and personal interest, we pay attention to the details: we sleep well, we eat properly, we exercise to the exact extent, we study the functioning of our bodies. All this to carry out our task masterfully, since it is the one that we choose for ourselves, of which we will be the result.

Furthermore, when we work for ourselves on what interests us, when and while it matters, we don't want vacations, we don't understand how one can want a vacation: we are the first to arrive and the last to leave, and that seems natural to us as breathing. However, nothing is more detestable than working as a mercenary who sells his effort to someone else's end. We are forced to lie all the time in an activity that competes with our intelligence - therefore, thinking ceases when business hours begin. Instead, we chose the opposite path: we worked because we couldn't think of anything more interesting. We don't separate life and work because we choose to exist for ourselves.

* * *

When we trade solitude like that for social prestige, we make a bad deal. We give our treasures to others to admire us, buying their flattery at the cost of our own indigence. Like clowns, we throw pies at our faces thinking it will earn your respect. Not because we like to prostitute ourselves, but not because of money: we do it all just for the honor of sleeping next to the gutter of their lives. If we prostitute ourselves in exchange for something so small, it will not be long before we will be despised because of it, because our value is something that we borrow from the opinion of others, such as someone who lives on crumbs.

Let us also add that, when presenting ourselves to others in splendid clothes, your favorable judgment about us will still not be sufficient to rid us of the boredom and misery of being a desert dressed as an oasis. In the best case, we will be recognized for what we are not, as impostors who wear false watches, regardless of knowing the time, or as someone who would remain still all night, just to convince others that they sleep very well.

Those who pretend forget the most important thing, that the essential thing in possessing a quality consists in enjoying the benefit of always having it at their disposal as something that counts in their favor. Qualities are only burdens for those who must pretend to possess them. Therefore, when we know we have a quality, it never occurs to us to demonstrate it for free. A contrary judgment will not take it out of our hands, nor will it interfere with our chances of success. Since it is independent of other people's opinions, we generally don't even want to know what people think about it.

So, since it makes no sense to defend our qualities, this is exactly what incriminates those who try to hide their weaknesses with exaggerations in the opposite direction. The qualities that an individual shows unnecessarily testify against himself, so that we would find within him just the opposite of what he appears to be: his constant effort to prove his worth indicates that he has none.

That's the reason why every flamboyance can be seen almost as a confession of incompetence: those who try hard to appear wise are foolish; those who struggle to be humble are proud; those who live to show bravery are cowards, and so on. It is enough to add a negative sign to the qualities they display to arrive at what they truly are.

That is why, in seeking from the outside of others what we lack internally, we are committing the mistake of allowing ourselves to be guided precisely by those who understand the least about the subject. We would do better to seek guidance from those who externally demonstrate the opposite characteristics to those we want, because in this they are natural masters - so much so that they had to invent an entire social facade simply to disguise it. We can, for example, be certain that no one has a better command of the art of being stupid than someone who pretends to be intelligent.

On the contrary, by being authentic, we are investing in the development of our own virtues, instead of wasting energy masking vices to gain the good opinion of others. Since we will never become masters of what we lack, it only makes sense to compensate for our weaknesses by exercising our true qualities, otherwise we will have only armored vices and anemic virtues.

✶ ✶ ✶

It is clear that the more we have in ourselves, the less we need the outside world to meet our needs. Material assets and social prestige will be secondary elements in our lives. Not that such things are unimportant. However, alone, they can do nothing for the one whose greatest disgust is to be himself. We just need enough wealth to live. Excess will also be harmful, as our efforts will be diverted to the work of maintaining our assets.

No wonder a wise individual will distance himself from society when society, in return, cannot offer him anything that is commensurate with what he finds in himself. Coexistence, in fact, would only impoverish you, since individuals who are socialized are, as a rule, bankrupt. They seek to live together just because they have nothing else. When contacting us, they cannot offer something in exchange that would compensate us for the boredom they cause us. They have empty pockets and just want to throw away time, both theirs and ours.

As there are only advantages to independence, it is almost inevitable that independent individuals will become unsociable. They don't need society and they're very grateful for that. Every day they realize how lucky they are to live alone, and not in the company of vulgar individuals with a perverse character and obtuse intelligence. When others don't see any use in us, when they can't find a way to exploit us for their benefit, they call us unsociable as if that were an insult. In fact, it's the highest compliment we could ever hope to receive: being useless to short, vulgar, and ignorant individuals is something that deeply honors us, it's almost proof that we're on the right path.

They are always networks of personal interest that lead us to contact each other. If men were sufficient for themselves, society would not exist. Men hate each other, all of them, without exception: they are undeclared rivals. They don't miss an opportunity to pillage each other when they know they'll get away with it. They are social beings, but they group together out of necessity, like porcupines in winter. They put up with each other just because they have no choice, because on their own they would freeze to death, otherwise they would turn their backs without blinking an eye. That is why socialization is a necessity for the inept, but a disgrace for the wise.

We know that, unless our insides are made of gold, no one will have the slightest interest in what is inside us. About us, the rest just want to know what benefits they can get, that's all. They may say otherwise, but we're not naive enough to believe in free favors. No good intention, because it is good, fails to expect compensation.

So, if we are lonely, if we are sufficient for ourselves, we must, in all fairness, ignore the call of the flock and walk our own path, knowing that being selfish in a world driven by selfishness is nothing more than a sign of intelligence.

BOREDOM

Boredom is an agonizing feeling of emptiness, of disgust, of annoyance. Everyone knows him, few really understand him. When bored, it's common to say that the cause of this is the fact that we don't have anything interesting to worry about. However, this is a superficial interpretation that confuses causes and effects. In fact, the opposite is true: we have nothing interesting to worry about because we're bored. As soon as boredom leaves us, we will find several interesting occupations, which will often be exactly those in which we saw no value while we were bored.

A bored individual sees the possibilities that lie before him as an anorexic sees a lavish feast. Expecting someone who is bored to have motivation is as ridiculous as expecting an anorexic to have an appetite. Bored, all possibilities disgust us, making us positively averse to any occupations. We know that eating is necessary, and that it can also be pleasurable, but without appetite there is nothing to be done.

Boredom is painful because it paralyzes us and renders us insensitive to any pleasurable impressions, reducing everything to a gray and insipid darkness. No matter how long the periods during which we experience it, everything is irrelevant in it, and such experiences will simply fade from our memories. Everything becomes phantasmagoria. This mental state that undermines our motivation dismantles our goals and can make life as morbid as depression or sleep deprivation.

Suppose we were bored. It occurs to us, for whatever reason, to read book x or finish project x. *In this situation, the idea of taking any x forward will seem simply unreasonable to us - and that's even if we were in the habit of dedicating ourselves to such activities on a daily basis, of our own free will.*

Immersed in boredom, none of *us* incites curiosity, we don't see any reason to achieve goals. We feel that the outcome, whatever it may be, will be irrelevant. We are prevented from using our own strength, unable to find satisfaction even in what commonly pleases us. We know what we want to do, but until the boredom is over, nothing can be done about it.

To draw an analogy, our situation is similar to that of a salaried employee who does not appreciate his job in itself, taking it forward solely on the basis of the money he receives for his efforts. As a rule, in a job, we dedicate ourselves to tasks that, if not for the salary, would seem absolutely detestable to us. We can be certain that, without such compensation, virtually all professional careers as we know them would crumble.

From this point of view, when bored, we are like employees aware that they will not receive any reward for their effort - that is the reason why we do nothing. We find ourselves subtracted from exactly what motivated us to work. In this case, the difference consists in the fact that the boss is called the brain and the payment are regular doses of pleasure.

Bored, we are in a situation where our boss sees no use in paying us to perform the tasks before us - in a kind of neurochemical unemployment. We want, very desperately, to continue nurturing our addiction. However, faced with this impasse, we are forced to change our professional strategy, the central problem being the fact that we do not know very well how this can be done.

The boredom equation, as we can see, is quite simple: in order for us not to be bored, we must stay busy; for us to stay busy, we must find satisfaction in what we do. The vicious circle is sustained or broken depending on the value we see in this occupation. Within that, the nature of the occupation, in and of itself, is irrelevant - it is enough that it keeps us moving, and we will be protected from boredom.

✶ ✶ ✶

Because boredom evokes the very real awareness of our nullity, occupations that inflate our vanity, our sense of importance, are something very useful to push it away. In that sense, it would obviously be useless to just praise ourselves: we know that this is cheating. We cannot simply print the banknotes with which to buy the pleasures of vanity ourselves. Only genuine praise, derived from public recognition, pays us to feel praised.

We believe, almost always without reason, that we are worthy of praise, but our brain is prudent in this regard — it never buys praises of dubious origin. Promises and words of honor are irrelevant to vanity: without an audience, the brain doesn't even bother to negotiate. He has always known how to distrust our honesty.

We want drops of pleasure, and in that our brains are fountains, biochemical oceans of inconceivable delights, but we will have to deserve them, every single one of them. Negotiations are open, but the conditions are strict: there is no possibility of loans, and the certain will never be exchanged for the doubtful. Even in biological drug trafficking, the golden rule is recognized: only cash payments are accepted.

This means that our vanity will never be inflated for free without any criteria. To do so, it will be necessary for us to present testimonies from trustworthy individuals. From ourselves, favorable testimonies are worthless. Testimonials from friends, because of their partiality, are similarly worthless. To be well paid, we must elicit praise from our enemies: the guarantee comes from the fact that they hate us.

This makes it quite clear how wise our brains are in this type of question. Knowing that free compliments are hollow nuts, and possessing a profound sense of reality, our brain only allows us to be deceived about ourselves to the exact extent that we can deceive others about it.

In this context, as can be seen, it is not enough for us to be successful individuals: we must also be recognized for this, so that we then feel recognized. That's why riches, by themselves, don't buy any pleasure. Not only rich, we must also place ourselves in situations that make us great because of this, otherwise we will be plunged into the boredom of a null and insipid success.

Thus, we are not physically but only psychologically dependent on each other — precisely because of those rewards of pleasure that we seek in each other. From this comes our social nature. For what purpose do we interact, if not the hope of convincing others of our value, of being praised, and thus feeling good? Imagine, for example, how disastrous it would be if there were complimentary capsules available to us: they would destroy the foundations of society.

This means that, strictly speaking, the others are not important, but only that they praise us, so that we distance ourselves from boredom. Lies, once reflected in others, are sufficient to convince and motivate us: this is the principle that drives society as a whole.

* * *

If we are given to philosophy, it won't take many years for life to soon take on the appearance of a foolish game. However, for our brains, or at least for the unconscious portion of it, this is no joke. He still believes in this task with a seriousness that we can only laugh at. Be that as it may, this means that we will not be rewarded for recreational purposes. We will be rewarded only for what, in any way, contributes to the satisfaction of the items that are included in the official list of biological needs.

In this context, our brain — an educator with the thankless task of cultivating functional consciousness — employs boredom as a very modest punishment, at least compared to the other forms of suffering that it has at its disposal. It is not a sign of imminent danger; boredom is like a miniature grief, a friendly invitation to rethink our priorities - before the seriousness of the situation becomes something capable of overwhelming us.

Thus, alongside pain, boredom takes the form of a preliminary warning, of a friendly and well-intentioned rebuke. Boredom is calculated from a quick outline of biological expenses, representing just a warning not to lose sight of what matters. Furthermore, there is no immediate charge, other than that we do our part as soon as the opportunity arises. However, if we don't pay attention to boredom, soon our attention will be paid to pain—and that will wake us up very quickly. Lucidity is born of pain.

* * *

Boredom arises, then, when we have no reason to believe that we will be applauded by carrying forward any of the possibilities that we have before us, evoking the awareness of the nullity of our value. How can this be explained? The world is a stage of incessant competition. Our brains make us victims of boredom in order to protect us from bankruptcy.

Of course, when we talk about our own brain in the third person, we're actually referring to instincts. Nevertheless, designating him as the "master" of our consciousness is still quite correct. Consciousness, endowed with a rather limited perspective of the organism as a whole, has the aspect of a servant of instincts. Left to herself, she doesn't know what direction to take: she needs a teacher to guide her. Thus, although relatively independent, consciousness and instincts are two forces designed to work together.

Instincts, enclosed in their grandiose but primitive cabinets, do not deal directly with practical reality, limiting themselves to stipulating orders and deadlines. It is up to conscience, its sole employee, to find acceptable solutions and results. Thus, in setting objectives, the conscience generally has little say, and is limited to distinguishing the best means of achieving them.

Often, by virtue of this hierarchy, we feel as if we are being trampled on by incoherent orders. Nevertheless, it is fair that the conscience does not have much choice, since its sight is short and its motives, as a rule, are petty. Your concern is always the same: the next dose of pleasure — ignoring everything else in the equation. We can be sure that consciousness, alone in control of our lives, would be certain death.

Nature, as we see, established this dual and hierarchical structure of our minds, and that has always guided us. There is, however, a modern alternative to satisfying our addictions: changing suppliers. We learn to mint counterfeit coins, and with them we trick the brain — that is, we reward ourselves artificially by injecting false value into our systems.

Because of its blind evolution, nature could not foresee this possibility - otherwise it would be forbidden to us. Because our brains think that they are the only narcotics suppliers we have access to, this opened a window of interesting but dangerous possibilities for us. For example, suppose that, to circumvent boredom, we have carried out a chemical fraud. What will be the result? Believing that they are banknotes issued by itself, the brain does the math and, seeing the sudden profit, is satisfied: flooding us with pleasure is the fairest payment. It results in the feeling that the problems, all of them, are solved.

Because fraud is a seductive shortcut, we incur increasingly large debts. The reality, whatever it may be, is ignored - because our instincts are celebrating.

However, it is not long before our companies become extremely unstable, because, instead of striving to legitimately consolidate them, we simply dedicate ourselves to leisure, without having been guaranteed any safety through work. In this situation, addiction quickly transforms us into shell companies. The countless cases of lives destroyed by addiction make it clear that our brains were right to not allow us to directly handle the notes with which to buy pleasures.

In the company of our bodies, nature fixed the fair position of secretaries for us. Conscience, with just a few decades of experience and limited vision, does not have sufficient competence to make important decisions regarding the body in which it is installed. Coupled with instincts, conscience is a child — it has no maturity for almost anything, least of all to compensate itself with prudence.

Our instincts, on the other hand, although somewhat outdated, are highly qualified in the task of managing bodies, as they have been doing this for billions of years. Your diploma is our genes, emitted by natural selection. Instincts may not see the now clearly, but what they do know reflects the most universal needs when it comes to survival - and within that the fads of consciousness are irrelevant.

✶ ✶ ✶

From the point of view of introspection, we have described the nature of boredom well enough, and the way in which it dulls our sensitivity. We try to discern, albeit vaguely, the relationship between boredom and our biological needs. Although this required the use of a predominantly subjective language, we will now move on to a more objective stance.

Let's summarize everything that has been said so far as follows: boredom is an affliction of a chemical nature. In a word: abstinence. Starting from this, let us return to what the understanding of boredom reveals to us from a broader perspective: the chemical nature of everything that moves us.

To avoid confusion, since there are many taboos involved, let's first look at the issue as follows: our *DNA* has the recipe for building a brain capable of synthesizing stimulants, painkillers, painkillers, hallucinogens, anti-inflammatory drugs and everything else we can imagine in this sense. It is, in fact, a very complete biological pharmacy at our disposal. Such substances, as needed, are produced by the body, making a veritable cocktail of natural drugs circulate in our bloodstream.

We know the usefulness of all this for survival, but what is the purpose of these elements for consciousness? Allow the adjustment of our sensitivity to particular circumstances, making our perception of reality adjust to our needs. This, in turn, has the obvious function of adapting our behavior to the situations in which we find ourselves.

To illustrate the practice, suppose the following: we are walking somewhere and suddenly we stumble upon the image of a lion. How do we know, faced with this image, what we should feel or think? To see it, we use our eyes - and to judge its meaning? We use sensitivity, we use emotions and feelings — which are regulated by brain chemistry. The mere image of the lion, by itself, tells us nothing about what we should feel — but fear tells us that running is exactly what we should do.

Thus, given any situation, it is the specific configuration of the chemicals present in our brains that determines how we will feel that situation, in what sense we will think about it, on what information we will focus our attention. Brain chemistry is what allows us to feel situations, just as our eyes allow us to see them. It is what gives colors to our affective world. In this sense, just as we can have different versions of the same song, our mental machinery, under specific chemical influences, creates different "versions" based on the same facts.

Let's draw a parallel to better understand this process. We know that when reality stimulates our senses, it creates a signal, like a string instrument being played. The audio signal, in turn, can undergo various types of processing, but we only hear the final result, what the speakers produce: sound vibrations that, once ordered, gain meaning and become music. The same occurs in our brains. Our perception of reality is modulated by a chemical orchestra, and we only experience the final result of this, which is what allows us to experience the meaning, the "background music" of the situation.

On a daily basis, when we are motivated, pursuing our goals, we are under the action of constant pleasure rewards. So when we're unmotivated, feeling the weight of boredom, what are we experiencing? A framework of natural abstinence. Boredom, from this point of view, could be understood as a symptom of chemical abstinence, and we do not make such a statement in a vulgar sense, referring to addiction to synthetic drugs, but to our dependence on natural drugs, created by our own body.

Artificial drugs, whatever they may be, only work because our brain is designed to respond to similar natural drugs. Clearly, if there were no receptors in our brains for such substances, they simply wouldn't work. Thus, we must bear in mind that natural drugs are part of the "language" that builds our affective world.

Our brain can naturally create everything we feel with synthetic drugs: it is enough to know how to manipulate it. Similarly, everything we feel naturally can be reproduced with synthetic drugs: it is enough to know which one to inject. Just as love can be caused by a person, it can also be caused by an *ecstasy* pill; just as a challenge can motivate us, so can an amphetamine capsule.

One sensation induced by synthetic drugs is not "false", just as another, naturally induced, is not "authentic". Sensations are concrete facts, neurochemical phenomena—and in that equation there is no room for moral considerations. Between natural and artificial addictions, the only tangible difference lies in the fact that the brain, as a supplier, tends to be more honest and reliable than most individuals, doping us in the right measure and only with substances of good origin, since it synthesizes them itself.

Thus, drugs are elements that nature itself developed with the purpose of orchestrating our affective lives. They are not "optional". Without such substances, we would not be, as one might think, socially responsible individuals, but inert vegetables, insensitive to any experience endowed with meaning.

∗ ∗ ∗

Now we can calmly affirm that everyone is dependent on drugs. There is no escape from the fact that, by nature, and without exception, we are all addicted. In this sense, it is irrelevant whether a certain dependency framework was established naturally or artificially. *Equally addicted are those who seek euphoria by parachuting, playing video games, or using stimulants.* Equally addicted are those who seek peace through meditation, physical exercise, and the use of opium derivatives.

From this point of view, believing that drug use is immoral is as unreasonable as believing that there is something immoral about someone exercising or falling in love. Morals can only be inserted into the equation to judge the social consequences of these facts, and giving different names to natural and artificial vices is a purely political issue. If we do it, it's just for convenience, because those who manage to govern life depending only on endogenous drugs tend to behave more stable and predictable. The unavoidable reality of our addiction, however, remains the same.

In view of this, it is not surprising that natural vices can entail consequences as disastrous as artificial ones; it is not surprising that we can fill natural deficiencies artificially, or vice versa. Whether the substances are of internal or external origin, the activated reward and punishment brain mechanisms are the same.

What, for example, we call "nostalgia" is usually nothing more than romanticized boredom. Otherwise, let's see: nostalgia refers to the absence of something that gives us pleasure. We get used to using a certain person as a source of satisfaction and, in the absence of that person, we become anxious, sometimes desperate, seeking in every way to find them again, without being able to get them out of our minds for a moment. Of course, once we find it, the nostalgia disappears. Doesn't the same thing happen with any other drug?

It is enough to replace "nostalgia" with "abstinence" and "loved one" with "pack of cigarettes" to understand that both cases are reduced to the same process. In fact, when we view nostalgia as a condition of abstinence, it is obvious why the best way to overcome a person's absence is to replace them with another. We know from experience that this works, but only now do we understand why.

* * *

With that in mind, let's return to the case of boredom. It seems to us that the best way to circumvent it naturally would be to acquire the capacity to manipulate ourselves voluntarily, to use intelligence to find practical ways to lead our brains to reproduce the mental states that please us. This is because, if our brain is capable of naturally producing all the sensations that we experience, it would be enough to develop techniques that would allow us to control it precisely, and happiness would be before us as a real and free possibility.

At first, it seems like a promising idea, but does it work? Well, of course it works. In fact, in the art of self-control there are a lot of options, and they all work. Not only practical techniques, but also self-deception gives results; we know that. It is an undeniable fact that the placebo effect, despite being based on false beliefs, releases very real substances. However, by putting this seemingly revolutionary idea into practice, we would not be accomplishing anything new, since religion has been doing this for thousands of years. The "divine sciences" are specialists in this regard: it is enough to connect the dots to understand it.

Religions are always involved with the "transcendental" and with "parallel realities". They value authority, trust, and the beyond. Why? We know that, by doping ourselves through artificial procedures, we induce an alteration in our brain chemistry, our view of reality is rapidly distorted. For simple individuals without any notion of how the mind works, what is the result? The impression of having entered "another" reality, or of having captured certain "hidden energies". The beyond can, from this perspective, be understood as a symbolic interpretation of these hallucinatory experiences, and theology is the area that theorizes based on this type of fantasy.

It seems evident that religion exists as a popular wisdom involved in the use of these calculated vices, all indirectly linked to the benefits of the placebo effect, and none of this was ever related to the origin of the universe, to the mystery of existence, to gods or spirits. All of these are backgrounds. Our traditional religious ideas such as salvation, bliss, enlightenment, relationship with God, revealed truths, divine interventions, and inspirations are just allegories that revolve around the use of the placebo for social, recreational, and motivational purposes.

The history of faith, of religions, of metaphysics could almost be reduced to the methods that we invented over time to naturally doped ourselves. Thus, if faith comforts, if meditation calms, this occurs purely and simply because praying and meditating are means of inducing mental states that we consider pleasant, drawing specific rewards from our brains. Within this, God never went beyond a grandiose pretext, because the fact is that revealed truths do not reveal anything to us - they only give us "good feelings". We envy the mystical catharsis of the Saints the same as we envy *junkies* with needles stuck in their veins: free pleasure. And when addicts overcome their addiction through faith, it's not a miracle: they just changed drug dealers.

All of this may seem like a delusional argument. However, if the purpose of religion were not to doping individuals, hallucinations, mystical experiences, peace in the soul, success, and personal happiness would not be seen as arguments in favor of the veracity of religion. Nobody, when seeking religions, is seeking truth, but for happiness, and this makes it perfectly clear that having faith is about maximizing the chances of success in employing the placebo effect.

Since the effectiveness of the placebo is inextricably linked to our capacity to believe — not to know — the veracity of religious belief becomes irrelevant in this regard. The content of belief is simply free, since it is nothing more than a metaphor, a symbolism to which conviction can be fixed to achieve the desired result - something that will be of any practical benefit, since it is obvious that, if they sought knowledge, they would dedicate themselves to study.

Many criticize, not without reason, the blindness caused by faith. However, considering that the effectiveness of the placebo effect depends precisely on the firmness of the conviction, it makes perfect sense that faith should not give importance to facts, since its function is not to know but to exercise control over our mental world. For this reason alone, doubt is a sin in religion, and that is also why "detachment" is preached in relation to the material world, as well as submission to authority. Believers want results, not explanations.

It is enough to have faith: do we now understand what this means? God exists to make faith possible, not the other way around. Miracles are the cases in which the placebo effect worked, and that is sufficient proof of the existence of God. Atheists cry, but belief works, otherwise there wouldn't be so many faith addicts. Let's just note that, like heavy *LSD* users, those who use a lot of faith hardly return to reality. Unable to manage their addiction, depending on their character, they become saints or fanatics.

✳ ✳ ✳

With these observations, we better understand how brain chemistry governs our daily lives. We were able to distinguish how, in practical life, our actions and beliefs revolve around a vague and intuitive understanding of how we can extract rewards from our brains, using their potential to our advantage through indirect procedures, with religion being a great example of this. However, before we close the matter, let us make a few more comments, not about the foolish, but about the wise.

We were somewhat perplexed to see how often great wise men claim to be envious of the ignorant. However, as we become wise, we discover that this occurs because optimistic delusions are simple, cheap, and efficient narcotics. To a greater or lesser extent, we know that when we rationally unravel an illusion, when we stop believing and begin to understand, this dispels much of the comfort it provided.

From this perspective, considering how much we depend on delusions, it is natural that nihilism, when carrying out its sober and inflexible oversight of reality, takes the form of an extremely threatening stance against those who depend on divine drug trafficking. We know how distressing it is to see reason throw our beliefs into private, because without them we are left with only a regrettable and empty existence. Thus, our passionate attachment to delusions is not really about the need to believe in the content of our convictions, but about our inability to remain sober indefinitely in the face of nothing.

Whether we like it or not, deluding oneself is necessary, and it is remarkable how discussions on the subject miss the mark. Belief or disbelief in gods, for example, has nothing to do with our curiosity about the origin of the universe. If God hadn't created the world, it wouldn't matter. So, if we are careful to analyze the reasons why, without any evidence, the existence of God is accepted as a fact, this will make it clear that God comes from our need to believe, from effectively depending on that illusion to carry life forward, like someone who has the active principle in faith, the excipient in the dogmas and in his particular religion the bottle of pills for the miseries of existence.

It doesn't really matter what the superstition is: no belief supported by faith has its value measured by how much it makes sense or by its explanatory nature, but by how much it comforts. So much so that religious people change beliefs without any difficulty, since the color of the pills changes, but the active ingredient remains the same. The important thing is to have faith, no matter what God.

Some religious people are, while others are not, tolerant of other types of beliefs. However, everyone is intuitively and uniformly intolerant of unbelievers. It greatly amazes those who depend on beliefs that one can live without one, and that people like that are not monsters. To live without faith seems as absurd to them as to live without friends - but that perspective is something perfectly understandable, even predictable. We know that God is a pretext for firmly deluding ourselves, not a source of enlightenment, and we know that chronic addicts do not have the option of giving up their addiction voluntarily, nor of being impartial about what they hold on to in order to live. In practice, it doesn't really matter what you hold on to, as long as you remain attached to something. That's having faith.

This perspective will be even more clear if we are careful to observe that religiosity, like atheism, is not in fact a voluntary choice that one makes. Atheism only becomes possible when belief in God becomes unnecessary. Solitude, for the same reason, only becomes possible when friends become superfluous. Of course, once atheists, it seems inconceivable to us to believe this kind of thing - at least until we realize that there is no choice between believing and disbelieving. Like smoking, religiosity doesn't make any sense, but both are acquired addictions that give pleasure, and are equally difficult to give up.

✶ ✶ ✶

Rational individuals never chose to be incapable of doping themselves with childish delusions, just as religious individuals never chose to have faith. Neither of you has the freedom to voluntarily change the way your brain has always been accustomed to functioning. However, since we need illusions to live, each one, according to their intelligence, is forced to employ different methods to support existence.

It's useless to insist: we can't have faith. Our only alternative is to seek solace in enlightenment, but how? Only lucidity in the face of a miserable world causes misery. Then, if we are unable to overcome this problem by involving ourselves with absurd delusions, then we begin to engage with sensible delusions, which satisfy our intelligence.

Lies just don't captivate us—they disgust us. Thus, since we cannot deceive ourselves with falsehoods, we delude ourselves with its opposite: the truth. We find in knowledge what fools find in faith, we seek in honesty the same as others in deception, we understand with open eyes how the blindfolded are comforted.

We learned to endure life in our own way. If today we have a clear conscience in the face of the fact that we don't need to have faith, this is because pharmacies and libraries are enough for us. Our miracles are in *blisters*. We conclude instead of believing, we reflect instead of begging.

The fact is that we would never have accepted God's death so calmly if we didn't have reliable means of replacing him. In place of the Garden of Eden, we have placed the garden of philosophy, and both serve only to distract us, to hide the nihilistic gorge. We know that, in our lives, philosophy, abstract reflection, plays the same role as religion, and both are merely means of escaping from reality.

We recognize that neither philosophy nor religion will get us anywhere—they will only distract us from boredom. It doesn't seem like much, but it's enough. We're human, and a decent existence is all we expect. Since we have pharmacies, self-deception has become dispensable. Because we have intelligence, we find comfort in reflection, and we feel full because we can carry forward our natural inclination to honesty.

From this perspective, philosophy would be like an "atheist sister" of religion. Religious and philosophers, each in their own way, have their consolation wherever they find it — in mystical or intellectual contemplation. This makes clear why, while rational, philosophical considerations about reality are often empty and irrelevant.

Like religious people, philosophers largely lose themselves from reality — and they like it. Philosophy amuses us, but it hardly enlightens us about the world, since it is just an empty exercise in thinking clearly, like playing chess. For this reason, it is rightly said that it is the science with which or without which the world continues as is - nothing could be more correct. It was only the scientists who were best able to protect themselves from this type of loss, since they had the enlightenment to combine the useful with the pleasant through a method that keeps their thoughts with their feet on the ground.

The conclusion is as follows: faith comforts ordinary individuals; reflection comforts intelligent individuals. The difference is that only the latter can confess it: the search for truth is the pretext of intellectuals. In this situation, since thinking rather than faith is the condition of our well-being, we need to cultivate doubt: it is our salvation to keep our brains active, with philosophy being the area that best fulfils this function.

Therefore, not to believe, we need to doubt: backwards believers, any certainty would asphyxiate us. Thinking dangerously can be viewed as an extreme sport, as a therapy, as an escape — that depends on the point of view. We just can't deny that it's pleasurable and a great meaning for life - otherwise there wouldn't be so many who compulsively dedicate themselves to the activity.

Immersed in reflection, we like to think dangerously, and doubts seem irresistible to us. However, over time, instead of just being distracted by reading, contemplating the intellectual adventures of others, we set out on our own: we risk daily problematizing existence. And since intellectual problems are the most urgent for thinkers, seeking their solution becomes a very important task - and thus we distance ourselves from boredom.

The pleasure of reflection is similar to that of stepping your foot off the deck on a winter's day. Once that's done, we dedicated ourselves to finding a way to warm you up under the cloak of truth. The challenge is to be able to do it on time and rationally, without allowing doubt to keep us discovered for a long time. Thus, once discovered, thinking becomes urgent, and we begin to seek solutions, even if temporary, to the problem that we ourselves invented - even because final solutions would be disastrous, the end point of a game that we were unable to abandon.

In this process, we only need two things: doubt and a pretext to overcome it. That is the search for truth, a useless adventure that we embark on voluntarily in order to distract ourselves from boredom.

* * *

As we see, it makes a lot of sense to see the search for truth as a sensible alternative to belief in God. Because, unable to deceive ourselves, we replaced the placebo with the drug. Unable to believe, we delude ourselves into knowing. That is the meaning of life for intellectuals. Knowing is just a pretext. Technology is just a consequence. The goal was always to have something interesting to do.

Therefore, if our nature gives us an affinity for this, study and reflection prove to be a very promising way of becoming self-sustainable addicts. With an empty room, a full library, a curious and creative brain, we will have before us the opportunity to seek the pleasant vice of the intellectuality.

Once this state of dependence on reflection has been reached, it will be up to us to maintain the vicious circle that frees us from boredom. We will be out of their reach as long as we are able to keep our brains active, something that, at first, we can easily do with readings.

In this situation, instead of talking to ourselves and reciting ignorant superstitions, we talk to enlightened philosophers and educated scientists who captivate our intelligence, and that will guarantee our daily dose of the anti-boredom vaccine. When we need miracles, there will be no need to be deceived: it will be enough to go to the pharmacy.

The only problem with intellectuality is the fact that this habit usually leads to loneliness, and this will cause us boredom due to the initial phase of abstinence from praise. There are, however, considerable advantages in submitting to the artificial reeducation of vanity that makes loneliness possible, because in this way we can replace two addictions with just one: we will have books as friends and reflections as an activity. Only then, even if alone, will we feel accompanied in our intellectual addiction.

Of course, at first, such a stance may seem impractical, but it is not. We know that life is unjustifiable. However, without vices, it also becomes unbearable. To endure it, we need vices, vanity being just another of them—a vice that, like any other, can be replaced. Living together is not a necessity, just a vice that we have the habit of overcoming using other people. This is natural, but not necessary. Resorting to friendships when we don't know what will end our lives is as arbitrary as resorting to cigarettes when we don't know what will happen to our hands. In either case, all we have is a pattern of dependency that is difficult to break.

In any case, if we want to have friends, we can have them; however, if we don't want to, we don't have to. We don't need cigarettes either; however, if we want to smoke them, we can. Intellectuality will not make us misanthropes, incapable of any friendships, just as it will not make us allergic to tobacco. Cultivating friendships will always be a possibility. However, if we don't have them, they simply won't be needed. In this sense, the point to be emphasized is that a vice that is independent of the opinion of others makes us independent of it, a very considerable advantage from the point of view of the sustainability of our well-being.

* * *

Perhaps we will understand this position more clearly if we draw a distinction between what we actually need and what we just feel we need. The idea is as follows: there are needs that have underlying realities, such as hunger, thirst, sleep, breathing; and there are needs that are merely representations of realities, such as sex, friendship and leisure. Hunger, for example, cannot be circumvented under any circumstances, because it reflects a real need - our bodies don't work without energy, and there's even no point in considering the possibility of living without food. Then, even if we suppressed the hunger signal by living in a pleasant state of constant satiety, we would eventually die of starvation.

Now let's think about needs that are mere representations. If we suppress leisure from our lives — or sex, or friendships — in such a way that this lack is not felt because we have suppressed that signal — in the same sense that hunger can be suppressed — there would be no consequences. In that situation, with such needs satisfied, we would live with the feeling that we are "tourists", and it would never occur to us to think that maybe we needed leisure. Equally, we wouldn't have sex because we would already feel sexually satisfied all the time. So, if we are already living satisfied, what lack would such things be missing? None, because they are not really needs. Rather, they are needs that our own brain creates, and that our own brain decides when they have been satisfied.

Keeping this in mind, we can conclude that, except in his first years of life, man does not need society, not literally. But then why do people seek socialization? To satisfy some kind of need, of course. Let's try to illustrate the idea with a practical view. Imagine that we're feeling lonely. What does that mean? Nothing; a feeling of malaise; an anguish. Hoping to solve the problem, we took to the street. We talked with some acquaintances and, some time later, we started to feel good. What does that mean? Nothing; a sense of well-being; a pleasure.

Now imagine that instead of going out looking for company, we had gone to the movies. We sat down in the armchair, watched the movie, and eventually started to feel good. What does that mean? Nothing; a sense of well-being; a pleasure. In this situation, we can see that our satisfaction does not really depend on the people themselves, but merely on the fact that they provide themselves as an object that we can occupy ourselves with, just as we can deal with books and movies. So if we have this need to get busy, people are a medium, movies and books are another medium. If we have cultured friends because we like to debate ideas, and if books give us that same pleasure, it doesn't matter if we use books or people.

To socialize is to take care of people, and we like this not for the company, but for the relief of boredom, which is exactly the same pleasure that intellectuals find in reflection - which is the reason why both things tend to be mutually exclusive.

It will be inevitable to think that, although functional, this vision is devoid of meaning. However, the lack of meaning is something we should already be familiar with: meanings are beliefs. Our social needs are all purely psychological. So, if we can satisfy them on our own, loneliness turns out to be a perfectly tangible possibility and emotionally equivalent to socialization.

* * *

The journey we took seems to have been quite enlightening, allowing us to reach some conclusions that are certainly worth noting. There would, of course, be many other possible ramifications to be explored. However, for our purposes, that would be to dwell unnecessarily on small details. From the perspective we have outlined, it is wiser to allow everyone to draw, according to their interests, the relationships that they deem most pertinent.

As we have seen, nature has always forced us to achieve our small doses of satisfaction through hard work. However, over time, we discovered that we can find additional doses in religions, in hallucinogenic plants, in dark corners, in pharmacies, and even in philosophical systems. It seems obvious that humanity has always lived to be doped up, even if we prefer to call it "the search for happiness", "living intensely", "dreaming big".

When meeting, for example, an individual inflated by romantic daydreams, let us realize the curious fact that the "meaning" of their life is similar to the tortuous journey of an addict in search of a perfect drug whose effect never ends. This fact has always deluded us, and from this was born our belief in "true love", "true faith", "true knowledge", etc. We believe like fools that, if found, such things would give us eternal satisfaction, ignoring the fact that eternal satisfactions are biologically impossible.

Thus, although we like to be comforted by impossible dreams involving eternal satisfactions, the fact is undeniable, the reality that our dreams, once satisfied, do not satisfy us is undeniable. The philosophical finding that we should not expect our dreams, once fulfilled, to make us eternally satisfied beings is analogous to the pharmacological finding that we should not expect a dose of narcotic, once injected, to become eternally doped beings. Only in fairy tales can you live happily ever after. Satisfaction, natural or not, only lasts a few moments, because drugs, whether in ampoules or in brains, all have a limited half-life. Today's dose will not free us from tomorrow's abstinence, and that's the reason why we need to continue dreaming, even if our dreams have already been fulfilled.

Faced with this reality, we cannot see as something bad the fact that living is a vice, because it is because of that, and that alone, that we live. The fact that everything is chemistry, instead of being viewed negatively, should, on the contrary, give us some hope, because perhaps in the future there will be a sufficiently advanced technology for us to be able to control such chemistry with much more satisfactory results than the current ones.

Thus, if we are able to put aside our prejudices, we will see how enlightening it is to realize that our behavior is, and has always been, guided by the chemical treats that our brain offers us on special occasions. Considering that our consciousness was born and lives locked in the attic of a narcotics factory, the result could not have been different.

V

ON THE USELESSNESS OF EXISTING

SUICIDE

The fact that someone kills themselves is not wrong, in the same way that someone does not kill themselves is not wrong either. This may seem confusing, but it stems from the simple fact that morals don't exist. This may seem strange, but it can be easily explained as follows: values don't exist. This may now seem illegal, but it cannot be alleged that the laws do not exist, since they are actually registered in white blocks of environmentally friendly cellulose, all sliced in official dimensions and weights. We can read them in the form of traditional linguistic symbols of the culture in force in that particular geographical space dominated by a certain population of civilized hominids. Books of this nature say, based on values that don't exist, what we cannot do if we, who are not free, want to remain free, that is, to obey outside the chain. Its ultimate purpose is to determine, generally in *Times New Roman* size 12, the parameters for life in society, for morals... *inutilia truncat...* in short, for the good of all. Circular reasoning stops here. If someone wants to continue to legally twirl around in relativistic philosophies until they induce vomiting, go ahead.

This may seem insolent, but we can deny its existence with a concrete caveat: there are no laws, but only legislated behaviors. What does the law, after all, have to do with the matter? In essence, nothing. Basically, the fact is that killing yourself isn't wrong, but it's wrong, and it can be explained like this: one monkey rules, the other trembles. The law must behave like this, because what general would allow his army to kill itself before the war? Only the one who does not have the power to be one, since a general without an army is impossible. The moral logic against suicide, from a legal point of view, consists in the fact that leaders prohibit it in order to remain in control, as it always was, since, even shaved, we remain a hierarchical monkey. It's not about social welfare. Every time someone fills their mouth to talk about the great common well-being, they are hiding some other equally grandiose lie, whether on a personal or national level. Nobody believes this nonsense, least of all those who defend it. Just as priests are much closer to atheism than the faithful, legislators and lawyers believe much less in laws than ordinary citizens.

In and of itself, death is not morally reprehensible just because it is biologically inevitable. If dying were an option, not a necessity, natural death would also be prohibited. Dying or killing oneself, despite the fact that they correspond to the same objective reality, are subjectively different things, at least for the spectators, from a moral point of view. For the deceased, this makes no difference, as it is already far from the question, with its nirvana guaranteed forever and ever. Be that as it may, we should be thankful that they cannot punish us after we are dead. However, if they could provide a metaphysical arrest warrant, they would pull the feet of the suicide bomber who was ascending to heaven, bringing him back to the world just to lock him in a cell. If you doubt that our perversity can reach such a proportion, consult some books on reincarnation; you will see that we are even spiritually vindictive.

The fact is that legal punishments prove nothing, just that the leaders have an interest in us staying alive. But why do those controlled, on a daily basis, anonymously, surely, prohibit each other from committing suicide? Because they're bad and selfish, just like their leaders. When the death of the individual does not directly harm them, this can be explained by the same logic as the anonymous complaints of chocolate theft in supermarkets: envy of those who are more selfish, freer, more immoral than themselves, of those who would have gotten away with it if not because they were targeted by a resentful citizen. In their explanations, they state that they fear that this anarchy may one day harm them, who are orderly and follow all laws impeccably. This, however, is not the kindness of a good citizen, but the resentment of an envious monkey. Because of his complaint, he wants to be considered an everyday hero, aiming to improve his social image. It's easy to see the reasons for this: since they are forbidden, but they cannot take revenge on the oppression of their leaders, an impotence that eats away at them, revenge is diverted to their equals free of charge, to those who have nothing to do with their private interests. His speech is "punish all the immorals, all the criminals themselves, all the cowardly monsters that do what I cannot do, that achieve the peace that I cannot have". It doesn't matter what they say: deep down, they're nothing more than hard fingers.

In practice, we can understand them as orchestrated ants, sharing the burden of carrying civilization leaves to the anthill: they want them all to share the same misfortune, since none has the right to be free from the suffering of which they are mandatory victims. Thus, if there were three ants carrying a leaf and one of them released it, increasing the effort of the other two, they would readily incarnate, full of resentment and envy, what they detest most, their own subjection, and would oppress it until it became as disgraced as themselves, and would continue to carry the leaf indefinitely, towards a natural death.

✷ ✷ ✷

Whatever one may say, suicide, like death in general, is not a mistake, but a biological fact. Even if it's illegal, seeing the matter from that perspective doesn't clarify it at all. So let's look at it this way: if suicide were wrong in and of itself, when we cut our wrists, the blood, instead of gushing, would give us a moral lesson. Since that doesn't happen, we have to admit that killing yourself is a perfectly tangible possibility.

To begin our reflections from a more sensible perspective, let's compare the words of a suicide bomber and those of those who try to convince him otherwise:

— Living isn't worth it. Since I was born, life has always been a series of disappointments. No dream made me happy, no achievement satisfied me. I would have said *no* if they asked me if I wanted to be born and yet, without any permission, I was thrown into the maelstrom of the world. All I've done since then is run in circles, and I realized that the wisdom of life is nothing more than a way to avoid calluses and blisters. My only consolation is that life has an end. Without that, I would have gone crazy.

— Of course it's worth it, don't be crazy! Life is a wonderful experience that we will only have a chance to enjoy once. Of course, after that, we'll all die, but it's not right to leave it incomplete. There are so many mysteries to be unraveled, so many unforgettable experiences to be experienced, a world so curious and full of possibilities. How can you let go of all this? Of course, there are difficulties, but we must strive to overcome them. Therein lies the pleasure of living. Life may not only be made of flowers, but it is also not pure suffering.

— Let me try to illustrate exactly the situation in which I find myself. Perhaps this will help you understand why such words are useless. Some people like math, others don't. Is that your case?

— No, I think it's a dull issue.

— Well, if your life, instead of being practical, were made up only of mathematical equations, what would you say? Your lunch, one formula; your love, another. I would have sex through numerical simulations. Your friends, everyone, sets of mathematical symbols. Your dreams, equations to be developed. What would you say about leading a life of this kind, in which all existence is reduced to numbers, and the struggle, within four walls, is waged on the blackboard with a chalk in your hands?

— I would prefer death!

— Exactly, and not even the greatest mathematician in the world could convince you otherwise.

This illustrates the issue well enough. If we want, it will be easy to find arguments against suicide, but none of them are based on intelligence. They are all based on a kind of hypocritical compassion, on the foolish affection of those who have nothing to say, but still fill us with useless advice.

Nobody suffers more from the pity of others than the suicide bomber. They unload on him all the lies they tell themselves. In everything they claim, we've never found a motive against suicide that isn't infected with obvious and ridiculous fallacies. Someone who would simply be silent when faced with the issue would be much more worthy of respect and, perhaps, would still represent a last hope in life, since at least they would show that they understood that opening their mouth would mean betraying the truth and insulting their interlocutor.

The more people speak out against suicide, the more this makes it obvious how comfortable most individuals are to lie for a *long* time — imagining that their intimate reasons are above suspicion. In this sense, we must choose to endure life's misfortunes with composure or take immediate action, because nothing is worse than being a victim of the free compassion of those who are willing to love our lives when we ourselves can't. There is nothing to say, since they will only realize the futility of what they say when they are, themselves, in the same situation, and if they find themselves completely unable to find solace in the wise words they addressed to us.

Faced with the obvious lack of arguments, the final accusation against the suicide bomber is one of "cowardice", although it is not exactly clear what is meant by that. Where is there cowardice when someone no longer wants to continue an effort in which they see no value? This is equivalent to saying that if we were merchants, we should choose to starve to death rather than declare bankruptcy and abandon the business. Such an accusation can clearly be interpreted as an *ad hominem* for those who are unable to establish a position based on logical and consistent argumentation. This is an insult, not an argument. However, if the suicidal individual is bluffing, it is very common for them to take the bait. Thus, in the face of this attack, he must prove that he is not a coward, and the only way to do so is to remain alive. People like that don't really want to die, although the fact that they're still alive for such flimsy reasons also doesn't lead us to believe that their lives are worth living.

In general, this happens because many think of suicide just because they don't have the courage to lead the life they really want. However, they soon realize that death is not what they are looking for. What they are looking for, in fact, is a solution to their problems. In this case, the individual, by placing the barrel of the gun on his head, will immediately abandon the idea of suicide. You will feel with perfect clarity how small your fears are in the face of a perspective as radical as death, you will perceive the countless possibilities that life as a whole offers you. The glimpse of that freedom will be enough to overcome the fears that led him to consider suicide - which requires much more courage than he actually has. Perhaps his sudden bravery can be attributed to the release of adrenaline in the face of imminent danger, but he demonstrates how his motives are easily circumvented through modern pharmacology.

Since killing yourself, in essence, is something extremely simple, we can't really believe that so many individuals fail in this endeavor for a mere lack of intelligence. A suicide attempt is not a failure, but a stupidity. If they really wanted to die, they would try again as soon as they opened their eyes, but that hardly ever happens. In turn, those individuals who sit on the edge of buildings and start whining are not suicidal, but idiots seeking attention. Such a little theater is what is called a "suicide attempt", which should be called success in ridiculing oneself.

The characteristic sign of authentic suicide bombers is not a blatant revolt, but the discretion of a profound disregard for life. They kill themselves without hesitation, in the blink of an eye, leaving no room for another individual to stop them. They don't keep up the clock, whining as they scratch their heads with the barrel of the gun. Those who are determined to take their own life do not stop at nothing, do not waste time with rituals or farewell notes. Dying becomes a personal interest. The decision has already been taken once and for all and, with the calculated coldness of a *serial killer*, he seeks only the most convenient way to fulfill his will, without anyone being suspicious.

✳ ✳ ✳

Life advocates remain steadfast in their conclusion that suicide is a "mistake." However, faced with such firm positions based on such clumsy argumentation, we should have imagined that the real issue is never brought up, as this would reveal that the prohibition is not based on profound compassion for the suffering of others, nor on a belief in the value of life, but solely and exclusively on selfishness, in an attempt to preserve one's own well-being. At best, we try to alleviate the distress of the potential suicide bomber because his death would make his pain our problem, and we don't want that. Even if we didn't have a shred of affection for the deceased, we would at least have to fulfill the thankless task of burying him with all the ceremonies that are required on that occasion.

Nobody is really concerned with someone else's life, but only with the consequences of that individual's death on their own lives. Here we have the key to understanding the purely selfish motives involved in this issue—that is, the real motives. Nobody, for example, would worry if someone on the other side of the world jumped off a cliff. There are billions of people on the planet, and we don't have enough time to become close to but a handful of them. It's no surprise to realize that we would only revolt against the suicide of this restricted group of individuals that concern us personally. The reason for this can be reduced to the fact that we only care about the people we invest something in. Everything else is perfectly indifferent to us. If this were not the case, as people die every second, we would spend our entire existence agonizing in whining and convulsions.

When there is a death, the real damage is on the part of the living. The dead didn't lose anything, but simply left the game, falling into oblivion. Those who will have to live with the consequences and the pain of this are those who cry over the casket - meaning that wakes are not really for the dead. From this perspective, we can understand that the prohibition of suicide is nothing more than an attempt to protect the investments we make in each other in life in society. It's not really a "moral" issue in the sense that we're really concerned with the "value of life", but an economic one, relative to the cost of maintaining society.

Of course, if we have family, friends, they will suffer from our death. It's normal for those who were close to us to feel guilty or responsible. However, they really feel guilty not for having ignored our suffering, but for not having

247

stopped us in time. Only now, because they are suffering, do they blame themselves for the imprudence of not having protected their investment. Our pain, our true motive for suicide, is something that does not reach their souls. No tears will be shed because of the pain that consumed the suicide bomber. Everyone cries because of the explanations they invent in their heads, for what they lost in their lives, not for the life lost.

This makes it perfectly clear why no one has good reasons against suicide: against suicide there are only personal interests. As can be seen, the real motives are so petty that, if revealed, they would, on the contrary, constitute an invitation to suicide. In the form of an argument, we could put it this way: "your suffering is not and will never be sufficient to justify suicide because *I would* suffer from it". Very moving.

It is ironic that, after so many fiery speeches about the value of life, of courage, about the importance of enduring our own suffering, the true cowards reveal themselves to be those who, with our death, would not bear their own. Therefore, out of kindness, out of the same compassion that they themselves cannot have in relation to our pain, we must remain alive.

✶ ✶ ✶

Once we understand the reason why individuals oppose suicide, let us turn to the issue from a personal point of view to investigate the reasons in their favor. First of all, we must understand that suicide is not a "solution" to life's problems, but only the end, a letter of resignation handed over to existence. If we don't like the experience of living, we can simply abandon it.

The question is simple: do I want to stay alive? The answers are *yes* or *no*, without compromise, without reasons, explanations, or conditions. Existence has no ears for our conditions. Living is that, or nothing. Let us review the matter calmly, for as long as we deem necessary. Once the choice has been made, let's take action. Once and for all, let's choose to just live, or just die. There's nothing more pathetic than the cowardly blackmail of those who flirt with death whenever they run into difficulty. And there is nothing sadder than someone who is dead inside and is not firm enough to assume themselves as such.

To a greater or lesser extent, everyone fears death. In logical terms, this doesn't make any sense, because after we die there will be nothing - just as there was nothing before we were born. Many wonder "where do we go after death?" , and the answer is simple: probably to the nearest cemetery.

Our fear invents incoherent things like "heavenly paradises", "spiritual im-mortalities", thinking that the denial of death would solve something. However, if we were eternal, that wouldn't change anything. Life would continue to be what it always was, just indefinitely. As a rule, those who seek security through the idea of spiritual eternity don't really consider the implications of that vision—they just want a pretext to set the matter aside until the next life begins. They don't want to die for the same reason they don't want to be fined or arrested. They see death as a kind of inconvenient interruption of their daily activities, which will be incomplete, as if dying were equivalent to being shot with a tranquilizer dart and then teleported to the afterlife.

In fact, if you think seriously, it's hard to believe that anyone would actually want to be eternal, at least in this world we're in. Many say the opposite because they never honestly thought about the matter, as a real possibility, but only as a poetic escape. Living eternally more seems like the definition of hell. *If an ephemeral existence is already bitter, an eternal one would be terrifying — in desperation, we would cut off our heads over and over again, only to see them reborn ad infinitum.*

What prevents us from dying voluntarily is not laws, it's not morals, it's not our consideration for others: it's the survival instinct. We fill our future with impossible dreams so that this pretext will keep us alive, hiding the fact that, although life is not worth living, we are too cowards to die. We invent a thousand excuses to leave suicide until tomorrow: we will only carry it forward after our impossible dreams are fully realized, detail by detail, in the order imagined. First, don't even think.

We fooled ourselves with a lot of creativity. We don't give up on life easily. It takes an extraordinary reason for us to be able to see death as the most desirable option, and this explains why most suicides are committed during periods of crisis. For example, an individual going through a depressive phase clearly feels that their life doesn't deserve to be carried forward. In that situation, it really doesn't work. However, if you are not experiencing your first experience of existential nausea, you will be aware that this feeling is fleeting, despite the clear impression that everything will be like this forever. Even in the following depressive crises, the present feeling contradicts the past experience: it always seems that, this time, the pain will never pass. But the individual knows that, in fact, this has nothing to do with the value of life. It wasn't existence that ceased to have meaning, but your brain that is probably chemically imbalanced, so much so that your depression can be cured quickly with medicine. Problems with neurotransmitters are major reasons for suicide.

Neurochemical pain, however, hurts like any other. What is desperate in this situation is not the present suffering itself, but the overwhelming prospect of a lifetime immersed in this deplorable situation. Suicidal ideation places death as the only viable solution because, in that circumstance, it really is the case. Nobody would choose to live if that were the only condition of existence. However, the fact is that, in one day, the whole world collapsed. In the other, we danced on the wreckage.

We know that the whole drama unfolds inside our minds. However, that doesn't make it any less real or worth considering, because, after all, everything happens in our minds - where else would it occur? Even if our suffering comes from the situation in which we find ourselves, what causes us to suffer are the repercussions of this in our minds, the way in which we feel those external factors.

Thus, it doesn't matter if suffering comes from adverse internal or external conditions: there comes a point where the pains of life simply supplant the terrors of death—and no word will convince us that all the distress we feel is an illusion. Whatever argument we use to claim that suffering is illusory, such an approach will, with even more reason, reduce happiness and everything else to the same ghostly existence, in which life is a painful fantasy.

Even more ridiculous than denying the reality of life is to suppose that its existence is conditional: it becomes real when we are happy and imaginary when we are sad. It makes no sense to deny the value of just one side of the issue, imagining that it will balance the scales of our satisfaction. It doesn't matter whether we consider life a real or imaginary theater: it is in it that we exist, without any guarantee that we will be making the best choice by remaining alive.

* * *

Life is a personal matter, not a public one. Knowing that, in this regard, no one will have to satisfy others, we are aware here of our full freedom to resolve the matter by ourselves. We can decide whether, in our point of view, which is exclusively ours, life deserves to be lived or not. The position of the others in this regard does not matter, because it would be petulant on their part, and stupid on our part, to believe that they have the right to give an opinion on this matter. In life in society, we may owe satisfaction in various matters, but this is not one of them. *Since only we know first-hand what our life means, it's up to us to decide how much pain we're willing to endure to the point where we say enough is enough.*

This is an intimate and personal decision. We know why we want to die, and also what still holds us back to life, and the only people who care about that are us. Nobody is in a position to make that choice for us. The problem is ours, solitarily ours, and we have to solve it on our own. Placing such a choice in the hands of someone else would be equivalent to placing a scalpel in the hands of a butcher who, in addition to being incompetent, still has an interest in keeping us alive - there is no way to expect the surgery to be impartially successful. The result, whatever it may be, will be rude close to what we could accomplish with our own hands.

Even from a personal point of view, the issue of suicide is not related to the "meaning" or "value" of life: we know that it has neither. Living is a great effort that doesn't pay the investment, it never will. No matter how much we smile, what we receive will never be enough to compensate us. Since life is a private non-profit initiative, the question is just how much harm we are willing to tolerate before giving up. There's no need to suffer for free, there's no merit in that. However, since we can choose death, when we are still alive, we lose the right to raise our voices with the discourse of injustice. Even though we knew that the odds were against us, it was only our choice to submit to that kind of existence and carry it forward. The facts are before us, the conditions are in

251

place. We know what life wants from us. If we sign your contract, we promise to endure it without opening our mouths. We can't claim ignorance. It's already a big thing that we have a choice, something that no other animal seems to have.

* * *

Under certain circumstances, our lives seem worthwhile. Not under other circumstances. As long as, in general, we think it's worth it, let's continue. As long as our living conditions are not something deplorable, living is not a shame, just an irrationality. However, when the disgust for life takes on such a proportion that nothing arouses our interest, when every step is a pain and every breath is an anguish, and all we want, honestly, is the blessing of sleeping and never waking up, suicide may well be what we want.

In this situation, we don't want attention from others, we don't want them to suffer, we don't want to destroy the world or save it, or the publication of a suicide note. We don't even want to see our own wake. We don't turn our backs on life expecting it to apologize to us. We would just like to disappear, as if life were something that had never happened.

So if we want to live, let's live; if we want to die, let's die. This has nothing to do with those around us. Suicide is not cruel to others, because when we die, we do not inflict any pain, we only fail to satisfy the needs of those who rely on us. We will only be needed in that sense. To the rest of us, we are important on the outside, as poles, not on the inside, as human beings. Nobody cares about anything other than their own belly buttons. So if ours asks for death, we gave him what he wants: it's the best we can do for ourselves.

* * *

Suicides aren't delusional. On the contrary, when they die, they probably know much better what they want than we do when they stay alive. Aware of their condition, they only declare the inevitable bankruptcy of their lives early, and perhaps the truth of their allegations is simply something that we all have to protect ourselves from in order to remain alive.

If we agreed to be at least reasonable on the issue of suicide, we would have to let them go and, in addition, we would be tempted to go too, since their motives also apply to us. There is no point in carrying out a task in which one feels no pleasure, and it is unfair and cruel to demand that the victims of this existential frigidity pretend that life is a multiple orgasm until some natural fatality takes them away in a socially acceptable way.

Approaching the issue from this perspective, we were able to perfectly understand the perspective of those who no longer wish to live. It may be difficult to conceive everything you feel, but your motives are more than evident. Only a fool would not prefer to die if he were forced to lead a life that seems absolutely detestable to him, especially when the experience has already been sufficiently clear to demonstrate that there is no prospect of improvement.

HAPPINESS

*We go through life cluttered, anxious, not knowing what we're looking for —
or, if we do, we can hardly answer why without stuttering.* In no moment do we
stop our existential flow in a present *flash* and say "this is what I'm looking for
in life - really everything I'm looking for". At best, our moments of happiness
are just a good dose of well-calibrated hormones that lead us to *think how
beautiful, right?* Those happy moments are engraved on us, but not by the
goodness of destiny. This phenomenon can be explained by the fact that one of
the main criteria for our memories to be fixed consists of natural *overdoses*,
that is, floods of substances released by the body itself in circumstances
emotionally relevant to the subject, ensuring that our existence has them
eternally as references, that we are always the full-scale version of the rats that
we created in the laboratory.

Considering that maintaining well-being is one of the most important goals
of the organisms, it makes sense to remember the strategies, the behaviors that
were positive in this regard. We memorize happy moments so that we can
repeat them, not in the name of happiness; we memorize what caused us pain
so that we can avoid it in the future, not in the name of suffering. In this
schema, we see that the objective is not pleasure or pain, but the simple
maintenance of the individual. That's the reason we don't remember the long
periods of boredom, which constitute the biggest chunk of our lives. They're
not recorded because they haven't taught us anything important.

The interesting thing here is to see the point where both things — happiness and our lives — intersect: memory. In other words, joy only crosses our
path when there is no longer any possibility of encountering it. The very fact
that we believe that endogenous *overdoses* have something to do with the
meaning of life already makes it clear how we were carried away by the nose on

254

this issue. So, in the absence of photographic film, if we want to remember any moment for the rest of our lives, and then call it happiness, we just have to do something that the rat inside us would never dare. We will gain a memory for life, a dose of narcotics for a few moments. That's all we can expect from the present.

From the future we expect impossible things, such as the existence conspiring to establish our ideals or the cessation of will to fulfill some dream imagined as important - which will be a dividing mark between the now distressed and the long and prosperous future full of fantastic things that will make us happy. Things that we don't know are because that never happened, although we insist on the belief that one day it will inevitably happen and it will be as good as one day we know we will know.

The problem is that we don't recognize the arrival of that future until it has become an old memory. This is because our dreams can be imagined as immense mosaics: from afar, they are very beautiful, composing fabulous figures that captivate our imagination. However, as we get closer, the details become increasingly rude, until, upon reaching them, we no longer recognize in them the image that seduced us. We will only begin to see the figure again when it becomes a distant past, filling us with nostalgia and cramps.

Seeking happiness directly in these places is an obvious impossibility that generates frustration. On the one hand, all the happiness we demand from the world doesn't fit in the present. On the other hand, when the future arrives, we never find in it the happiness we expected. We need, however, to live with some sense of dignity in our brains full of special twists. What is the "cat jump" to circumvent this mismatch? We falsified the memory. Nobody has more happiness than in the past: it's where we imagine that all the joy that we've been reaping like crumbs during our lives is stored, ready to be evoked and justify some more insipid idiocy that, in the future, will be the cause of nostalgic memories.

When in doubt, we are always left with an *interpretation* of the facts, never with the raw memory of those facts: we reinvent them, color them, fill them with greasy things. Then we spew that adulterated memory into our present consciousness, and that proves that we are happy. That's the only reason why we think of childhood as a happy time. Being the farthest and most vague thing we can remember, the lack of data makes us suppose that we didn't feel the full weight of existence when eating a rotten candy. Of course, if we could visit our own childhood in a time machine and ask ourselves directly about such things, the contrary testimony would *still* not convince us, generally under the pretext that our immaturity did not allow us to recognize happiness when we saw it, leaving it to go unnoticed - even if, in that sense, we remain as immature and blind as we ever were.

✳ ✳ ✳

The happiness of our lives is supported by a constantly false perspective. We dream about the future and say: "ah! , how happy I will be..." We looked back and sighed: "ah! , how happy I was..." Now we regret: "ah! , how disgraced I am..." At present, we are unhappy beings surrounded by great happiness, all of them distant, but close to which the current suffering seems despicable. It is as if we were living on an island of unhappiness surrounded by a sea of joy - but the fact is that we will never dive into that sea, because it is just an illusion that we invented to justify our misery.

Even if we never feel it, we are absolutely convinced that happiness exists - and wherever it is, it awaits us. It doesn't matter that, in this regard, our lives boil down to a series of disappointments: we never admit that everything is sand. We can be certain that if happiness were a person, they would be stuck - but that doesn't prove anything to us. Happiness smiles at us like a mirage, and we believe that this time it may be real: *let's believe the one that always fooled us!*

The present always seems unhappy to us. The future, in turn, seems beautiful to us for the same reasons as the past: we cannot predict details of the future or remember the details of the past. Life, then, becomes something as simple as the idea we have of it, and the present is just a temporary state of anxiety. The difference is that we have already been in the past and, since time does not go backwards, there is no chance of being denied, and it is, therefore, the safest place to deposit our most precious personal lies.

If we have doubts about this, let's do a practical test. At any time when we're deeply unhappy, let's take a picture of ourselves smiling and keep it for a while. We can even write down behind her exactly what we were feeling at that moment. When we have forgotten the specific details of the circumstances in which we were taking the photo, without a clear idea of what saddened us, let's look at the smiling photo. Seeing her, we remember that we thought we were unhappy at the time. However, we have the clear impression that, deep down, a fund, any background, we were happy, weren't we? Well it is.

In youth, all the unhappiness of past generations proves nothing to us, other than that they were unable to enjoy life — and we, obviously, will be the first exception in human history. In old age, we limited ourselves to daydreaming about how many times we were happy even though we felt miserable. However, experience, often wrongly interpreted as the wisdom of life, does not give us the right to push our lies to those who still know nothing about life, as if the mere fact of being old made self-deception respectable. Many swear that if they returned to their youth, this time they would be happy, but this is just another of the countless lies we tell ourselves when the future is already too short to accommodate our delusions of achievement. It's hard to imagine how many times an individual would have to live to confess something so obvious - and perhaps that would only result in even more unreasonable theories about the happiness of the hundredth reborn.

* * *

There are several ways of justifying to ourselves that, in general terms, we are happy, even if we don't feel any happiness.

One of them is to say that there are countless people who suffer more than us and that, therefore, simply because we are not even more miserable, we should be satisfied. If we have an ingrown toenail, there are those that don't have feet; if we don't have feet, there are those that don't have legs; if we don't have legs, there are quadriplegics; if we are, there are still quadriplegics with terminal cancer; if we are quadriplegic with terminal cancer, there are also quadriplegics with terminal cancer and a damn speck in the eye. Therefore, an ingrown toenail is negligible.

Of course, it doesn't stop being. However, it is only relatively insignificant and, in addition, the parameter that allows comparison is a pain that does not concern us. As the suffering of others does not diminish ours, it does. We are not comforted by the fact that we suffer only a portion of all the ills that we could suffer, because we are also not as happy as we could be. This type of reasoning, in general, is just a way of making us stop pestering others with whining. Nobody really takes you seriously.

Another strategy is to claim that the moment in which we are feeling unhappy is just a "passing phase" of life. Young children just don't express their unhappiness because they don't know how to speak coherently, although their constant crying is a good indication of that. However, a short time later, explicit complaints begin. The greatest desire of children, then, is to reach a certain age, confident that there they will be able to enjoy certain benefits that will make them happy. So, let's say, a boy wants to become a teenager so that he can enjoy the nightlife. Seeing that this was not satisfactory, she imagines that, when she becomes of legal age, she will be happy because she will be able to consume alcoholic beverages and drive. Such freedom, he thinks, will save him from his misery; error. Frustrated, he imagines that he will be full once he achieves his financial independence. However, seeing that there has been no change, he assumes that, over time, he will receive professional recognition and hold high positions. The presidential chair, however, does not console him. Then she imagines that she must get married and have children; another disappointment. He ages, becomes ill, and reaches the final phase.

Only then does he regret not having taken advantage of the small chances he had, since he considered every season of his life to be a "passing phase", thinking that, after any of these phases, the "great chances" and the "great joys" would appear. He went through existence in white, waiting for "true life" to begin with drums and trumpets. He let opportunities slip out of his hands because he was unable to recognize that suffering and dissatisfaction are intrinsic to life.

The anxiety caused by the dream of positive happiness leads us to rush through life, to see the present as something despicable compared to what the future holds for us. It is imagined that unhappiness will pass when we reach a certain age, at which current problems will not afflict us - and that in fact happens. However, new problems will arise, making unhappiness the only constant in life.

The idea that life is made up of "phases" cannot, therefore, be used as a pretext to ignore the present. Those who do not know how to recognize the benefits and ailments of their own age will suffer even more because they do not live up to their current condition. With your eyes fixed on the future, stumble on the now. In this way, your present will be even more disgraced, and in the future a disappointment awaits you.

In this continuous process of self-deception, we consider ourselves happy, not because we feel happy, but because we take for granted the promise of future happiness that, however, never arrived. It will never come. Everything was nothing more than a dream.

We also have entertainment as a very dubious way of trying to achieve ghostly happiness. It basically consists of the idea that, by being distracted at public events, we are enjoying life, and that means being happy. For example, let's imagine that entertainment is attending the performance of one of our favorite bands. Of course, in our homes, we sat in our armchairs, turned on the stereo and, relaxed, enjoyed the music. Everyone attends the event convinced that the situation will be even better, as they will have the artists in front of them, in a magnificent live performance. Let's see, however, how things actually happen.

We bought advance tickets and traveled to the city where the show will be held. Tired from the trip, with backaches, we have to face kilometer-long lines. Hours later, now also suffering from foot pain, we entered the room. If we haven't bought special tickets, with reserved seats, we wait standing or sitting on the floor until the event begins. In the meantime, we listened to a number of other beginning bands that don't interest us, which probably had the opportunity to open the *show* because they are the comrades of one of the main band members who, out of pity, decided to give them a chance to become known. Now, also with a headache, we can barely stand up, but we have to get rid of the tiredness because the event will finally begin.

The crowd desperately crowds, poking their heads in the hope of seeing their idols pick the instruments tens of meters away. In the process, we are squeezed everywhere by a mass of sweaty and drunk individuals, who climb above each other and shout uninterruptedly, following the songs with the most out of tune possible. The closer we get to the stage, the more extreme the situation becomes. Unfortunately, when we're almost able to see something, our bladders make us feel the call of nature. We have to cut through the crowd in a hurry. Relieved, we retraced the entire journey to where we were. With pain in the back, in the feet, in the ears, in the head, we will not escape the elbows, and we will still have to endure having our feet stepped on dozens of times. Unless we have morphine pills in our pockets, we won't be able to ignore all these annoyances and enjoy the music as we did in our homes. Negative factors override any possibility of aesthetic appreciation.

Like us, each individual is full of expectations of achievement, anxious to experience the happiness that they imagined for themselves at that event, but are unable to. Their exaggerated expressions of enthusiasm reveal no pleasure, but desperation. They look at each other bored, gesture in an attempt to attract attention, sing the most unknown songs in a very loud voice, certain that they will be demonstrating to others their profound knowledge of the most irrelevant aspects of the musical career of their stars. They jump at the lead singer's command, raise their arms, clap their hands. Every effort is valid, because they are forced to take advantage of that moment, whatever the cost. They will be happy, and it doesn't matter how much they have to suffer. At the end of the event, they tear themselves to pieces in an attempt to grab a miserable pick thrown by the musician, like someone who saw the Holy Grail of Happiness in it.

Finally, they return to their homes and, almost dead, filthy, full of bruises and cramps, are filled with painkillers, take baths and sleep like someone who fell into a coma. The next day, when asked about the experience, their raspy voices say: *the show was fantastic, I listened to my favorite song!*

In tourist trips, we have basically the same situation, and it is not necessary to describe other ways in which we become even more miserable in the hope of being happy. Suffice it to say that if there were a place so wonderful that just being in it would make us happy, the whole of humanity would be focused on that single point, and would never think of leaving it.

* * *

On the other hand, there are those who, instead of seeking happiness, blame the world for their unhappiness. Rebels, revolutionaries, or simply idiots, develop extremely sophisticated theories about predatory organizations that are dedicated to making us miserable and blind. Because of this "global conspiracy", the "true realities" in which we could find happiness are hidden from us. In his view, everyone is manipulated like puppets, and the only way to overcome this condition is to engage in utopian social struggles in which we will combat what is vaguely designated by the term "power". This is so that the next generations will be happy - we are already doomed.

Thus, we have, for example, the socialists, who blame capitalism for everything that is wrong in society, as if the multinational soft drink companies were villains that corrupt our lives by bottling carbonated syrups. They take comfort in thinking that they were victims of unscrupulous politicians who cleverly instilled false needs in them, against which they now stand up. They love to paint themselves as poor devils crucified by the system. They regret that everything today is driven by money, that our lives are disposable like cans of sardines. They talk about the infamous "programmed obsolescence", without suspecting that it works because we accept it as a measure against boredom. Plastic cups are not, as they say, the result of diabolical minds. It's our needs that are disposable. It was our frivolous way of living and consuming that created and nourishes this industry of obsolescence. It wasn't the products that made us like that, we created industries like this with our ordinary needs. Let's at least admit it: we love buying trash.

The desire for profit, in turn, is not the cause of human greed, but quite the opposite. If profit were abolished, we would find another way to exploit each other. Considering that in the old days this was done with nails, we are doing very well. If capitalism were overthrown, we would not become "brothers", as implied by the affectionate nicknames with which they treat each other. In a world where everything is driven by competition, there will always be those who lose, and that is not injustice, but the nature of life, even civilized life. If capitalism works, if it stubbornly resists every onslaught of egalitarianism, it is because it incorporates at least some of the rules of the game that drives us as living beings.

Even with a lot of encouragement, socialism has always failed. Capitalism, for its part, has always worked on its own, almost naturally. Not that human nature corroborates capitalism, because as far as we know, it doesn't corroborate any side, but there is a big difference between a system that works poorly and another that simply doesn't work. Furthermore, this peace that socialists preach is nothing more than a childhood dream. We will never become "brothers" or "companions" unless we have in mind the inclusion of *diazepam* in basic food baskets. There is a lot of talk about justice, but in practice, justice is a theory whose best job we could find is to get dressed up to solemnly decide whether or not we are going to cage the monkeys that disobey us. The speeches they give may be inspirational, but they are just that: speeches. Speeches whose practice implies a glaring contradiction with everything that constitutes us as human beings — are a joke to our most basic instincts and an insult to the intelligence that guides them.

Others point to environmental imbalance, pollution, deforestation, and the extinction of species as the central source of all the ills that affect humanity. They propose a life in harmony with nature as a solution to problems that have nothing to do with it. Even after Christianity has demonstrated, in every imaginable way, that free compassion doesn't work, they still want us to believe that piety toward animals or the planet will bring us some benefit.

The issue is not, and never has been, the importance of greenery, nature, colorful plants, and humming whales that our grandchildren will never see. The issue isn't that the planet is getting hot or cold and the polar ice caps are going to melt or increase. None of this is new. What draws attention is the devotion with which the followers of this reinvented environmentalism defend their ideologies, always with that tone of politics mixed with threats from an apocalyptic future. Green irrationality, which was once restricted to a few "chosen ones", has now spread to the volunteer *couch potato* who needs a dictionary to explain what life is, but who gives himself the right to preach because he planted a lemon tree in the backyard.

It's not hard to see the similarity of this movement with a kind of militant pantheism installed on people who are angry at the boredom of their own lives, and who want someone to blame for their own misfortune. Like any religious group, they are ambitious. Saving endangered species so that they could smile at the camera became too small. With fanatical followers around the world, why be content with such mixarias? They can embarrass everyone to respect any crap containing a *DNA* molecule and call it "recognition of biological tradition", or something equivalent, because all the children of nature have the same right, despite the fact that no right existed for 3.5 billion years.

The retro trend of these proud amoeba descendants is to extend the humanitarian nonsense of dignity — which never even worked in humans — to the intimate feelings of the grass, so green, that feeds the kittens that don't deserve to suffer to become hamburgers in the mouths of terrible, horrible human beings who go so far as to the absurdity of expressing their predatory nature instead of becoming resigned followers of greenness, eating soy meat, but not before asking the plants for forgiveness as well, promising advances in research Genetics for a Day they also have chloroplasts that generate clean energy and thus end the indiscriminate killing of vegetables by planting human beings, who are worthless.

If we were dependent on this type of conservationist mentality, which raises the flag of nature and pretends that it evolved at *Disneyland*, the continents would still be tied up to conserve Pangea — whose disintegration, in some way, should also be attributed to man — and we would live with the dinosaurs that, after being protected from extinction, were moralized to the point of becoming effeminate reptiles, ashamed of their sharp teeth, regretting wearing leather, eating tofu and treating themselves with heavy antidepressants to endure the unhealthy unnaturalness of this lifestyle justified by ideals so hollow that they only find parallel in the Gospel.

This humanist benefactor that acts as the moral representative of the planet — something which life never needed — took away from species the right to disappear with some dignity, victims of their own adaptive incompetence, which was always the fundamental principle of life maintenance. Allowing a bunch of fanatics hallucinated by the ideal of an impractical altruism to place sick and doomed to failure species in the foreground because they feel guilty of human interference on the planet is the recipe for the most ridiculous imbalance that ever existed, with the Earth looking like an infirmary where we find all the little birds that fell from the nest — but were rescued by the environmental unconsciousness of our species.

We are very creative, sometimes almost epic, when it comes to evading responsibility for our personal dissatisfaction. In this case, the strategy was even original: realizing that human happiness is impossible, they transferred their useless dreams to the animals that, poor things, now have to bear the burden of being happy for us.

There are also those who blame the modern media for the extirpation of our "true nature" — whatever that means — because they reduce us to mere commercial puppets unable to think for themselves. When watching movies, for example, our personalities are deformed to such an extent that our ideal becomes a life inside television sets. Furthermore, the influence of television invades our minds and subverts the notions of reality and fiction, so that we begin to consider the superman real and the baker as imaginary. This has very real consequences. Many people jumped from buildings thinking that *Clark Kent* would be there to save them. When we turn on the radio, we give up our individualities and embrace a massive lifestyle, imposed by the announcer's musical selection and by the commercials for toothpastes that suggest that we have to brush our teeth. Now, any self-respecting subversive individual knows that bad breath is a myth invented by the ruling elites. Also, when buying products *online*, we lose contact with social reality, as we stop interacting physically with the retailers. Our souls become progressively empty as we stop standing in lines and hearing nonsense from smiling vendors. Of course, in our eyes, none of this seems like a loss. However, as we are alienated by the technological frenzy, we are unable to realize how much we are losing.

Slowly, without realizing it, we lost contact with ourselves, stopped "creatively constituting ourselves as original individuals" —another incomprehensible idea—and accepted being constructed according to models imposed by the fictional world forged by the entertainment media. Who would have thought that watching the cartoon *Tom & Jerry* would have such devastating consequences to our existential authenticity! The warning is given: whoever has ears should listen. It is not clear, however, what kind of happiness we would achieve after leaving our modern means of communication. Perhaps we will only understand the relationship between happiness and all of this when we return to communicating using smoke signals.

Spending the money we earn on honest work, in turn, is "consumerism", through which we lose sight of the things that "really matter", although we cannot say what those things are or why they would make us happy. We should apply all our savings only to what is absolutely necessary. The rest must be stored under our mattresses or donated to charities. We are wrong to spend it on superfluous things, with the sole purpose of entertaining us during leisure time.

The need to have fun buying what we like is alienation, the result of our immersion in a consumerist culture. Why buy clothes if we can dress up with potato bags? Now, the craving for luxury and ostentation was implanted in us artificially, through contact with *billboards* and promotional brochures. Who would buy shoes if they discovered that they could replace them with the scraps of leather discarded by tanneries? Nobody. But that the "system" doesn't want us to know. Our consumerist impulsiveness, as can be seen, was ideologically constructed by the advertising industry, which installed fictitious needs in our minds, which is the only reason why we bought orange squeezers. May fate keep us from—woe to us! — buy things with our own money that make our lives easier!

Irony aside, we know that, free from natural hazards, the essence of the human being boils down to dreaming silly things and having fun with useless things — so much so that the Brazilian Indians were immediately fascinated by the trinkets brought by the Portuguese, and this without any "insidious advertising" to manipulate their minds. The main rule that guides industries is to meet the needs of their consumers. If our needs extend to imbecility, wouldn't it be more worthy to simply admit it? We remain unhappy after buying things that we don't need, and not buying them would make any difference, except that we would have to manufacture our own superfluous props, for which we would certainly also be criticized.

Such examples suffice to illustrate our pretexts. Of course, when we allow ourselves to be deceived by obvious deceptions, by impossible promises, we know that very well. We just want to have someone to blame for our unhappiness. We place our dreams in the hands of others and curse them for not being able to achieve them.

Our quest for happiness is a bottomless pit dug by ourselves. We will only let go of the shovels when our arms succumb to exhaustion. Until that occurs, we will continue to insist that it may be just ahead. The only thing that's certain is that it's not with us.

* * *

We've already ridiculed our motives well enough. Let us now return to happiness itself. What is its essence? Properly analyzed, happiness has the aspect of a theological concept, such as omnipotence — something possible only to angels. We can, without much difficulty, realize that it is a fiction distilled from pleasure, the idealized version of any satisfaction, multiplied by a thousand as many times as necessary to make the pain, in contrast, seem insignificant. It is enough to scratch an insect bite and multiply the resulting relief millions of times: we will have before us a very accurate conception of the happiness that is sought. From this point of view, it is reminiscent of a homeopathic remedy: a drop of it dissolved in the ocean of our lives is enough for us to begin to believe, but not feel, that our lives are a sea of joy.

So it doesn't matter that everyone says they're happy in unison: they're not, none of them, because being happy is impossible. Happiness is an empty word with no reality behind it. Those who say they are happy say something as absurd as claiming that they can fly by waving their arms. Faced with this impossibility, it makes no sense to redefine the meaning of the word "happiness" as we please, as a superfluous synonym for what pleases us personally. If we think that happiness is pleasure, if we think it is peace, why don't we call it pleasure or peace? We seem to like that word more than we like our lives. Happiness as a pleasure, for example, is a dead end. A fully full glass is satisfaction — happiness would be to fill it even more without overflowing. Happiness as peace, on the other hand, is the same as inanimate matter, the same as being dead. There doesn't seem to be a way out.

If we investigate the question from a practical point of view, we will see that the only materially plausible argument in favor of happiness is a smile. So if we want to be happy, we just have to inject morphine into our veins, cut off our lips, and go out into the world spreading joy. We won't feel happy, but maybe we'll convince some lunatic of this, leading him to suffer to achieve the happiness he imagined seeing in our uninterrupted smile. When we convince a large number of individuals that we have achieved happiness, we are only one step away from joy: it will be enough to hit our heads on a rock.

From this point of view, happiness becomes a matter of public utility, not a personal one. A sign that we display externally to demonstrate that we are healthy, docile, able to live in society. To do so, the forced smile of an attendant suffices: that is happiness. Be willing to pretend, to act, to do whatever is necessary to carry life forward, dancing according to the music.

We know that behind our smiles, there is no happiness. If we don't find happiness in our own smile, why should we believe that we find it in someone else's? Your happiness is a smiling facade, just like ours. Being happy is just social professionalism, an ability to make yourself pleasant, a dental arch in a constant position of meaning. It's worth as much as knowing how to type, calculate taxes, or dress well. Outside the work environment, this farce earns us friends, that is, informal partners that provide security to our investments.

In our society, not believing in happiness is taboo, as is not believing in deities. It doesn't mean, however, that such things exist. God is to the mystery of the universe as happiness is to a smile. Both are believed through faith, not through life experience. We only know happiness by sight, only what is said about it. Nobody, for example, believes that a nighttime gas station attendant would be amazed to be a doormat for everyone who wants to fill up the tank in the middle of the night. Even if such an individual doesn't feel happy, he smiles and says: *come back often!* She seems happy: that's what matters. He doesn't sit around all night waiting for clients because that is an immense pleasure, but because he wants money, and this can be achieved by smiling and doing the will of the customers. He shows himself happy for money, like a prostitute, like everyone else. Between friends, the difference is that there is no charge in sight.

✶ ✶ ✶

We never experience, in real life, the happiness that we believe exists - our belief in it is justified by the smiling facade of others, just as they believe in ours. That's why it's common for so many to live based on the happiness of others. Everyone always smiling, everyone always unhappy. They make mistakes and live for each other in the name of a happiness that no one feels. Because we think that happiness is the only thing capable of justifying life, we become obsessed with being useful. We seek to believe that others are happy so that this justifies our miserable lives - at least as a means to the immortal happiness that is always hidden from us. That's why we insist that happiness exists. We would never confess the universal nature of unhappiness, for it would implode us.

Happiness, then, is never in us, nor in the other, only in the way *we think* of others. It's about projecting our expectations onto others, and that's the reason why happiness is always found "on the other side" — we think that only others can be happy as we would like to be. Knowing this, we turn to others, do them some favor, and they smile at us as proof that happiness exists. We are part of it because the favor came from us. Our lies, once reflected in others, become truths.

Let's think of a happy person: they don't exist. Whoever she is, it's just in our imagination. If we want proof of this, it will be enough to address the person in question and ask them about the idea we have of them: they will immediately open a smile of compassion, moved by our innocence. Even the people we admire, whose lives seem absolutely fabulous and worthy of envy to us, are actually like us, and the fact that we ignore that truth is the only reason we believe that happiness is possible. To understand it, we just have to think about how certain individuals admire in us things that often don't even exist and, even when they do, don't bring us any happiness - but they envy that in us, they really envy it, and they imagine that, when they achieve it, they will be happy like we are not. At the end of the day, if we admire a person, it only proves that we know them poorly. We can be certain that we would immediately abandon our admiration if we could, for just one minute, live under your skin.

To recap: we feel miserable, our lives are worthless. What is the solution? To live for others - because they, for whatever reason, must be worth something. But others think the same way and, like us, they are worthless to themselves. They feel miserable, but they believe that we are happy. The circle closes. If they live for us, and we live for them, where is the happiness, the reason why we live? It's in that myopia. Loneliness is unbearable to most individuals precisely because it reveals this truth to us - it reveals that the same actions that we direct to others, thinking that this makes them happy, when directed at ourselves, do not bring us any happiness. The circle is broken because we can't fool ourselves by smiling at ourselves — and loneliness falls on our heads as irrefutable proof that no one is happy.

REPRODUCTION

Faced with all the perplexity involved in the fact that we exist without reason in a disgraced world and that this, as a rule, means being unhappy and suffering for free, those who shy away from this issue like cowards boldly say to those who care about it: why don't you kill yourself? The question, of course, is a fair one. However, let's ask another slightly more interesting question: *why do you reproduce?*

First, let's look at the issue as follows: what currently constitutes our bodies has been wandering around the universe for at least thirteen billion years, and we would hardly find anyone complaining about that period of non-existence. On the other hand, this same subject, after becoming a man, accumulates enough pain in a few decades to fill all the hospitals and psychiatric clinics in the world. If the universe were self-aware, the only possible conclusion would be that it detests itself, because it decided to become a legion of survival machines that tear each other apart as breadwinners. But the only conscious things, as far as we know - and to a certain extent - are us, who believe, through a kind of demented tradition, that there must be a glorious next generation, who will be the happy heir of our achievements.

The reasons for this tasteless scheme to set in so naturally are obvious, and are explained in any basic biology textbook. In other words, like any species, or almost all, we are programmed to reproduce, care for our offspring, and then return to the dust with an impalpable, almost conventional feeling of accomplishment. Of course, if we depended only on rational deliberations to guarantee our perpetuation, we could nurture the benign hope of seeing life go extinct with a serene and confident smile. However, the issue is linked not to rationality, but to our greatest reference for pleasure: sex. A decoy created by nature with such perfidy that it would leave the Devil himself looking like an amateur when it comes to leading individuals to do bad business. This bait, in itself, is so efficient that it does not need any encouragement, any justification, since it appeals to what is most basic and energetic in our nature.

Human animality, therefore, is responsible for almost all the tortuous motives of procreation, and this without any mediation by reason, since its power to persuade or dissuade an excited monkey is simply null. When, out of miraculous wisdom, reason has the opportunity to utter some prudent words in this regard, they are almost never in favor, but explicitly against, suggesting contraceptive methods and narrating horrifying stories about sleepless nights filled with screams and excrement, whose protagonists later evolve to the stage of parasitism and remain there until the monetary cord is cut.

It's understandable that most individuals allow themselves to be guided by their basic instincts. Sex is good, it gives us free pleasure without negative consequences as long as we take basic precautions. Many become parents by accident, either because of inconsequence or because of the failure of contraceptive methods. It happens. We know the risks. Regrettably, the morals of most societies prevent us from choosing or not to carry out an unwanted pregnancy without making us criminals. Of course, from a rational point of view, it's strange that we feel such fixation on copulation, which basically consists of repeatedly penetrating a self-lubricating meat hole with a tube that throws out liquids filled with swim cells. However, if we want free pleasure, that's how we find it in nature. We're programmed to find healthy bodies exciting, and that makes us want to copulate; we can't help it. It's very easy to understand why such a system works in nature, and why children are born for that reason. On the other hand, if there were no pleasure in copulation, the future of our species would be somewhat doubtful, since there seem to be no rational reasons to justify the spread of life, but only genetically programmed instincts. If we doubt that, let's ask a chair what advantage it finds in human perpetuation.

* * *

However, contrary to everything that touches common sense, let's look at the reasons that are normally presented in favor of intentional procreation. A certain individual, after being cursed by the previous generation on the condition of being alive, begins to feel a certain emptiness in their existence. Assuming the most favorable circumstances, he was born into a good family, was educated, graduated in the area of knowledge that he likes most, gained professional respect and financial independence, married his beloved, bought most of the things he wanted, visited the most curious places on Earth. In short, he has sought every kind of achievement in the world. Nevertheless, he remains dissatisfied with his condition; he feels like a wretch. He begins to suspect that March of the World is a bad joke, but he refuses to confess it to himself. He continues to seek some external solution to his unhappiness. Seek relief in friendships, games, sports, betting, extravagances, parties, sex, drugs. But the next morning, reality whispers her failure in her ear.

The feeling that something is missing continues to tighten her chest and, after very little thought, she remembers the saying: *write a book, plant a tree, and have a child.* As the first two feats are palpable lies, ignore them with the same logic that should make you laugh even more at the last one. But through some lame reasoning, such as, for example, "if it's not that, what will it be?", she is quickly convinced that the solution to her miseries lies in procreation. From then on, it limits itself to daydreaming about how many pleasures will result from the formula *ejaculation* + nine months = happiness. Well, she has a son and innocently casts her plagues on the poor devil. Obviously, she does so with the best intention, dreaming of a bright and joyful future for her offspring. You can't imagine that the same blind impulse that led him to fight for the conquest of a life that, although stable, remains insipid, now leads him, like the outcome of his comedy, to perpetuate it simply because he cannot bear the frustration of everything he achieved in life, having been of absolutely no use.

Always, all the time, his desire was just to run away from himself. However, now, it does so by projecting the fulfillment of its life project on the horizon of the next generation. By doing so, he resigns himself to his long-dreamed, profound and stupendous personal happiness - which, of course, would come - and passes the baton forward, thinking that by doing this he is doing what is most "noble" on Earth. Faced with such regrettable reasoning, it is fair that nature has placed parental love as a kind of compensation for the innocent who has just appeared in the world without having done anything to deserve it.

If we can describe human existence by the maxim: *life is boring, and then you die,* reproducing means: *life is boring, you have children to forget about it, and then you* die. Can anyone see any trace of goodness in this? *When we solve personal problems through a child, we forget that the child, when arriving at the same situation as his parents, will be faced with the same problems for which he was a solution that, however, does not work.* As you will inherit the same intelligence as these, the cycle will end in rampant dementia.

✷ ✷ ✷

Let's look at the issue from the perspective of inanimate matter that is about to become a human machine fueled by illnesses and shortages. What does a handful of atoms have to gain by becoming a living being? The same thing that led the living to *flee* from themselves, that is, anguish, boredom and pain, all masked behind magnificent dreams that, inevitably, culminate in disappointment. The work of seeking unrealizable happiness at the cost of a thousand penalties and a thousand dangers for, in the end, nothing. Considering that the center of the universe is the navel of each one, giving up one's own life to create another is equivalent to the admission of one's own incompleteness of living, of the impossibility of being fully realized on one's own, of what would have been more valuable to have never existed.

But this painful silence that leads to extinction is something that the proud parent cannot admit. The individual feels aware of his very high value, although he is the only one who believes it. He feels that he cannot deprive the world of his legacy, of someone who continues his undertaking so decadent, so bankrupt, demanding the maintenance of his unsustainable condition. He thus throws into the future a hope so clumsy and cross-eyed that it seems more like revenge - but this is something that must be echoed for eternity as a testimony to his imbecility. Every sprout that appears in the family tree of the human species attests that our intelligence has not made us less irrational than any other animal.

As can be seen on a daily basis, most individuals are endowed with such a short vision and such unstoppable selfishness that they do not even think about the possibility that the other individual, created from nothing, despite the best intentions, will be as disgraced as himself. Thus, ignoring everything he learned with his own life and with all past generations, he bets that, in his case, for the first time in human history, love will make things different. His son is already born cursed by the burden of realizing a happiness that proved impossible to all who existed before him.

The proud parent does not see or even suspect what degree of cruelty is involved in the act of transforming a dust that has been dead for billions of years into a living being simply because he is dissatisfied with his own life. Therefore, instead of feeling proud, he should justly be affected by a deep and poignant remorse for the perversity, for the cowardice he has just committed against what, in the end, he himself would like to be: nothing.

Perhaps, after a while, when your children cease to be appendages to him, he will come to understand that it has only multiplied the pain that exists on Earth. It is true that sometimes he is sincerely bitter when he sees his offspring suffering in the whirlwind of the world, but he hides in the depths of his heart the guilt, the awareness that he is the only one responsible for it. Blame the world, invent a thousand explanations about the need to learn from one's mistakes to become a grown man, but one never honestly asks the question that the real mistake was the multiplication of the pain it caused.

Understanding that no one deserves the punishment of being born in this miserable world is the true lesson to be learned from a miserable experience. *Thus, his own life experience - of which he is paradoxically so proud - should have led him to conclude that he himself is nothing more than another error caused by a misunderstanding of the pathetic human condition - an error that, at least out of a minimum of compassion, should have caused him to stop at it.*

However, this kind of consideration never crosses the minds of these successful breeders - not even when they face an indefensible I *didn't ask to be born, something that should make them cover themselves with shame for an act as petty,* as ridiculous as taking from inanimate matter the peace that they themselves sought by cultivating the dream of having a child, ignoring that this can only be achieved with death, with the end of this regrettable succession of tragicomic events.

* * *

Even in the face of such evident facts, we tend to just shrug our shoulders, implying that it is a purely personal choice, that we must understand both positions as acceptable and justified, since one has a solid biological foundation and the other, intellectual. This, however, is a misconception: a mere appeal to nature does not subtract from reproduction its disastrous and immoral character.

As rational and lucid individuals, we cannot help but sympathize with the good taste of those who insist on being the last chapter, the end of this silliness. As minimally decent human beings, we cannot hide our disgust at the cruelty of those who choose reproduction, as if seeing this as an indisputable right, regardless of how much pain is involved.

Thus, so that there is no justifiable shadow of doubt left over the perspective that we have presented so far in defense of voluntary extinction as the only sane and moral stance towards life, let us leave aside the subjective tone of the discussion and see its purely concrete face.

Let's start from the assumption that to live is to suffer. What we call happiness, in fact, is the temporary suspension of pain: satisfied for a long time, we suffer again, this time with boredom. It is an objective observation regarding the nature of our subjectivity: no one escapes it. The fact that such an individual will suffer is as true as having two eyes and one mouth. We are talking about something that is an unavoidable physical reality. The only personal choice involved, in this case, is whether or not to have children. We have no options as to the realities involved in this. The implications follow inexorably, whether we like it or not. Therefore, regardless of the opinion we have in this regard, they will not make any difference as to what, in fact, occurs when a new consciousness appears to walk over this world.

When understood in a context that takes into account the logic of life, suffering is not necessarily undesirable. It exists because it fulfils a biological function, just like pleasure. Despite being a subjective component, it is determined as a function of an objective task, that is, the maintenance of the organisms. Pain, like pleasure, does not exist by itself, but only subjectively.

275

From an objective point of view, suffering is a phenomenon like any other, just like pleasure.

Non-living matter, being purely objective, is alien to the subjective phenomena that torment living creatures, that is, free from any and all suffering, in a state of perfect serenity. It doesn't make sense to try to be "mean" with inanimate matter. There is no way to torture stones by throwing them off cliffs, hammering them, etc. There is only one way to make matter suffer: to transform it into a living being. It follows that, even from an objective point of view, we can find moral implications in reproduction, since it condemns matter to suffer uselessly in the form of a living being driven by illnesses and deficiencies, only to then return to the same situation in which it found itself, without any sense or benefit from it.

From this point of view, we do not say that reproduction is wrong, just that it is cruel. We affirm that, objectively, living is a shame. However, we did not draw any subjective conclusions from this. Whether or not living is worth living is a distinct and subjective issue, which refers to the value we attribute to life. Immorality lies in the fact that the value of life is an issue that can only be considered by those who are already alive. When we reproduce, we impose our personal conclusions on someone who can't even defend themselves.

Of course, this is not a transcendental and absolute moral, but one related to life. It can be understood as objective in the sense of referring to something that necessarily occurs, by the very nature of life, by the conditions imposed on subjective existence when inserted in the determinations of the objective world. Therefore, let us not confuse this observation with moral preaching about right and wrong, right and duty, etc. We are only concerned with objectively describing the physical consequences of the equally physical phenomenon of bringing into existence a new consciousness to be haunted by the restlessness that drives life.

From this perspective, reproduction makes us solely responsible for creating suffering in the world. Without us, there would be no pain. But there is, and it's our fault. Objectively, pain is not a bad thing, but subjectively it is. We, as living beings, have pain as the supreme reference for everything that is undesirable. Our objective, biological nature imposes this condition on us. Just as pleasure is good, pain is bad — whether physical, emotional, or psychologi-cal. So don't let the relativists stand up with their crazy theories about the "arbitrariness" of the issue: we would like to see them believe this while we insert nails under their fingernails. The presence of pain as something positive-ly undesirable is an essential requirement for life to be sustainable. It is a condition objectively imposed on the survival machines that we are. Pain makes us efficient organisms, and without it we wouldn't function properly, we would just die painlessly because we ignored the dangers that surround us.

This means that when we cause all the pain that exists on Earth to appear out of nowhere, when we place matter in the only condition in which it can suffer, that is, when we transform it into a living being, we become positively evil, responsible for the spread of suffering. Thus, intentional reproduction makes us perverse and immoral beings, and this in a purely objective sense, since it is a universally valid judgment, regardless of the circumstances in which we find ourselves. As long as there is pain in existence, as long as life involves suffering, the act of reproducing yourself means collaborating with your growth, perpetuating that disgrace, actively striving to make the world a more painful and regrettable place.

Obviously, we have the freedom to be as bad and selfish as we want, but we cannot deny that we are guilty of this, there is no way we can be exonerated from this accusation. Originally, that life didn't exist, it never existed, and it would have been so, if not because we had the admirable idea of ejaculating in a womb and making it appear out of nowhere and then affirming that your suffering "is not our problem", that we are not responsible because it is some-thing "natural". Now, not even a theologian could take such a lame apology seriously.

The objection that this does not necessarily make us bad because suffering occurs in life in a natural and inevitable way is not justified because, although we cannot alter its intimate constitution, we have the choice to reproduce or not. The one who is born, on the other hand, has no choice, just as we didn't. We may or may not have children. However, when we decide to have them, the choice makes us positively evil, freely cruel. We, like an insomnia of matter, attack what sleeps deeply just to share our lack of sleep, to feel less bored with our embarrassingly futile existences.

Undoubtedly, the reproductive impulse has deep biological roots, but that doesn't free us from guilt either. Of course, we weren't the ones who invented life and its rules, but we were the ones who propagated it. We created a life intentionally, in circumstances in which *we knew that suffering would be* inevitable. Often the impulse of aggressiveness leads us to commit crimes, but we still consider it reprehensible. It is something equally instinctive and natural, ingrained in us as deeply as the sexual urge. The difference is that our aggression will take place nine months later, like someone planting a time bomb in the heart of nothing.

* * *

The situation we have is basically the following: an individual deliberately inflicts great physical, emotional, and psychological suffering on others in the hope of diminishing their own, and the victim will never be able to defend themselves against such aggression, except through suicide. Logically, the pain will not be caused directly by us, but by the circumstances in which we place the individual. However, this could have been avoided with any cheap condom. Causing great pain to an innocent person, just to achieve a small reduction of our own, is a vile and revolting attitude. We could, without a doubt, feel entitled to demand compensation for such injustice, for having been placed in this undignified and degrading situation. It would make sense to receive compensation for the inconvenience of having been born, but this is something that, as stated, nature has wisely provided in the form of an instinct to protect the offspring. Fatherly love is the compensation that children receive from their parents for having placed them in the world.

Let's look at some more illustrations. Suppose that, by some miracle, we had attained a state of perfect peace and serenity. We live happily and satisfied by the simple fact that we exist. No pain bothers us, no desire torments us; everything is fine. Then an individual full of heartbreak arrives, bored of existing, and forces us to leave that state of wholeness, placing us in the same deplorable situation just to not feel alone. What would we think of the character of such an individual? For the price of not feeling bored, or at least not so much, the other person must pay with all the pain they will have to endure throughout their life, from birth to death. Admittedly, we are all driven by selfishness. However, when there is a great disproportion between the interests and the benefits that each one receives in the relationship, we stop being simply selfish and become scoundrels.

In another case, we have a quiet individual at his residence, relaxing in the nirvana of inanity. It is surrounded by possible dangers, but the door is securely locked because it is unlikely that they will hit it by chance. Such dangers can be illustrated by hordes of wild and perverse animals, such as men, for example. We, with the best of intentions, will come to your residence. We don't ask for permission to enter. We do not consider whether, in the same situation, we would like to be visited. On the contrary, with excessive insolence, we knocked down the door with axes and tore it out of the house by the hair so that it can share its existence with us, so that it can live up to our expectations, so that it can delight in being exactly what we hate. What are our reasons for this? As a rule, fear of loneliness, boredom, or mere lack of creativity. The individual is now exposed to all the dangers and pains of life simply because we, as arrogant imbeciles, believe that we have the right to speak for anyone who cannot defend themselves.

It should also be added that there is no remorse for the pain it causes. We simply apologize with the idea that such suffering is "natural." However, it's natural for us, that we don't have a choice. We're already alive, and all the suffering we have to endure is of absolutely no use. We strive day after day, we face a thousand sorrows, only to repeatedly fail to achieve any peace, and nothingness enjoys perfect serenity, not for a few seconds, but for all eternity. Then, filled with envy, we avenge ourselves, transforming him into a similar person, into a sufferer who will be nicknamed with our last name.

∗ ∗ ∗

When, guided by this understanding, we sympathize with the idea of voluntary extinction, we are faced with the only moral perspective in favor of compassion that can be objectively supported. Because we know that if we have children, they will suffer. If we stop having them, there will be one less pain on

Earth. This, of course, is not a heroic call to free kindness, to headless charity, or to paranoid compassion. Those who are alive suffer, and will continue to suffer until the end of their days. We can't change that, at least not without fleets of water trucks filled with morphine. However, if we have the slightest aversion to gratuitous cruelty directed at innocent people, we will be able to admit how repulsive there is in reproducing ourselves. It's as atrocious, as degrading as physical torture. Like a psychopath who rejoices to kidnap an innocent person, lock him in his basement, and torture him for years, decades, until he dies of natural causes.

Furthermore, the amount of suffering that we stop feeling when we fulfill our desire to procreate is never greater, not even remotely equal to the magnitude of the suffering that will be inflicted on the one who is born. The end result will always be a greater proportion of pain than relief, an inflation of suffering. Therefore, even if the idea of having children represents for us a great dream of personal fulfillment, we must understand that, no matter how good our intentions are, we are not able to, we have no resources to guarantee the happiness of the one we place at this end of the world, no matter how rich, dedicated, or affectionate we are, no matter how better the living conditions we provide them. We simply don't have the powers to do that.

As parents who want to form a happy and prosperous family, suppose the best possible circumstances, that is, with our intention of having a child, we are truly sincere in our desire to raise him in the best possible way, doing everything in our power to see him happy. If we really have that goodness in our hearts, that lavish wanting well, the following reasoning will be sufficient to convince us that the greatest goodness will be in not carrying our dream forward.

When we give up having children, we give up a small and dubious personal satisfaction to prevent the onset of great suffering. If we manage to exercise a minimum of compassion in relation to what, according to ourselves, will be the only object of our love and dedication, we will see that, by not reproducing ourselves, we will be putting into practice the only possible goodness in relation to our children. Let us console ourselves with knowing that, because they were not born, in our dreams they will always be sleeping in their rooms, under blankets as soft as the embrace of the one whose love would never allow them to suffer and, for that very reason, protected them from existence. They remain comfortable, serene, at peace, with a half-smile on their lips because they have never tasted the bitterness and disappointment of life. They will always remain pure, eternally free from the dangers of the world. That is the true meaning of giving up one's life in favor of that of one's children.

In this situation, we don't engage in real cruelties in an unsuccessful attempt to nullify pain with good intentions and imaginary happiness. Assuming that our interest was really the well-being of our children, that would be nothing more than common sense, the application of the most elementary principle of decency, that is, not doing to others what we would not want them to do to us. Recognizing our limitations, our kindness led us to the only possible way out: to spare them the suffering of existing.

We have already demonstrated that the best thing for children is not to be born. On the other hand, for fathers, it is also more advantageous not to have them, since the personal benefits of fatherhood are practically nil. Considering that our children will not make us happy, since happiness is just the dream of those who have forgotten the brain in the heart, leaving procreation aside reveals only wisdom. Otherwise, we are filled with fanciful expectations that will inevitably be frustrated by reality. Sooner or later, we will see that children are nothing like we imagined. However, after they are born, we will have to lie about this so as not to hurt them, so as not to make them feel like a burden. Thus, with fatherhood, we are wrong about our children and then we have to deceive them as well.

∗ ∗ ∗

As we can see, even the most optimistic perspective proves to be unsustainable, even if we are quite generous in accepting palpable lies as reasons in favor of reproduction. To demonstrate how unfounded and fragile such positions are, there was not even a need to refute the ideas of "selfless altruism" or "unrestricted kindness", exposing them as the obvious impossibilities that they are. Since even poetic ideals cannot lend sufficient coherence to such a stance, honesty will only serve to reduce it to a joke, like someone kicking a dead dog.

However, let's kick it so that we can finally bury it.

When we investigate what our true motives — that is, the selfish motives — are for reproduction, the implications are even more revolting. We find ourselves acting only out of our own interest, to the great detriment of others. Motivated by an illusion that, in addition to being foolish, is also impractical. We often employ the discourse of altruism to justify reproduction, but that is simply social automatism. To be minimally honest, we have to admit that, with reproduction, we would only be able to distract ourselves from our own suffering by alleviating someone else's, in a kind of occupational cruelty. In other words, we place an individual who suffers upon the world just to feel virtuous and useful in trying to reduce their pain. We actually become bad just to feel comforted by mitigating the consequences of this—do we need to say more?

It is clear that when we have children and justify ourselves with the discourse of goodness, this makes us as absurd and perverse as the Christian God, that is, an entity that, like us, came from nowhere and, for lack of something better to do, creates living beings and tortures them, because it loves them.

✳ ✳ ✳

Everything that was discussed above could have been scientifically explained in terms of *DNAs*, natural selection, perpetuation, competition, instincts, etc. However, everyone already knows this, or at least should. It would be unnecessarily repeating what has already been exposed by countless specialists. As long as we have a minimum scientific education, we understand why we reproduce. Any child knows that the meaning of life is to be born, to grow, to reproduce and to die, *ad* nauseam.

We, on the contrary, were more interested in investigating the human reasons that lead us from point a *to* point *b*, from incoherence to atrocity, and with that we arrived at much more curious and thought-provoking conclusions, which almost make us puke. Now, just to finish, let's see how our story would be told in the light of the motives that drive us.

The beginning was simple: a clump of matter exploded, as if coughing out of nowhere. It wandered in the void of space for billions and billions of years, without any boredom or trauma. At a given moment, some of that matter ended up constituting a planet lost in the confines of a galaxy also lost among billions of others. On this planet, great seas filled with organic compounds were formed, and on them the molecules were floating happily in the unconsciousness of the being - but something terrible was about to happen. A virus appeared in this chemical soup, and matter became sick and began to suffer because it existed. Enslaved by selfish spirals, she was forced to organize herself, taking the form of survival machines, all condemned to suffer needlessly in the name of an equally useless perpetuation.

Soon after its appearance, the entire surface of the planet was flooded with blood and tears, and it agonizes in excruciating and endless pain. We, on the crest of this wave, represent a major technological or, better to say, pathological innovation. By building machines with rational brains [sic], such viruses became more contagious than ever. Now, organized in large societies, machines are engaged in tasks that, unconsciously, are at the service of their own perpetuation.

One of these human machines, in its painful feeling of experiencing an ephemeral, miserable and unreasonable existence alone, seeks ways to alleviate its ills. She is constantly coerced by pain and need, always unhappy with her condition, but she remains convinced that there is a solution to her discomforts, and all that remains is to discover which one. That machine doesn't really know what to expect from its own existence. However, desperate, frustrated from head to toe, unable to discern a solution, she is seduced by the mirage of impossible happiness, which she believes she is creating another machine just like herself. She doesn't really believe that, but her instincts tell her otherwise, because the virus has done its homework and has mastered the art of manipulating the bodies it inhabits. Thus, trapped by circumstances, unable to think clearly, thirsty for a minute of peace, she inoculates the germ of her misfortune into another machine equipped with an incubator. For nine months, this symptom feeds on healthy matter, and when expelled from the womb, it is already completely and solidly ill. The curse of life has been cast.

The parental infectious agent believes that, by doing so, he will be freed from his own curse, although he cannot explain why or how this will occur, since, in exchange for reproduction, the virus did not promise him anything other than an orgasm. He just clung to that clumsy hope like a clumsy shipwrecked man who, trying to hug a canoe, knocked down the black and muddy sea of life also the one who was in it, oblivious to the situation. Your life then gains a purpose: teaching your victim how to swim. Even if she hasn't found the peace she wanted, now at least she has someone to talk to in the ocean of her helplessness; she has a companion of misfortune with whom she shares her desolation. It will teach him everything he knows, namely, that, in the rough seas of existence, we must find solace even in sticks that help us float; that, if we are wise and prudent, if we work hard, one day we may even be able to conquer a piece of board on which to rest our heads for a few moments; and that in another life, who knows, maybe there will be a place where everyone will have their own canoes.

The victim must be eternally and blindly grateful to their aggressors, honored to represent another link that leads to the perpetuation of this sandwich. After being educated in the morbid art of existence, she will follow the example of the most serious illnesses, inspired by the dream of one day becoming incurable. Give yourself body and soul to the mission of proliferating exponentially, until the entire universe is transformed into an inoperable tumor mass.

* * *

Life is irrefutable proof that even inanimate matter is not safe from stupidity. At any moment, you can be condemned to the torments of a sordid and useless existence by any ingenious individual who decides to give meaning to his life through ejaculation. Summoned as another member of the Infantry Army of Disquiet, matter is given the eternal mission of suffering in order to exist and to exist in order to suffer. Their battle cry is *Grow and Multiply*.

When we inject the emptiness of our lives into the nothingness of existence, another wretch appears in the world. By our own hands, emptiness and nothingness meet — *ad majorem doloris gloriam*. While the newborn cries almost prophetically, the others celebrate this unsustainable dementia of being, the arrival of another shipwrecked child in this nihilistic paradise.

God, religion, morals, the origin and meaning of life, free will: in *Atheism & Freedom*, fundamental issues are brought to the light of reason, in an attempt to clarify some of the lies and truths that surround us. Controversial, frank, revealing and bold, *Atheism & Freedom* is an invitation to reflection, to free thinking, and to the search for a rational and coherent explanation of man and the world.

The exploration of the underground, of the taboo, of the humanity that we prefer to hide from ourselves: *The Emptiness of the Machine investigates some of the most uncomfortable topics brought to light by the emptiness* of existence. Nothingness, absurdity, loneliness, suffering, suicide, hypocrisy are some of the main topics addressed throughout the work. We know how far we can go with our modern knowledge - it finally remains to use it.

This book is an attempt to justify the transition from atheism to nihilism based on modern science. It presents an interpretation of nihilism (existential nihilism) according to which it follows from considering the implications of our main scientific discoveries, simply revisiting classic existential issues in the light of current knowledge. Thus, the idea is that once we become atheists, nihilism follows.

Joe is an essentially introspective novel, in which an attempt is made to construct a vision of the world from the character's eyes. The idea that animated the production of this work was to illustrate, not in theory, but in the context of practical life, all that perplexity that takes hold of us when we turn our eyes to the world from a perspective, so to speak, "existentialist", and we are overwhelmed by the sense of the absurdity of existing.

Insomnia of Matter is a collection of poems written between 2002 and 2007, corresponding to the interval between the writing of *Atheism & Freedom* and *The Void of the* Machine. The atmosphere of perplexity and unease that permeates almost every poem can be seen as a reflection of the anguish felt when we try to deal with a problem that still escapes us - such as a ghost that haunts us, until we can put it on paper.

ISBN: 978-65-00-73904-6

9 786500 739046

Printed in the USA
CPSIA information can be obtained
at www.ICGtesting.com
LVHW042159270724
786704LV00007B/382